THE SPIRIT AND
FORMS OF
PROTESTANTISM

by

LOUIS BOUYER

Translated by

A. V. LITTLEDALE

THE NEWMAN PRESS

Westminster, Maryland

1956

First published 1956

Nihil obstat: RICARDUS ROCHE, D.D.
Imprimatur: ✠ FRANCISCUS, ARCHIEP. BIRMINGAMIENSIS
Datum Birmingamiae, die 28a Novembeis, 1955

Library of Congress Catalog Card Number: 56–10001

CONTENTS

Letter to the author from G. de Broglie, S.J.

Dear Reverend Father,

Though you are now one of my colleagues in the Faculty of Theology in Paris, you have requested, with a modesty both honourable and touching, a preface from one of your old teachers. However, the excellence of your book on the subject of Protestantism stands in no need of my recommendation. Your own repute is warrant enough to your readers for the immense interest of the work and the soundness of its doctrinal views.

As you have asked for my opinion, I will say that you are practically the only person in France today capable of dealing adequately with the subject. Admittedly, we have plenty of theologians equipped to argue on theoretical lines, but it is almost impossible to bring an exact and balanced judgment to bear on a religious movement in the concrete, if one knows it only from the outside, without being personally involved. We Catholics are at once aware of this whenever we come across some general account of our religion written by a Protestant; yet we do not always allow that the same holds good in the reverse sense, and so we remain puzzled by various aspects of Protestantism. You, however, are in a position to treat of the two religions, not solely as the result of investigation, but as a living experience; and that gives your work its exceptional value. It makes it one of the most important works that has yet appeared on the subject of Protestantism, being the fruit of some twenty years of study and reflection.

You have adopted as your guiding principle that it is impossible to reach a just estimate of the work of the 'reformers' in all its complexity, if it is viewed merely as a more or less extended list of condemned propositions. What is needed is to penetrate directly to what was, and remains, its living principle, to the depths of the motives prompting Luther and his first followers to break with the actual forms of thought and devotion embodied in the customs and institutions of the time. From this line of approach, you have no difficulty in showing that the very source of the movement was a genuinely religious reaction against a theology bordering on Pelagianism and against forms of devotion which tended to stifle the essentials of religion with the merely accessory. Then, after clearly defining the legitimate and valuable element in their aims, you go on to show, with equal clarity, how the nominalist attitude characteristic of Luther and most of his contemporaries distorted, from the very beginning, an impulse which, in a different climate of thought, could, and indeed ought, to have resulted in nothing but good. Consequently, what was first intended to be a simple reform was bound to develop into a heresy, as a result of the flat denials of traditional teaching entailed by the application of a disastrous and misleading philosophy.

It is this innate opposition between the positive elements—the true source of the Protestant religious life—and the corrosive negations inextricably involved with them that you elucidate so cogently; this makes your work so original and valuable. You trace out the stresses of this internal opposition as they show themselves in the whole course of Reformation history, the true key of which you would seem to have discovered. From this duality of elements so clearly perceived we may anticipate what will be the reactions of many readers. Your early chapters will surprise more than one Catholic, perturbed at your commendation of the religious feeling of a Luther, a Calvin, or a Karl Barth; while, on the other hand, your final ones will affront many Protestants, disappointed that a work so promising in the beginning should conclude on a note of severe criticism. My own opinion is that no serious person, provided he take the trouble to read the entire work with attention, could entertain any doubt that it has been inspired throughout by a constant care for sympathetic understanding and frank objectivity. Nearly all will ultimately be grateful to you for having obliged them to reflect on a problem one or more of whose aspects had doubtless escaped their attention, and so for bringing a better understanding between Catholics and Protestants. Works of this sort are of particular service to the great cause of Christian unity, since, far from trying, on the pretext of charity, to gloss over differences of doctrine, you aim at setting them forth with the greatest precision, tracing their causes to their ultimate roots.

In addition to this, your readers will derive from your book other benefits of a more general nature. To my mind perhaps the most salient one is the great help it will give our Catholic theologians to reach a better understanding of one of the fundamental principles which should always govern their discussions with the heterodox. Actually, we are too much inclined to blame the blind obstinacy of our opponents for the failure of our arguments to convince them, whereas this is often due to the narrowness of our aims and vision, even, nay especially, when we have recourse to the utterances of authority to conceal our defects of method.

Admittedly, the teaching authority of the Church has its particular function in this connection, and it discharges it admirably when, in stigmatising a heresy, it selects for condemnation a list of propositions containing its chief errors. The harm arises when the apologist imagines that his task consists simply in taking these condemnations one by one and vindicating them by a series of sound arguments. Such would be an excellent method of procedure only if heresies arose, as a general rule, by the spontaneous generation, in the souls of certain people, of a pathological taste for a collection of erroneous propositions. But their genesis, in actual fact, is quite otherwise. In the religious domain, as much as, possibly more than, elsewhere, the only errors to which people of some education are liable are those which assume the mask of some truth with such plausibility that they insinuate themselves with it, without their being aware of the difference between them. For this reason, if we want to convince a person of his error, it is seldom enough to refute in themselves all the false propositions he has accepted; what is more important is, by a close historical and psychological inquiry, to lay bare the positive motives for which such innovations have found acceptance. Only when we have come to estimate exactly the strength and the weakness of these motives will we be in a position to show those we want to convince that they are not required in the least to abandon their legitimate desires, but only to recognise that these can be met under conditions less drastic than they supposed.

Many controversies of the past would have been far more profitable, had they been conducted from this point of view. How much more effective, for example, would have been the arguments against the traditionalism of Lamennais or, later, against the modernists, if it had been admitted, from the beginning, that there were excellent reasons for wanting to break the narrow bounds of Cartesian rationalism, or to overthrow a pseudo-scientific conception of faith and apologetics; but insisting strongly that to return to a theology more completely Christian in inspiration did not imply such extreme corollaries as were thought! In this aspect, your work will help us all to discern more clearly all the advantages to be gained from more frank and comprehensive methods of controversy.

There is yet another, and most opportune, lesson to be learned from your book: the importance, for the defence of orthodoxy, of a sound philosophy.

For, if the source of the Protestant heresy is not to be found in some sudden and monstrous growth of moral perversity or intellectual insanity, but solely in the rigid and relentless application of a nominalist philosophy to a movement prompted by genuine religious feeling, it is a terrifying thought that the theology of Occam and Biel, so esteemed by generations of devout thinkers, should have contained in itself so powerful a poison.

Yet the blindness of such thinkers is not without its explanation. At the close of the Middle Ages, when, in practically the whole of the West, the Christian faith seemed destined to a long prosperity, it needed the insight of genius to perceive how menacing to the faith was a system which, in its seductive 'clarity', boasted of being its buttress. Even the ecclesiastical authorities of the time seem to have shared, at least in part, the general illusion, a matter of surprise to those only who mistake the infallible magisterium for an imaginary charism of universal insight. What is really shocking, and almost incredible, is that the Church should have been unable to profit by the lessons of subsequent events, repeated on various occasions right up to our own times. If the Church in the nineteenth and twentieth centuries, without indeed claiming a mission to teach philosophy, has shown an increasing solicitude for the sound philosophical training of its theologians; if it goes so far as to pass judgment on systems of philosophy (not in themselves, but in their concordance with dogma), and to assert boldly its own preferences, an investigation like yours is of the greatest help to us in realising how such action comes within its rightful province.

Everyone who reads your work intelligently will have no difficulty in acknowledging that the Church can no longer hold itself completely impartial to the rival philosophies of Occam and of Thomas Aquinas.

I have enumerated some of the benefits to be expected from your excellent work. I congratulate you most heartily on your achievement, wishing it all the success it deserves.

G. DE BROGLIE, S.J.

Introduction

THIS book is a personal witness, a plain account of the way in which a Protestant came to feel himself obliged in conscience to give his adherence to the Catholic Church. No sentiment of revulsion turned him from the religion fostered in him by a Protestant upbringing followed by several years in the ministry. The fact is, he has never rejected it. It was his desire to explore its depths, its full scope, that led him, step by step, to discover the absolute incompatibility between Protestantism as a genuinely spiritual movement stemming from the teachings of the Gospel, and Protestantism as an institution, or rather complexus of institutions, hostile to one another as well as to the Catholic Church. The study of this conflict brought him to detect the fatal error which drove the spiritual movement of Protestantism out of the one Church. He saw the necessity of returning to that Church, not in order to reject any of the positive Christian elements of his religious life, but to enable them, at last, to develop without hindrance.

The writer, who carved out his way step by step, or, rather, saw it opening before his eyes, hopes now to help along those who are still where he started. In addition, he would like to show those he has rejoined how a little more understanding of the others, above all a greater fidelity to their own gift, could help their 'separated brethren' to receive it in their turn. In this hope he offers his book to all who wish to be faithful to the truth, the truth, first, of the Word of God, but also to the truth of men as they are, not as our prejudices and habits impel us to see them.

CHAPTER I

The Positive Principles of the Reformation

THE Reformation is generally considered to be a negative movement, not only by its critics, but also by many of its partisans. The very word 'Protestant' at once suggests the idea of a rejection.

Most people, if asked point-blank for a definition of Protestantism, would say immediately: 'A Protestant is one who does not believe in Our Lady, the Saints, the Real Presence, and so on.' Many Protestants even would react in the same way. To judge by many of the books devoted to the exposition and defence of Protestant ideas and practices, such as the popular catechism of Pastor Nyegard, one would think that there lay its essential nature.

It is still less surprising if Catholic controversialists see Protestantism simply as a rejection of the Church and, in particular, of its authority. They are doubtless aware that the Protestant rejects it on Scriptural grounds, but, for the most part, Catholics consider that their separated brethren use Scripture not as an authority in itself, but as a basis for their own arbitrary interpretations. Hence the well-known saying: 'The Protestant, Bible in hand, is his own Pope.'

The whole aim of this book is to show, in the first place, that authentic Protestantism is far more than an unbridled and negative individualism, though that is how it may appear at first sight. There is, it is true, abundant evidence, both in past and present Protestantism, to justify this negative view. What in our day goes by the name of liberal Protestantism is, in fact, just such a system; it proudly claims what was originally a reproach. But, even before it made its appearance, there were some who, outside the ranks of Protestantism, adopted the same line of defence. Bossuet condemned the Reformation as the victory of private judgment and its resultant anarchy; Michelet commended it for practically the same reason. In his view, the merit of the Reformers consisted in having sown the intellectual and spiritual seeds of the great Revolution.

1

Still, we must not overlook that even liberal Protestantism, while claiming as a merit what had been levelled as a reproach, does not admit the purely negative character of private judgment. It claims rather, in the celebrated phrase of Sabatier, to be the religion of the Spirit as opposed to the religions of authority. None the less, the fact remains that the Spirit in question is, properly speaking, the spirit of man, even though it be granted as self-evident that its liberation is bound to let in the action of the Spirit of God. Thus, it has to be admitted that the affirmation which lies at the root of Protestantism, if this 'liberalism' is its true and final expression, must be the self-assertion of the individual. This involves an individualism which rejects, not only the affirmations of the Christian community of tradition, but any divine revelation not made directly to the individual consciousness.

All the same, while acknowledging that this liberalism is rooted in the very origin of the Reformation, we would be making a serious mistake to see in it the true face of Protestantism. Wherever liberal Protestantism has gained the upper hand, 'Protestantism is but an aggregate of different religious forms of free thought', to quote a revealing phrase of Gabriel Monod. To take that for living Protestantism is to be entirely mistaken.

No religion, or religious movement, is to be judged on the basis of its theoretical expositions. It is something living, and has to be looked for in the communities where it has its life. Any discussion on Protestantism which does not start from this point risks ending up in spinning logical webs which bear no relation to reality. On the other hand, if we make the acquaintance of Protestantism in the souls where it is alive, all these reconstructions and expositions dissolve in the light of a reality with which they have little or nothing in common.

Let us try, then, to grasp, not this or that theory of Protestantism, but the living religion: to enter, if we can, into the ordinary life of a parish of the Reformed Church of France. We will soon find that Protestantism, for its members, means, not private judgment, but Biblical Christianity, incomplete or illogical it may be, but yet authentically religious.

The life of the parish centres round the Sunday service. French Protestants, whatever Catholics may think, do not call it a service of preaching (*le prêche*). They call it simply 'worship' (*le culte*). This austere, rather abstract, term expresses, none the less, what is bound to impress a Catholic, namely, an essentially religious act, in the exact sense of what is called the virtue of religion; that is, the constant recognition, dominating every thought and act, of the majesty of God. The sermon, it is true, is the most prominent feature, even, perhaps, the longest one; but it is preceded by readings from Scripture, and stands in a framework of prayers and hymns quite alien to the spirit connoted by the words 'private judgment'. The most usual subjects are the articles of the Creed, prayer, meditation, obedience, Christian renunciation, the duties of the Christian, particularly that of living according to the truths of faith.

There are, besides, in the parish a number of very interesting organisations for the preparation of the young, who, as their first communion does not take place at an early age, undergo a long period of instruction. In addition to learning the catechism, they are trained in the practice of religion by what are known as 'Sunday school' and 'Thursday school'. Both of these, by means similar to those used in the adult service, furnish a thorough and detailed knowledge of the Bible, especially the Gospels. The catechism revises and co-ordinates this knowledge by the study of the teaching, acts, and person of Christ. All this provides the context for the teaching of Christian spirituality and conduct, more or less closely linked up with doctrine, and based on the Gospel.

It cannot be denied that hostile references to Catholicism constantly occur in the sermons and instruction. On occasion this may be the theme of a whole sermon or lesson. What would strike Catholic susceptibilities would be not so much anything in the nature of heresy as the caricature set up for attack. In fact, it is noteworthy that, while the accusations levelled against the Church would seem to have little or no foundation, the things censured would, as a rule, be equally repugnant to a well-informed Catholic as to a Protestant. In other words, a Catholic would view the ordinary, domestic Protestant polemic against the Church as based on factual, rather than doctrinal, error. For example, the worship of saints and the veneration of images are denounced as idolatrous; but it is held that Catholics adore the saints in the same way as God, or instead of God, and that they actually pray to images. Or else exception is taken to Papal infallibility, which is taken to be a kind of omniscience; or to the infallibility of the Church, which is thought to mean some kind of sinlessness in ecclesiastics. A pagan element is attributed to Catholic worship, simply because it is thought that the Church regards the efficacy of liturgical prayer or the rosary as independent of the spirit in which it is said; or else they attribute a magical element to the Catholic belief in the sacraments, on the supposition that they do not require faith, contrition, etc., on the part of the recipient.

In general, when we have become familiar with these stock accusations which recur, from time to time, in Protestant preaching and instruction, we become aware that they all derive from a view of Catholicism held as self-evident, namely, that it is an organisation for practising religion by proxy, God, in his absence, being replaced by an all-powerful agency. This ultimately, and nothing else, is the object of attack; and it is against this absurd and mythical organisation that one hears, not 'private judgment' (*libre-examen*)—which is hardly ever mentioned in church—but 'liberty of conscience' extolled. This, even when commended in the highest degree, is viewed as the necessary condition of worship 'in spirit and truth', rather than as something merely negative.

This rapid summary may cause some surprise to Catholic readers. None the less, we believe that they would receive the same impression of Protestantism if they could share for a time the life of a parish, or, as it is called for preference, a 'Church'. They would come to feel that a wall of fantastic prejudices is what separates this 'Church' from the Catholic Church, and that the ideal aimed at is surprisingly close to the interior life based on the Gospel, a little on the austere side, it may be, but for the most part the same as the Catholic.

This conviction is reinforced when we come to examine the personal life, both of the young and their elders, formed on this pattern. In every case where the Protestant religion is more than a routine of church-going, personal devotion bears a clear and strikingly Biblical character. The basic act of religion on which pastors or parents insist for a young man or woman is daily reading of the Bible, or at least of the Gospels. To be exact, a meditative reading, closely akin to the *lectio divina* of the monks of the Middle Ages; in other words, leading on to prayer, private and personal. By this is meant prayer that is generally spontaneous in form, the traditional formulas of Catholic devotion being viewed with mistrust. Yet, in spite of this bias, the devout, in Protestantism as elsewhere, have at their disposal set formulas to facilitate their personal prayer—their hymns, in the first place—and they have no hesitation in using them.

What do they seek in this reading and in the prayer it inspires? We answer categorically: God speaking to the soul, and acting in it.

This form of devotion is, in fact, intimately associated with a spirituality of grace—grace, we must insist, considered as efficacious, productive of forgiveness, regeneration, newness of life. The main preoccupation of the devout Protestant is with sin, actual sins forgiven, as the initiation to a life of holiness, the life of Christ himself in the redeemed soul.

It cannot be denied that the recurring antithesis, sin–grace, gives Protestant devotion a somewhat oppressive air. The prayer of the Protestant tends to become a perpetual *Miserere*. However, the assurance of forgiveness through Christ, a certainty to which the devout Protestant is bound, opens the way to holiness and commits him irrevocably to it, with the constant support of grace, and that is what lifts and sustains him. At times, with particular sects, this certainty degenerates in practice into quietism. As a rule, though, it leaves the Protestant humbled before his judge rather than presumptuous in the justice he has acquired by faith.

Whatever the original sense of the expression, Luther's *semper peccator, semper justus* is certainly not now generally understood as an inescapable doom to sin combined with the definitive possession of a salvation already achieved. Rather, it is held to imply a continual struggle in which every defeat inflicted on the natural powers of man has to be repaired by a victory wrought by divine power acting through human weakness.

This analysis will suffice for the moment, without going into

further detail. What conclusions can we draw? The facts
established will surprise, agreeably or otherwise, both the free-
thinking historian and the Catholic controversialist who equate
Protestantism with the exercise of private judgment. Nevertheless, we repeat, they form the tissue of the daily life of a Protestant 'Church', as of the individual Protestant.

Doubtless, those avid of systematisation would account for
them as a mere survival in Protestantism from the Catholic past.
On this theory, the religious life of the Protestant parish, the
spiritual life of the individual, continue in spite, not because,
of Protestantism. The Protestant draws his spiritual life, not
from his fidelity to his principles, but from half forgetting them.
The Protestant 'churches' enjoy their vitality, not in virtue of
their Protestantism, but from possessing a few valuable remains
carried away, as if by an oversight, from the sanctuary they
abandoned.

Obviously, that line of reasoning could account for anything.
But consider the improbabilities such a theory entails.

Undoubtedly, Protestantism as currently practised includes
many discordant features left over from Catholicism. We are
not, however, concerned with incidentals, but with the normal
structure of Protestant worship and spirituality. If the distinctive principles of Protestantism are not confined to their
written exposition, we must make it our concern to detect and
grasp them in their application to life.

That is what we have done so far, but we can go further and
attain greater precision. The features we have sketched, so far
from becoming blurred according as a community or a private
individual aims at strict fidelity to the original spirit of the
Reformation, actually stand out more clearly. On the other
hand, they fade away or vanish altogether in those cases where
the Reformers are treated as ancestors to be venerated and subsequently ignored. Whenever Protestantism returns to its
original spirit, they recover their strength.

Protestants for whom their movement is merely rejection of
the Church's authority, the Reformation simply the first
triumph of the principle of private judgment, may certainly
extol the work of Luther and Calvin. Their action is analogous
to those historians of republican views who praise Richelieu and

Louis XIV for having paved the way for the Revolution in crushing the independence of the nobility and the Parlements. In other words, their commendation is consistent with a profound antipathy to the real aim of the Reformers. The latter, for their part, would not have hesitated to brand liberal Protestants, with characteristic force, as infamous heretics.

Among other types of Protestant, those who remained, or became anew, faithful to the guidance of Luther and Calvin exemplify best the kind of spirituality described above. Those who read these two writers in no carping or critical spirit, or, at any rate, those formed by ministers who look on the Reformers as leaders in thought and life, are, as a rule, the most closely modelled after the pattern described. For them Christ remains the Son of God made man, who died for our sins, and rose for our justification. They look on the Christian life as essentially a life of union with Christ by meditation on his words, by prayer, by obedience in faith and charity.

In the course of this work we shall examine, in all their complexity and diversity, the periodic movements of return to the first Reformers. At the moment, our task is to prove that the religious life whose outlines we have sketched is maintained or renewed with the same consistency.

To understand Protestantism, it is of the first importance to try to grasp the attitude of Protestants to their heroes, especially Luther. If we persist in confronting the Protestantism faithful to its forebears with the portrait painted by Catholic or sceptical historians, we will remain strangers to the soul of Protestantism. We shall fail to perceive, though it is essential, how Protestantism, for its authentic followers, is not, in the first place, a negation, but an affirmation, positive and Christian. In other words, how is it that, as we have shown, Protestants lead a real Christian life, not in spite, but because, of their Protestantism? To answer this question, we must start by seeing Luther with their eyes. Later we may criticise their view at leisure. But the first requirement is sufficient flexibility of mind to enable us to reach a deep understanding of what we wish fully to elucidate.

There is no question of making our own some sort of hagiographic interpretation of the Reformer, as was the fashion in Germany before Denifle's *Luther*, and as Felix Kunn's work still reflects. It is a typical mistake of Catholics to think that Protestants, particularly those most attached to their heritage, look on Luther as a saint. Their usual attitude is quite different. Luther is not looked on as a model in every detail of his life and teaching, but only in the manner in which, at a certain period of his life, he resolved a particular spiritual problem.

Let us see how the ordinary Protestant views this event. We need not detain ourselves with a long preliminary dissertation on the spiritual decline among people in general in early sixteenth-century Christendom. It was not only the humanists of the time (among them subsequent enemies of the Reformation), but also churchmen, even those most enamoured of tradition, who lamented the ignorance in an appalling number of Christians of the elementary doctrines of their faith. The great majority acted as if salvation depended on a mass of pious practices, regardless of the spirit in which they were performed, or even of their relation to the redemptive work of Christ.

In this connection, what interests us first about Luther is that, in the early part of his life, he was himself an outstanding instance of this disorientation, which yet was not incompatible with a real fervour and sincerity, both in his case and, no doubt, many others.

For Protestants on the whole, Luther, in his Erfurt days, is regarded neither as a religious genius nor, alternatively, as a wretched prey of concupiscence. He is simply a Christian, a monk very seriously concerned with his salvation, aware of his weaknesses, whose vivid awareness of his sins threatened to exclude all other religious sentiments. To bridge the gulf between his daily falls and the attainment of salvation, he saw no other means than his own strivings, whose weakness he felt so keenly. He longed for holiness, knowing that was the aim of the whole Christian life. He became a monk, seeing in the monastic state the most effective means to sanctity. Yet he was well aware that he was not a saint, but a sinner. The most common daily experience—there is no need to conjecture extraordinary vices, or even temptations—was enough to convince this fervent, scrupulous monk of the sad truth uttered by St. Paul: 'The good that I will I do not, the evil that I hate I do. . . . I delight in the law of God according to the inward man, but I see in my members another law contrary to the law of my mind which holds me captive.'[1] The tragedy was that he insisted on fighting against himself, as if he could triumph unaided; but the struggle only reinforced his conviction that he was powerless.

He had at his disposal any number of means to sanctification. All of these, however—prayer, fasting, monastic discipline, the Sacraments even, still more his own accumulation of petty devotions—he regarded merely as auxiliaries, or rather, stimulants, to his own will. There, precisely, is the point which he saw too vividly ever to forget—namely, that the powerlessness of the human will, in the matter of salvation, is not merely relative, but absolute. It is not that man lacks resources, even powerful ones, to strengthen his will so as to achieve salvation, it is his will which is purely and simply incapable. A feeble workman may achieve great effects with appropriate tools. In the hands of a dead man the most powerful machines are useless.

Luther's situation at this time was highly typical of the *impasse* to which a cramped spirituality was to lead so many. That explains why the exit he found was so generally adopted.

His first reaction was the semi-Pelagian, or even Pelagian, one of so many of his contemporaries confronted with their actual state of sin and the holiness which was their aim. He stands out from the rest only by his vivid awareness of the basic impotence of man, who was urged, none the less, or urged himself, in the words: 'Save thy soul,' or, at best, 'Heaven helps those who help themselves.'

We start, then, with an idea of salvation in which man is the chief agent, or at any rate an equal partner in association with God. Whether God's part is restricted to blessing the work accomplished by man, or whether he is associated with the work, man must always be capable of sustaining his part. The divine partner may crown the human achievement, even complete what is wanting; he cannot compensate for its total absence. Man is not saved; he saves himself, either alone or with the help of God.

Luther's experience had taught him that whatever success man may achieve in the physical and intellectual spheres, in that of

[1] Rom. VII, 19, 22–23.

eternal salvation he cannot succeed even partially; his failure must be total. On the high seas without boat or sail, whether the wind blows or not, one is equally helpless.

At this point the Catholic reader will be tempted to interrupt: surely the idea of salvation opposed by Luther is also condemned in principle by the Catholic faith. The very words Pelagianism and semi-Pelagianism indicate heresies that were summarised and condemned by Councils of the Church. Denifle had no difficulty in showing, as against Lutheran historians, that at the height of the Middle Ages Aquinas's doctrine of salvation was a clear and crushing refutation of these errors.

That is quite true, but the question needs to be pursued further. The salient characteristic of the early sixteenth century, with its nominalist theology (to be examined further on), was the complete collapse of the very principles on which St. Thomas had systematised the traditional teaching on the respective parts of God and man in the work of salvation. Once again, it is quite certain that the changed theology in which Luther had been educated accompanied, even reinforced, a striking change in the pattern of spirituality. In fact, nominalist theology won its victory in a world where religion seemed merely a matter of pious practices, prayers to recite, indulgences to be gained, relics to be venerated; and in all this people saw only acts to be done by man, supplemented, it might be, by the divine *concursus*, but only as a subsidiary.

In the eyes of Protestants, what characterised this period of Luther's life was his profound insight into man's incapability of any effective initiative towards salvation. Despair seemed unavoidable, unless some fresh factor emerged. This took the form of his reading the epistle to the Romans, on the advice or encouragement of his friend and Superior, Staupitz.

Unquestionably, with the lapse of time, Luther must have romanticised his discovery, more or less in good faith. It remains true, none the less, that his new view, to which this reading gave rise in the year 1513, changed his imminent despair to exultant joy. All his previous ideas were reversed, but his experiences remained valid; their fruit became embodied in another experience of a different order. In the course of working out his salvation as if it were the work of man merely crowned or completed by God, he came to see, in the brilliant light of evidence hitherto disregarded, that this salvation was, in fact, the work of God. He had sought to merit grace. He saw that if, as his experience had convinced him, this effort were vain, there was still no need for despair. This grace, far from having to be merited, was itself the only possible source of a merit which was not fictitious.

St. Thomas, it will be said, had never taught otherwise. Once again we reply that Luther had been trained on quite other than thomist lines. Till this moment all those parts of tradition and Scripture favourable to his new insight had been for him a dead letter, though he must have known them. If anyone is surprised at this, he has only to recall his own experience. We have all, at some time or other, had a sudden insight into the real meaning of expressions long familiar. We imagined, all the time, we understood them; but either our circumstances or our cast of mind blinded us to their profound significance.

The psychological process of this revolution in Luther's mind has been, and will ever be, a matter of endless examination. The fact remains that this phrase, 'The just man lives by faith', had abolished, once and for all, his Pelagian or semi-Pelagian idea of salvation, replacing it by one which gave the initiative to God alone. From now on, the antithesis between the 7th chapter of the epistle to the Romans, an exact picture of his own experience—'The good that I will I do not, the evil which I hate that I do'—and the 8th chapter of the same epistle—'Thanks be to God who has given me the victory in Christ Jesus'—threw a new light on the word 'grace', hitherto without effect on his heart and mind.

All historians of Luther's thought, both Catholic and Protestant, are bound to recognise that his whole conception of grace, though occasionally *simpliste*, is of considerable complexity. At the moment its details do not concern us; there can be no doubt what was its point of departure, its initial impulse. That was the positive certainty he at last attained that God, not ourselves, is the prime author of our salvation. Consequently, we have no call to be despondent at our powerlessness to save ourselves by our own exertions; for it is just to this powerlessness that the Gospel gives the answer. What we could not do, God, in Christ, has done for us.

A consequence, or, better, an implication, of capital importance seemed to him to follow of necessity. If we are not saved by ourselves, but by another, our immediate duty, in view of salvation, is to believe in him. Salvation is a grace, a gift of God, not the work of man. Therefore, man can be saved by faith in God the Saviour, and by this means *alone*.

How is this to be understood? It means, in the first place, that when Luther had reached the point of despairing of salvation—understandably, since he thought it had to be the fruit of his own efforts—faith came, not to deny the validity of his experience, but, while confirming it, to restore his lost confidence. This confidence, that had collapsed together with the human strength on which it mistakenly relied, now rested on the Almighty in person. The essential, for salvation, is to realise that God is its author, that it depends, not on one's own strength, but on God's. In this realisation, where a radical distrust of self is but the obverse of absolute confidence in God, consists faith; nothing else can possibly replace it.

In the next place, that faith *alone* saves us means, if it means anything, that we, on our part, have nothing to add to it, nothing outside or independent of it. Any such addition would result, of necessity, in a denial of the essential. For if, believing in principle in the saving action of God, we were obliged to add something of our own initiative, what would be the result? We would fall back at once into the impossible situation from which grace had rescued us; we would have to accomplish our salvation in part, in the hope that God would do the rest. But our actual state of wretchedness comes from our incapacity for any effective initiative, even incomplete, towards salvation; in short, we have not only to be assisted to save ourselves, we need to be saved.

In other words, either we are not saved by divine grace, acknowledged and accepted by faith, or this grace, which is in God, is the sole cause of our salvation, and faith, which is in us, the sole means of access to it. For if there is something needed for salvation which has a source other than grace received by faith, we are confronted again with the impossible task of the salvation of man by man. The Gospel, however, is the good news that someone else—God in Christ—has done for us what we could not do.

In the light of all this, we can understand the attachment of Protestants to Luther's rejection of salvation by faith and works. Later on we shall have to inquire into the ambiguity of this formula, both in its use by the Reformers and in Protestant tradition. What, in principle, it aims at rejecting is, alone, the idea that we have to add our personal quota that is something external to these two things, *grace which gives, and faith which receives.* Understood in this way, such an addition amounts to saying that we are saved neither by grace nor faith. Faith in divine grace would assure us that only a *part* of our salvation need no longer concern us. On the other hand, the insight of Luther, preserved in the type of Protestantism most faithful to its origins and most truly Christian, is that *all* is grace, and that, consequently, *all* in our salvation comes to us by faith. If this *all* is compromised, the very heart of Protestant spirituality is wounded mortally.

Here we reach the crucial point. Certainly it is permissible for the historian to discuss whether, as a matter of history, this is the correct interpretation of Luther. For our part, we hold that it does conform to his original and most significant phase. Even were it otherwise, the fact remains that, for the devout Protestant, this view expresses his sense of fidelity to his origins, a sense that Luther's experience is, we will not say a rule to follow (Luther is not looked on as an authority, as is a Doctor of the Church by Catholics), but a model to imitate.

At once we can see that Luther's view of salvation, so understood, is in perfect harmony with Catholic tradition, the great conciliar definitions on grace and salvation, and even with thomism. We shall have to return to this point for further elucidation; but we are entitled here to assert it with conviction, and to affirm that nothing could have countered so effectively the divagations of popular piety at the end of the Middle Ages, or those of nominalist theology—errors, we repeat, which at first infected Luther more than anyone.

It is only too true that the formula 'justification by faith

alone' was soon to take on aspects which we shall later
have occasion to examine and reprehend. What we insist
upon at the outset is the positive value it contributed to
Luther's religious development, as Protestants have always
understood him, a value in perfect accord with dogmatic
tradition.

A few years after its adoption by Luther, when its powerful
surge, first in an individual, then in a world equally chaotic, had
given rise to Protestantism, Melancthon drew up a systematic
statement of the essential tenets of the movement. It was he
who adopted the expression *sola gratia, sola fide* as the basic
principle of the Reformation. We must be quite clear on this
point—namely, that, if the various revivals in Protestantism are
invariably due to a return to the first Reformers, this is due to
the positive values which lie at the root of Luther's insight,
formulated into an axiom. Apart from these values, and their
presence in that first principle, the fact is unaccountable. There
lies the sole reason for the possession by Protestants of the kind
of spiritual life described above; it exists, not in spite of their
Protestant principles, but because of them—whatever objections
may be raised against other features to be found in the origin
of the Reformation.

However, to this basic, or material, principle Melancthon
added, as a necessary presupposition, what he called the formal
principle—namely, the supreme authority of Scripture. As is
implied by this quite appropriate distinction of formal and
material cause, the two are closely united, both on the plane of
fact and on that of ideas. For if, as Luther found out at Erfurt,
salvation is a grace, a pure gift to be received by faith, neither
our reason nor any human endeavour can attain in the realm of
thought what our will is powerless to reach in reality. Divine
revelation alone can make known to us the divine action; both
are equally gratuitous gifts.

In actual fact, as we have seen, it was through meditation on
Scripture, always looked on by Christians as the Word of God,
that Luther was led to his great discovery. It is easy to understand that neglect of Scripture—which either disappeared in
the medley of decadent scholasticism or, for the unlettered,
gave place to legends and popular devotions far remote from

revealed doctrine—accounts for that false idea of salvation which Luther, in the beginning, shared with so many others.

Herein lies the positive value contained, from the beginning, in the second Protestant principle: the supreme authority of the Bible. It signifies, primarily, a return to the essential. We can be saved because God has acted. We can believe in his action because he has spoken to us. It follows, easily and naturally, that the first impulse of the religious man should be to seek to know God's Word, to render it, not just an undefined respect, but the active worship due to it. Of this Word the Church is the guardian, set down in a book inspired, unvarying, yet impregnated with the life of its writers and of its divine subject. No other source has such an imperative claim.

Again, as in the case of the gratuitousness of salvation by faith, the original basis of this principle, so strongly felt, is undeniably positive. In the same way, whatever the role assigned to it by historical research into primitive Protestantism, the fact remains that the living Protestantism of our time sees here another link with its origins. And just as the expression *sola gratia, sola fide,* in the sense expounded, is nowise inconsistent with Catholic tradition, the assertion that Scripture, the Word of God, is invested with the authority of the Holy Ghost is quite in keeping with the status of the teaching Church; that, again, is one of the elementary doctrines of the Church. Consequently, the authors of the Confession of Augsburg could be, not merely in perfect good faith, but absolutely right— in broad outline, if not in detail—in concluding the positive part of their statement of principles with the words: *Haec fere summa est doctrinae apud nos, in qua cerni potest nihil inesse quod discrepet a scripturis, vel ab ecclesia catholica, vel ab ecclesia romana . . .*

The bald account we have given should suffice at least to show that it is no paradox, but simple logic, which serves to account for the fact we started with, and verifiable today: that Protestantism is Christian, not in its departure from the primitive and essential features of the Reformation, but in its adherence or return to them.

We will try to make this abundantly clear by a closer analysis of each of the two principles expressed by Melancthon:

justification by faith alone in divine grace alone, and the supreme authority of the Scriptures divinely inspired.

Once this fundamental truth is seen in a clear light, supported by indisputable facts and documents, we can approach our central problem: how was it that, starting from positive, orthodox, traditional principles, never abandoning them entirely, and periodically returning to them, the Reformation became something individualistic, heretical, and negative?

CHAPTER II

The Free Gift of Salvation

IT follows from what has been said that the true fundamental principle of Protestantism is the gratuitousness of salvation. In other words, salvation is not a work, or works, of man, but a grace, a pure gift from God, accessible to faith alone.

Melancthon was right in associating with this the principle of the supreme authority of Scripture, but it would be too pedantically logical to study this before the other. It is true that the Reformation, in its theological vindication, made the authority of the Bible, and its foundation, the *sola gratia,* a simple consequence of obedience to the divine word; but it is equally certain that it was Luther's religious intuition that illuminated his subsequent reading of the Bible, as it does still for Protestants. We shall only grasp their view of what is meant by fidelity to the word of God, when we have managed to penetrate the meaning of 'salvation by grace', or 'justification by faith'.

These two expressions, as is clear from what has been said, do not indicate two distinct principles, but two aspects of the same principle—the objective aspect being the gift of God; and the subjective the appropriation of the gift by man. None the less, the two aspects are not the same; though we may not separate them entirely, we have to study each in turn. Clearly, it is the first, objective, aspect that determines the second; so we begin with the study of the gratuitous nature of salvation. A later investigation into the part played in Protestantism by the faith through which salvation is appropriated will, moreover, bring to our notice a marked tendency, running through the whole course of Protestant history, to a separation, in effect, of 'grace' and 'faith'. In principle, however, they are intimately united, and it is quite certain that faith derives its content from grace, and not *vice versa.*

1. LUTHER AND THE *SOLA GRATIA*

Before anything else, we must subject the Protestant thesis, to which we have provisionally agreed, to a close examination and state our reasons for holding that. Luther's basic intuition was the gratuitousness of salvation, in the sense already explained.

Such a statement is called for because, as we have already indicated, there seems to be general agreement among Catholics, free-thinkers, and liberal Protestants in opposing this view, and assigning the most fundamental place to the principle of private judgment or, more generally, religious individualism.

We may remark that even those who disagree with our interpretation are bound to admit the obvious fact that the *sola gratia* is an important element in the original Lutheran creed. Yet in so doing they appear to regard it as merely a synonym or equivalent of salvation *without works*. For them, Luther, in teaching that we are saved by grace alone, meant simply that the works of piety which, in the traditional view, formed the fabric of Christian living were useless, contemptible, even harmful; that was its radical meaning. From discarding these chains as useless and stultifying he was led to reject their author, that organism of oppression, the Church. In this way we are always brought back to the conception of the Reformation which, to us, is a mere caricature, making it a simple movement of liberation, the escape of the individual from an authoritarian Christian society.

How can we tell what Luther's mind really was? He was by no means sparing in his accounts of his own early development. Leaving aside the question of his sincerity, much of what he tells us consists of recollections made in his old age, or at least in his late maturity; his view of the past is coloured accordingly. In consequence, the numerous studies based on these, influenced, in varying degree, by the views of their authors, have generally resulted in confirming their predilections. Many of them are not devoid of value, but they lead to no certain result.

There remain, however, two documents quite free from these objections, exempt from any preoccupation, whether apologetic or polemical. They do no more than express, with perfect spontaneity, Luther's state of mind at the moment he wrote them. It was precisely the moment when the great convictions which were to govern his life had just reached their highest pitch of lucidity and strength.

At the same time, while these documents bear the imprint of his personal experience, it is certain that they convey it just as it was given, with the least possible deformation. Their accuracy is vouched for by the end Luther had in view, an absolutely impersonal one. The first of these is the *Treatise on Christian Liberty*. In it he sets forth a programme for his followers, but it is certainly one he considers himself to have carried out. In the state in which he found himself after severe conflict, we can trace the outlines of his past condition, the crisis at last resolved. We perceive the past, not as Luther would have described it— he does nothing of the sort—but as it is implied by the present, whether he likes it or not.

The second of our texts is the *Great Catechism*, well known to be Luther's favourite; certainly the one most suited for providing for us in a single view, not every detail of his thought, but a survey of his considered account of Christianity. Here, better even than in the *Treatise on Christian Liberty*, the cate-chetical form, with its high objectivity, vouches for the authenticity of features revealed, almost in spite of itself, in the doctrine expounded with such absolute simplicity.

What is the first impression given by the *Treatise*? What, exactly, is this Christian liberty it sets before us? The Christian, we are told, is delivered from the yoke of the law, which, for Luther interpreting St. Paul, was the characteristic of the Old Testament. He is delivered from it by grace, the very heart of the New Testament.

Hear how Luther envisages this opposition and the deliverance which is its sequel. These are his words:

'. . . In the Scriptures, two things are to be distinguished— the commands and the promises. The former instruct us in the good; but it is a long way from being commanded to obey. They lay down what we are to do; they do not give us the power to do them. They reveal man to himself, convince him of his impotence for good, and lead him to despair of himself. They pertain to the Old Testament.

'Thus, the commandment which says, Thou shalt not covet, convicts us all of sin, since no one, however hard he try, can avoid concupiscence. This incapability of obeying the law of

B

God drives us to despair of ourselves and to seek in another the strength we lack. "Destruction is thy own, O Israel; thy help is only in me" (Osee, 13, 9).

'It is the same with the rest of the commandments; we cannot, in fact, keep a single one of them. When man realises his inability to rise to the height of what is commanded; when, in his distress, he looks for a means to fulfil this law which condemns him, no iota of which may be ignored, his eyes are opened to his meanness and nothingness; he finds within him nothing whereby to be justified and saved.

'At this point appear the promises of God. They form the second part of the teaching of Scripture, and show forth, in striking fashion, the glory of God. They are thus expressed: If you desire to fulfil the law and overcome concupiscence, believe in Jesus Christ, in whom you are offered grace, justice, peace and liberty. By faith, you possess all these; without it, you are a stranger to them all. What is impossible of attainment by the works of the law, so numerous and yet so ineffective, is easily accessible by faith, for to it the Father gives everything. The man of faith possesses all. "God has concluded all in unbelief, that he may have mercy on all" (Rom. XI, 32). The promise, therefore, gives all that the commandment demands, it accomplishes all that the law ordains. Both command and execution come from God alone; he orders and, at the same time, he fulfils. These promises make up the New Testament.' [1]

It is worth while examining these statements one by one. The text claims our close attention for two reasons. First, because, in setting forth the teaching of Scripture, and particularly what is definitely *new* in the New Testament, it places us, beyond doubt, at the central point of Luther's convictions. The liberation there described, which constitutes for him the essence of Christianity, is precisely the overt object of his reform, what he believed himself to have attained.

Secondly, the terms employed leave no room for ambiguity or false interpretations. It is especially significant that each

[1] Translated from the text quoted: *Le livre de la liberté chrétienne*, translated by Félix Kuhn, Paris, Fischbacher, 1879, pp. 29–31.

phase of the argument invites the use of those negative formulas of the customary interpretation of *sola gratia*, if that interpretation were the true one. In every case, however, we find he expresses himself in the most positive terms.

After such a vivid description of how the law shows that man is utterly powerless of himself, and the statement that this law is the Old Testament, we might expect Luther to view the New Testament, based on faith, as dispensing the believer from obligations now regarded as lapsed. If so, we would have failed to appreciate all the significance of the clause which says of this law that 'no single iota may be ignored'. Besides, no sooner does he mention the promises of the New Testament, in contrast with the precepts of the Old, than he describes them, in his opening phrase, as follows: '*If you desire to accomplish the law and overcome concupiscence*, believe in Jesus Christ . . .'

Even so, some may cavil at this and maintain that the function of faith is merely to silence the scruples of those who, in Luther's terms, 'desire to accomplish the law and overcome concupiscence', not by enabling them to do so, but by dispensing them from the necessity. They may argue that such is the sense of the following words: 'What is impossible to the works of the law, so numerous and ineffective, is easy to faith, for it receives all from the Father.' If so, let us see how Luther goes on to define the nature of this gift to faith. What do we find? 'The promise, therefore, gives what the law commands; it *accomplishes that which the law ordains*.' Then comes this sentence, which summarises better than we could the doctrine expounded in the previous chapter: 'The precept and its fulfilment come, then, from God alone; he who commands is, at the same time, he who performs.'

From the *Great Catechism*, too, we will cite only one passage, but of central and weighty significance. It comes from the beginning of the second part, which is a commentary on the Apostles' Creed, and its express purpose is to link this part to the first. Now the first part deals with the Decalogue. Consequently, we may expect to find there Luther's clearest formulation of his view of the relations between the Old and the New Testaments, between the law and justification by faith in grace alone. This is what he says:

'We have treated of the first part of Christian doctrine, the
law, which shows us all that God commands and forbids. We
now approach the second part, faith, which teaches us all we
may expect to receive from God; in other words, teaches us to
know it perfectly.' [1]

Then, without further transition, comes the capital definition
of salvation by faith.

'By it we *are enabled* to accomplish what we *are bound* [2] by
the law to do; for the latter is so high and of such range that no
human power is capable of keeping it. Consequently, it is
absolutely essential to teach faith, so as to know how we can
keep the law. For if, of our own strength, we could keep the ten
commandments as God exacts of us, we should need neither
Creed nor Prayer.' [3]

Is this not precisely the scheme we have already outlined?
Knowledge of God's demands; experience, confirmed by the
words of Scripture, of our powerlessness to meet them *of our
own strength*; acknowledgment by faith, of the gift of God—
that is to say, the discovery that *the force needed to effect what we
could not do of ourselves is given to us in Christ*.

The question is so important that we may be forgiven a
certain repetition. Before leaving these texts, the second in particular, we will recall the reasons for attributing to them an
authority hardly to be equalled. The *Catechism* does not come
from a period of transition, when Luther was still in search of a
doctrine; it belongs to a time when, if ever, he enjoyed perfect
mastery of his ideas. Nor is it something written to meet a particular emergency, when principles are liable to be deflected by
the circumstances and needs of the moment. We have in it,
rather, what may be called the 'master-work' for the spread of
Luther's gospel. Again we quote, not a subordinate section, but
the precise passage where he enters on the account of what, in his

[1] Translated from the text quoted: *Le Grand Catéchisme de Martin
Luther* (translator not named), Strasbourg, 1854, p. 97.
[2] Italics are not ours.
[3] He refers to the *Our Father*, which is commented on in the third part
of the catechism.

view, is the object of faith, and of what constitutes for him its entire value. Nothing could be clearer than his account; it is there for anyone to read.

The *Treatise on Christian Liberty* and the *Catechism* are both absolutely clear on the crucial point of Luther's teaching; their agreement is of particular significance in view of his fluctuations and inconsistencies in other writings. It seems, then, indisputable that the core, or the germ, of Lutheranism and of Protestantism in general lies in his insight as we have described it; the evidence is plain, however misunderstood by so many.

The texts quoted are important for the light they throw, not only on Luther and the origins of the Reformation, but also on all those Protestant sects which, at various times, used them as a court of appeal.

We all know that the *Commentary on the epistle to the Romans* had been forgotten until quite recently; his other commentaries, it is not too much to say, have been respected, rather than read, by pastors other than the erudite. That is still more the case with those controversial treatises occasioned by special circumstances, such as the *De Captivitate Babylonica* or the *De Servo Arbitrio*. By contrast, the *Treatise on Christian Liberty* has always been the classic work for traditional Protestant devotion, and the *Great Catechism* one of the chief sources of orthodox Protestant teaching.

All this accounts for the apparent paradox we have noted— namely, that those Protestants whose ideas in practice are remotest from the Protestantism described by Catholic controversialists, free thinkers, or liberal Protestants are, in fact, those who pride themselves, with good reason, on their fidelity to the first Reformers.

2. *SOLA GRATIA* IN PROTESTANT SPIRITUALITY

Luther's original conception is the basis of the real spiritual life of Protestantism; this is supported by a mass of evidence of all kinds. Its devotional literature, especially its hymns, the lives of persons acknowledged as its authentic exponents, its methods of education and spiritual training, all lead to the same conclusion.

All through the centuries we find the spiritual life of Protestants formulated and sustained by writings of all kinds, such as we find in every Christian community. The mode of devotional expression generally preferred, particularly in the Lutheran countries (Germany and Scandinavia) and the Anglo-Saxon ones, is the popular hymn. As a rule, the hymns are suited equally to public and private devotion. They are based on the Lutheran chorale, considered by historians of the Reformation as one of the greatest, if not the greatest, of the devotional creations of Lutheranism. Actually, the chorale originated long before the Reformation. Latin hymns on their first appearance, in the time of St. Ambrose and St. Hilary (they were only later incorporated in the Roman liturgy), were analogous to the chorale both in structure and purpose. They met the same need for a simple rhythmical chant which should express in popular language sentiments suited to the private devotion of all, as well as appropriate to the use of congregations. In the Middle Ages the Sequences served the same purpose; the same period saw, in German-speaking countries, an abundant crop of vernacular hymns. We may compare the Italian or Provençal *laudes*, particularly those of St. Francis.

This kind of popular chant, strongly encouraged by the example of Luther, very soon occupied an important place in Protestant worship. Quite a number of his compositions were taken from old Catholic hymns. Others were his own creations, the most famous being *Ein fest' Burg ist unser Gott*.

This has always been far the most popular hymn wherever the Reformation penetrated. It is, so to speak, the battle-cry of Protestantism; very few hymns express so directly and powerfully the truths dear to the heart of the devout Protestant. Historians have discussed at length the identity of the enemies primarily envisaged by Luther. Were they the Catholic princes who opposed the Protestant Schmalkaldic League? Or, more probably, the Turks approaching the walls of Vienna? Whoever they were, the great majority of Protestants have always looked on them as Catholics do the enemies of the Psalmist. The point is that this hymn, so much the most popular, expresses precisely the positive view of the *sola gratia* above described. It conveys the feeling of man's powerlessness, left to himself, and of his faith in the omnipotence of God, who, in the words of St. Paul, works, by Christ, his strength in our weakness. Here is the version by Thomas Carlyle.

> *A safe stronghold our God is still,*
> *A trusty shield and weapon;*
> *He'll help us clear from all the ill*
> *That hath us now o'ertaken.*
> > *The ancient prince of hell*
> > *Hath risen with purpose fell;*
> > *Strong mail of craft and power*
> > *He weareth in this hour;*
> > *On earth is not his fellow.*

> *With force of arms we nothing can,*
> *Full soon were we down-ridden;*
> *But for us fights the proper Man,*
> *Whom God himself hath bidden.*
> > *Ask ye, who is this same?*
> > *Christ Jesus is his name,*
> > *The Lord Sabaoth's Son;*
> > *He and no other one*
> > *Shall conquer in the battle.*

> *And were this world all devils o'er,*
> *And watching to devour us,*
> *We lay it not to heart so sore;*
> *Not they can overpower us.*
> > *And let the prince of ill*
> > *Look grim as e'er he will,*
> > *He harms us not a whit;*
> > *For why his doom is writ;*
> > *A word shall quickly slay him.*

> *God's word, for all their craft and force,*
> *One moment will not linger,*
> *But, spite of hell, shall have its course;*
> *'Tis written by his finger.*

> *And though they take our life,*
> *Goods, honour, children, wife,*
> *Yet is their profit small;*
> *These things shall vanish all:*
> *The City of God remaineth.*

The devil's power unleashed against the Christian is a frequent subject of Luther's, one of those which link him, through the Middle Ages and St. Gregory the Great, with the patristic tradition. This hymn has no trace of superstitious terror; its most striking feature is the virile, joyful defiance of the Christian sustained by faith. This faith is contained, we might say personified, in the triumphant Christ, the great conqueror whose power is all the more strikingly shown by the accumulated might of sin and death. It ends with the assurance that the Word which is Christ himself, the creative and saving Word, will finally triumph.

This hymn, admirable in its joy and hope, at once humble and triumphant, is an exact counterpart, lyrically, to the commentary of the *Little Catechism*, written by Luther for children, on the second article of the Creed:

'I believe that Jesus Christ is not only truly God, born of the Father from all eternity, but also truly man, born of the Virgin Mary; that he is my Lord, and has delivered and redeemed me from all my sins, from death, and slavery to the devil, after I had been lost and damned. He has truly bought me, not with silver and gold, but with his precious blood, his sufferings, and his innocent death, that I may belong entirely to him, and, living under his rule, I may serve him in justice, innocence, and eternal happiness; as he, risen from the dead, lives and reigns for ever and ever. This I firmly believe.'

The two texts we have selected for quotation are in most frequent use among Lutherans; they are the clearest expression of the exultant sense of liberation and religious vitality characteristic of the best Lutheran devotion; they recall the spirit of the early Church. The same principle underlies them both;

namely, that grace is all; a principle accepted by those writers who were most effective in reinvigorating Protestant devotion.

Let us consider German hymnody from this aspect. After Luther, the two most important writers are Paul Gerhardt and Tersteegen. They differ from each other as much as they differ from Luther; but at the heart of their personal devotion and poetry we find the same religious intuition.

Gerhardt (1607–1677) wrote a number of hymns which, in their evangelical simplicity, their joyful, almost childish, serenity, are in marked contrast with the turbulent period of their composition. They have achieved immense popularity in German-speaking countries. The most celebrated, deservedly so, is the *O Haupt voll Blut und Wunden,* a free version of St. Bernard's *Salve caput cruentatum.* Bach used it as the centre of his St. Matthew Passion; in France it is known in the adapted form *Chef couvert de blessures,* sung in all Protestant churches on Good Friday. The most popular of Gerhardt's original works among German Protestants is certainly his *Befiehl du deine Wege.* The circumstances of its composition, more or less embellished by legend, are worth recalling; they convey admirably the reason why this hymn is especially dear to Protestant devotion.

Paul Gerhardt, a native of Saxony, had been appointed pastor of the Church of St. Nicolas in Berlin. A few years later he refused to agree to the fusion, ordered by the Great Elector Frederick William, of the Lutheran with the Reformed (more or less Calvinist) Church, and had to go into exile. Deprived of his office and not knowing where to go, after a day's journey he arrived at an inn, where his wife, who was with him, had an acute attack of despondency. Gerhardt gently comforted her, repeating the verse of Psalm 37: 'Commit thy way to the Lord, and trust in him; and he will do it.' Then he went out into the garden, and composed these lines:

> *Put thou thy trust in God,*
> *In duty's path go on;*
> *Walk in his strength with faith and hope,*
> *So shall thy work be done.*

Give to the winds thy fears;
Hope, and be undismayed;
God hears thy sighs and counts thy tears,
God shall lift up thy head.

Who points the clouds their course,
Whom winds and sea obey,
He shall direct thy wandering feet,
He shall prepare thy way.

Leave to his sovereign sway
To choose and to command;
So shalt thou wondering own his way,
How wise, how strong his hand.

Let us, in life and death,
His steadfast truth declare,
And publish, with our latest breath,
His love and guardian care.

(Translation by John Wesley)

The account goes on to say that, while reading the last verse, Gerhardt was met by messengers from the Duke of Mersebourg, who had come to the inn to offer him the parish of Lusace, where he was to end his days in peace.[1]

It is deeply moving to discover in this idyll, dramatic if a little smug, the same sturdy conviction of the battle-cry of *Ein fest' Burg*.

Tersteegen (1697–1769), of Westphalia, was a different kind of person altogether. He belonged to the pietistic revival inaugurated by Gerhardt; we shall have more to say of it later. However, he was one of those who are not to be confined within the limits of a school. His life, more than any other, proves that Protestantism contains a very real vein of mysticism. He lived, in accordance with the evangelical ideal, by manual work; his trade was weaving. He lived a solitary, severely ascetic life, alternating with periods of light and darkness. He wrote in his

[1] On this subject, see G. Tournier, *A travers l'Allemagne religieuse*, Paris, 1912, pp. 158 and following.

blood, one Wednesday in Holy Week, an act of consecration to Christ, which clearly echoes some of the phrases of the catechism already quoted, and expresses the aspiration of the soul to sanctity in most moving terms:

'O my Jesus, I consecrate myself to thee, my only Saviour, my Spouse, Jesus Christ, to belong to thee completely and for eternity. I renounce from today, with all my heart, all the rights and powers to myself unjustly given me by Satan; for thou hast bought me by thy agony, thy conflicts, thy sweat of blood in Gethsemani; for me thou hast broken the gates of hell, and opened thy Father's loving heart. From now on, may my whole heart and love be given to thee in return; from this moment and for all eternity, may thy will, not mine, be done. Command me, rule me, reign in me. I give thee all power over myself, and I promise, with thy help, to shed my last drop of blood sooner than disobey thee deliberately or be faithless to thee. I give myself entirely to thee, dear friend of my soul, I desire to be fixed in thee for ever. May thy Spirit never leave me; may thy mortal agony be ever my support. Amen; may thy Spirit seal what, in all simplicity, thy unworthy slave here promises, Gerhardt Tersteegen.'

To this soul, essentially mystical, the *sola gratia* takes the form of the absolute sufficiency of God, who gives himself to it. The whole scope of its prayer is eternal union with God, exemplified in the famous pilgrim's hymn, *Kommt, Brüder, lasst uns gehen*. A foretaste of this union, in this life, is expressed in the hymn to the Spirit of life, as it were the *Veni Creator* of Protestantism, *O Gott, O Geist, O Licht des Lebens.* . . .

> *Oh God, Oh Spirit, Light of life,*
> *Light us in the shade of death.* . . .

At the approach of his own death he used words more expressive even than his poems of the genuinely mystical sense of the *sola gratia*, both for himself and, through his influence, for so many others: 'Poor, wretched Lazarus that you are! Yet the angels themselves are not ashamed to bear you away!'

A short time before, he had said that God, depriving him of all his powers, one by one, was like a mother undressing her child for the night, before it abandons itself to rest in her arms.[1]

The English Protestant hymns are no less important than the German, though as a rule vastly inferior in literary merit. They mostly belong to the Wesleyan revival, whereas the German owe their existence to the genius of Luther, equally great in the literary and the religious spheres; and it is unquestionable that, whatever its religious importance and value, Methodism as a cultural movement cuts a sorry figure by the side of the old Lutheranism.

Later on in this work we shall come to investigate more closely the English revival, so important in the history of Protestantism. Here it is enough to note that, in the course of the rationalistic and deistic movement of the eighteenth century, it appeared as a popular movement of return to an ardent devotion to the person of Christ. It originated with the great John Wesley. He was himself strongly possessed by the doctrine of salvation by grace alone, and, through his dynamic temperament, this doctrine gained a marvellous increase of vitality. At the same time, as we shall see, he set it in a new light.

John Wesley was the author of a number of hymns; but it was his brother Charles who, in his numerous compositions, was the first to set forth the revived Lutheran doctrine in even clearer relief than the German hymn-writers. This is of especial significance as the Wesleyan revival was to spread to the Continent early in the nineteenth century, to France and Switzerland in particular, countries ravaged by Deism. It was the cause of the rejuvenation of Protestantism there, which otherwise would almost certainly have died of the disease of rationalism.

We will look at some of the most popular and typical hymns of Charles Wesley. The first to be quoted is a tissue of Lutheran allusions expressed almost word for word. It contains practically all the words whose ambiguity lays them open to the most negative interpretation of Luther's doctrine. The hymn itself, however, explains them so exactly that there can be no doubt that they were understood in quite the opposite sense

[1] *Cf.* G. Tournier, *op. cit.*, pp. 225 and following.

both by the Wesleyans and all the Protestants who drew thence their inspiration.

It begins with the lines:

> *Jesus, lover of my soul,*
> *Let me to thy bosom fly.*

The last two verses, however, are the most significant:

> *Thou, Oh Christ, art all I want;*
> *More than all in thee I find:*
> Raise the fallen, cheer the faint,
> *Heal the sick and lead the blind.*
> Just and holy is thy name;
> *I am all unrighteousness;*
> False and full of sin I am,
> *Thou art true and full of grace.*
>
> Plenteous grace with thee is found,
> *Grace to cover all my sin . . .*

The verses in roman type are, as it were, a *résumé* of those celebrated passages of Luther which might lead us to think that salvation by grace meant exclusively or chiefly liberation from the Christian duty of personal sanctification. His sins 'covered', once and for all, by the works of Christ, his own might be thought superfluous. His faith in grace would be all-sufficient, whatever the traditional view of the need of works might be. In this way, the holiness of Christ would cover the sinner as with a cloak; it would not change him.

None the less, this is not what Wesley meant by salvation through grace, not even by the passages patient of such an interpretation. The verses immediately following are decisive on this point.

> *Let the healing stream abound:*
> *Make and keep me pure within.*
> *Thou of life the fountain art;*
> *Freely let me take of thee,*
> *Spring thou up within my heart,*
> *Rise to all eternity.*

In this form of Protestantism the grace of God in Christ is, certainly, everything. But this grace is viewed in the most orthodox light; it is a power transforming our whole life and being, not a substitute for this change.

Equally decisive, from beginning to end, is another hymn, as popular as the first, of Charles Wesley. We see in it the battle-similes of *Ein fest' Burg* as well as obvious allusions to St. Paul:

> *Soldiers of Christ, arise*
> *And put your armour on,*
> *Strong in the strength which God supplies,*
> *Through his eternal Son;*
>
> *Strong in the Lord of Hosts,*
> *And in his mighty power;*
> *Who in the strength of Jesus trusts*
> *Is more than conqueror.*
>
> *Stand then in his great might,*
> *With all his strength endued;*
> *And take, to arm you for the fight,*
> *The panoply of God.*

Then follows a passage whose meaning is as clear as could be desired:

> *From strength to strength go on,*
> *Wrestle and fight and pray;*
> *Tread all the powers of darkness down,*
> *And win the well-fought day.*
>
> *That, having all things done*
> *And all your conflicts past,*
> *You may o'ercome through Christ alone,*
> *And stand entire at last.*

Nowhere could be found more definitely stated the doctrine of salvation by grace alone in Christ. At the same time, in perfect consistency with that, this hymn embodies, without the least distortion, the traditional idea of salvation and of the Christian life.

The influence of these hymns has been enormous. Both German and English, in spite of their characteristic differences, agree strikingly in their teaching; they are the basis for all the modern Protestant collections. Now, the French *Recueil de cantiques*, the Scandinavian *Salmbok*, in the same way as the German *Gesangbuch* and the English Hymn Book, serve both for the public worship and the private devotions of Protestants. They form, in practice, the principal commentary on Scripture and a synthesis of its teaching. In consequence, they are unparalleled in their influence on the faith and life of the faithful in general.

Their effect on Protestantism as a living system is easy to deduce. It is confirmed by the study of what may be called the spiritual technique, or religious training, of Protestantism.

The first thing to be emphasised about this technique or training is that, by the very nature of things, it is the centre of the specifically Protestant religious life. Neither the teachings of authority, nor the liturgy with its Sacraments, have the importance for Protestants that they have for Catholics. Some Protestant communities are exceptional. Certain Lutheran churches, in Scandinavia or Germany, give a prominent place to the liturgy, an emphasis it has recovered in the Anglo-Catholicism of the past hundred years. These, however, are merely instances of the survival, or rediscovery, of parts of Catholicism. The same applies to their firm grasp of doctrine shared by some Calvinist communities; they are not typical of Protestantism. The essentially Protestant feature, shared by these churches with others which have no such preoccupation, is a special mode of religious training, a distinctive spiritual culture.

What constitutes the essential unity of Protestantism is its emphasis on the interior aspect of faith and worship; this emphasis is found even in those churches where external ceremonial and dogmatic formulas are prominent. All Protestants, as such, view sacrifice, worship, the mysterious relationship between God and man, as significant only in relation to the individual soul. The entire exterior side of religion has no other end than the interior life of the person. This is such a universal and typical feature of Protestantism that it will call for special treatment when we come to consider the subjective aspect of 'justification by faith'. Here we have simply to mark the fact and its significance. The devout Protestant either discounts altogether the idea of a priesthood, or of the external priestly function, or else relegates it to a subordinate place; he does this, not because he rejects the idea of consecration in religion, but on the ground that every Christian ought to be a priest in the secret sanctuary of conscience, the sole place of 'worship in spirit and truth'. We will not enter here on a discussion of this idea in itself. Our reason for mentioning it is that it explains the overriding importance, in Protestantism, of all that goes to form the religious conscience. There alone can we hope to discover the very essence of the Protestant religion.

On what grounds does Protestantism justify its emphasis on the 'interior' aspect of religion? It holds that man must be deprived of every human support, real or illusory. The believer must be brought, solitary, face to face with grace, that he may come to rest on God and on him alone.

We are not concerned now either to defend or criticise this view; we simply state the Protestant position. All the externals of religion, says the Protestant, whether we reduce them to the minimum, as is the usual practice, or whether their use is accentuated, as with some of us, whom we consider liable to lapse into Catholicism, are designed precisely to enable us to do without them. All authentic Christianity aims at bringing man to renounce all that is human, to find his sole support in God. This is the object of all our observances, in so far as we admit them: to set man in the presence of God, and to leave him there alone.

If we study the methods, and, at a deeper level, the tendencies, of Protestant spirituality, we will soon see that this is the end they envisage.

The reading and pondering of Scripture is the chief act of Protestant devotion. The reason is that the Protestant is convinced that God speaks to him directly in the words of Scripture, instructing him what to do, and making known His promises, without the obscuring effect of any intervening medium. He makes known His will and how he is to fulfil it, just as we have seen outlined in the *Treatise on Christian Liberty* and the *Great Catechism*. For the same reason, private and personal prayer is insisted on as the practice next in importance. By this means the soul sets forth all its needs to its Creator, and relies entirely on him to satisfy them.

The ideal cherished by all Protestant spiritual writers, and constantly urged by zealous ministers on their flocks, is the same as that portrayed by all the artists of the Reformation. We find the subject everywhere, from Dürer or Rembrandt to the most insipid productions of Burnand, the chief representative of what might be called the Protestant St. Sulpice. It is to be seen in nearly all Protestant homes; it is the most complete and eloquent expression of the essence of Protestant devotion. We allude, of course, to the picture of a man or woman praying, after the day's work, before an open Bible. Listening to God speaking in the Bible, answering him in prayer: 'From thee I await the strength to do thy will, as thy word has revealed it to me': there is the best possible summary of Protestant teaching. The life envisaged by Protestantism, and which justifies its existence, is one of obedience to God, who, in his turn, provides all the means to it, as long as we ask him for them on the sole ground of his promises.

From this it appears that gratuitous salvation, as we understand it, is no abstract principle, but the living centre of Protestantism.

All this is reinforced by the biographical literature of Protestantism, equal, as it doubtless is, in volume to that of Catholicism in modern times.

Throughout we find the same concern for the essential feature of Protestantism. This is the bond of union linking the various types of spirituality, the pietism of Arndt or Spener to the traditional Lutheranism of Löhe or Kliefoth; the conservative Anglicanism of Jeremy Taylor to the Methodism of Wesley; the Calvinist Evangelicalism of Adolphe Monod to the Lutheran Evangelicalism of Louis Meyer, and a popular preacher like Felix Neff to a thinker, perhaps over-subtle, like Alexander Vinet. They all agree perfectly in their essential attitude, however various the courses they pursue.

Of course, there are no saints, formally declared such, in

Protestantism. Protestants, for the most part, prefer it so, looking on canonisation as setting man in the place of God. That does not mean that in their eyes the ideal has not been, in a very high degree, realised by individuals, whose lives remain an inspiration to others. In fact, the spiritual biography is a form of reading as common with the devout Protestant as with the Catholic. Such works are innumerable. We have only to take them at random, and we will be struck by their agreement on the central point among their incidental differences.

Confining ourselves to French Protestantism, we will consider two examples of those 'servants of God' who are representative of the loftiest ideals of the two great non-Catholic spiritual groups of France. The two ministers, Adolphe Monod and Louis Meyer, already mentioned, stand out as perhaps the two most distinguished members, in the spiritual sphere, of the Reformed Church and the Lutheran Church in the nineteenth century. The pastoral activity of each covered a wide area. The fame of Adolphe Monod is due, above all, to his preaching, whose quality entitles him to the highest rank among Protestant preachers of any time. But his influence over others derives in even greater measure from a small book of his, one of the purest gems of the Protestant religion, and an inspiration to souls without number.

We refer to the book published by his friends after his death, *Les Adieux d'Adolphe Monod*, a simple and unpretentious work written in circumstances of exceptional interest.

Suffering from what he knew to be a mortal disease, Adolphe Monod used to gather together, Sunday by Sunday, a few of his friends, who met in his bedroom. As long as his strength lasted he desired to communicate to them his most intimate feelings, which seemed daily to grow in depth with his sufferings and the approach of death. These last words of his were written down by their hearers; and so we are enabled to follow, step by step, the progress of his thought as he approached the term for which his whole life had been a preparation, the end he eagerly embraced as he felt the imminence of death.

The truth he witnessed to as he lay dying, expressed with increasing lucidity, is all contained in the words of St. Paul: 'I can do all things in him who strengtheneth me.' In other words, the most categorical assertion of the nullity of human power before God, and of the complete sufficiency of grace, not as absolving from the necessity of effort and suffering, but as the power of God acting in the extremes of human weakness. In various places we find him repudiating the Catholic doctrine of the value of man's suffering for his salvation. But, as we have already pointed out in connection with declarations of that sort from the Protestant pulpit, he evidently misunderstood what is meant by the meritorious or expiatory character of suffering. Consequently, these passages only serve to bring out more strikingly the decisive character of what he goes on to say; namely, that the suffering of the Christian, though powerless of itself, when accepted in union with Christ becomes, through grace, all-powerful, and opens the gates of eternity to the dying. At the same time as he asserts uncompromisingly the doctrine of salvation by grace alone received by faith, he rejects, with no less decision, any idea that this salvation and grace remain external to the believer. Adolphe Monod's experience, purified to the utmost by his sufferings, was that salvation by grace meant the transformation of our sufferings and conflicts into those of Christ, so that the triumph of the Cross might become ours.

Here, grace is all, but not by a kind of legal fiction which dispenses us from action in consideration of our belief. It is an irresistible power set in action by Christ within those who give themselves to him without reserve. Consequently, in spite of their nothingness, more vividly felt than ever, Christ creates in them the new man who is renewed day by day in his own image.

Here is a passage on the sufferings of Christ and the Christian. Monod is careful to avoid any expression which would seem to weigh man's contribution over against that of God in Christ; all the more keenly transpires his intense conviction that the power of God manifested in the Cross of the Saviour must totally transform the weakness of those to be redeemed.

'Why did Christ suffer? To atone for sin. We see, then, that it is right that suffering should follow on sin. We ourselves cannot bear the weight of the sufferings of Christ; we shall be happy if, in a spirit of expiation and to satisfy justice, we carry our share. "Why should mortal man despair on account of his sins?" This passage of St. Peter, "Be you armed with this thought that, Christ having suffered in the flesh, he who has suffered in the flesh has ceased from sin", shows that, to break free from sin, we have to suffer. Sin and suffering must confront one another in each of us personally and of our own will, and suffering applied to the destruction in us of sin, not to atone for sin—this was done by Christ—but to teach us to unite suffering with sin, and to unite joy with sanctification and liberation. The thought that suffering is the fruit of sin is one that should strengthen us; it shows us suffering as a simple and natural way which neither can nor should be spared us.

'After all, why did Christ suffer in expiation of sin? It was to save us and to make us participants in eternal glory; that was his dominant thought in his Passion. Well then, our suffering has to be loving, not selfish, not turning our attention back on to ourselves, but turning it to God for his glory, and then to our neighbour for his good. There is a wealth of charity and its fruits in Christian suffering, by the example to be given by the sufferer, the patience God gives him to bear them. How comforting and heavenly is the thought that, in suffering, we can be of use to others, especially our brethren! What could make our sufferings more like Christ's? St. Paul meant this, when he said, in a passage I am fond of quoting, "I fill up in my flesh what is wanting in the sufferings of Christ for his body, which is the Church." This verse has its difficulties; I will not go into their explanation now. Certainly, St. Paul was far from thinking of expiatory suffering. He joined his sufferings with those of the Saviour, and, because he suffered to save us, St. Paul also suffers for the good of mankind. As he wrote to Timothy, "If thou dost these things, thou shalt save both thyself and those who hear thee."

'This is what supports the Christian in suffering. Jesus Christ suffered; the more I suffer, the more I shall resemble him; suffering is a privilege. Christ suffered for our sins; suffering is a necessary, a salutary fruit of sin. Finally, Christ suffered for our salvation; I must suffer to do good to men and to bring souls captive to the obedience of the Cross. Let all those who suffer make it their endeavour to go out of themselves, to put aside egoism in their suffering, which deprives it of faith, love, and also consolation, and to enter fully into the love of Christ; then their pain too will be as a cross set up on the earth, shelter-ing all in their neighbourhood, not in order to give them eternal life, but to show them the way that leads there, to the glory of God.' [1]

This passage conveys well the atmosphere of these last con-versations, so charged with suffering and, at the same time, joy. The next one expresses most movingly the all-sufficiency of Christ for the believer. It shows how the life of faith in the grace given through Christ develops, in persons of holiness, into a mystical identification with Christ; which implies, not a legal substitution of Christ for the believer, but the penetration of his life and being with those of Christ. Once again this comes out most strikingly through Monod's insistence on the complete rejection of whatever power might be attributed to man of adding to what God gives him in Christ.

'From time to time, we are inclined to imagine Christ as merely opening to us the gates of Heaven, and leaving us to enter by our own efforts. That would be to take a far too narrow view of what Our Lord has done, what he is, for us. St. Paul's view was a more lofty one: "I desired, when I was among you, to know nothing else but Jesus Christ, and him crucified." For him, God is completely contained in Christ, and Christ in the cross. Again he writes: "He has been made for us in God wisdom, justice, sanctification and redemption." So we see that Christ is not given to us just to wipe out our sins by shedding his blood once and for all, but, once we are reconciled to God by his blood, to guide us, to sanctify us, to fill us with wisdom, to work all in all. Once more: "All the fulness of the Godhead dwells in him corporeally." God dwells in Christ in the flesh, in a visible manner, but he dwells in him wholly, with all his glory and eternal perfections. Here is another passage, equally pro-found, of the same apostle: "All things are yours, and you are Christ's, and Christ is God's." It shows us God as head of a wonderful, an admirable, hierarchy, the whole organism of

---

[1] *Les Adieux d'Adolphe Monod*, Paris, 1929, pp. 76–78.

divine truth; he sends his Son, brings him to us. The Son, in his turn, calls and adopts us, that, in his name, we may have dominion over all things, that we may possess the entire universe by right of being members of him to whom the whole universe is subject. "All things are yours": this is the first degree; "you are Christ's": this is the second; "Christ is God's", first and last degree, that is, the supreme degree to which all the rest are attached and on which they depend.

'How greatly this differs from the view of Christ accomplishing but a single act, the principal act of our salvation! Jesus Christ is the God of man, as Pascal said so well in a passage where he treats, in a deeply Christian sense, of the place Christ holds between God and us. He is the God of man, the God who gave himself to us. He gave himself entirely and, once we possess Christ by real faith, we possess no less than God himself, and eternal life in him. "He who has the Son has life . . . God has given us eternal life, and this life is in his Son." So, whatever need of our souls, or, indeed of our whole life, here or in eternity, craves satisfaction, we find it in Christ. Is it a question of blotting out our sins? He has done that by his blood. There is in the world only one thing that blots out sin, neither our penances, our contrition, our alms, our good deeds, not even our prayers, but the blood of Christ: "It purifies us from all sin." Every sin covered by the blood of Christ is for ever annihilated before God. God himself sees it no longer. I could use much stronger words without departing from Scripture. "God himself," says one of the prophets, "seeks them, and finds them no more . . . He has cast our sins behind his back", so as to see them no more. "He has hurled them to the depths of the sea"; and, regarding us in Christ, he sees us as without sin like Christ himself, who "was made sin for us that we might be made the justice of God in him".

'Whether it concerns life and wisdom, strength and resistance to sin, this world or the other, all is in Christ; having Christ, we possess all things, but, deprived of him, we have absolutely nothing. . . . Am I poor? All the wealth of this world is mine; it belongs to Christ, who is God, who is able to give me, with him and beside him, all the wealth of the earth if it could be of use to me. If he gives me poverty instead of riches, it is because that is better for me; it is the result of God's choice. The whole world, all its honour and power are mine, for they belong to my `Father. He would give me them tomorrow, and could do so today, if it were good for me, for he can do with them as he likes. Am I ill? Health is mine, strength is mine, comfort and ease are mine, absolute enjoyment of all the good things of life are mine, for all these belong to Christ, and he belongs to God and disposes of them as he pleases. Whom would he use them for, if not for me, his child? So, if he refuses them today, for a fleeting moment gone as quickly as a weaver's shuttle, he has his reasons; these pains and anguish hide in themselves blessings of greater worth to me than the health so much prized and the ease so agreeable. If he withholds any thing, it is always to give me a better; that is my consolation, it is all contained in his love. Is it a question of wisdom and enlightenment? All right; were I to remain an ignoramus all my life, without any chance of cultivating my mind in this world, I would still be learned in Christ. With the knowledge of Christ, I have more insight, more penetration, into the things of God that any man in the world who has spent a life-time over his books; for I know the eternal, uncreated light to which he is a stranger, the light in which God himself rejoices, my unerring guide in all the dark places of life. I challenge you to think of anything of which I cannot say that it is my Father's, therefore it is mine; that, if he refuses it today, he will give it me tomorrow; so I commit myself to his love. All is mine, if I am Christ's.' [1]

We find exactly the same in the life of Louis Meyer. He was better known as a spiritual director than as a preacher, and he had an unparalleled influence on the whole life of the Lutheran Church in Paris. It is not going too far to say that he transfigured all the works he found already in existence; in particular, he informed with his spirit the greater part of those who, along with him, devoted themselves thereto. In addition to the biography written by one of his sons, of special value for its quotations from his journal and correspondence, numerous extracts from his letters have been published, where, quite unconsciously, he reflects and portrays his own spirit. On reading

[1] *Les Adieux d'Adolphe Monod*, Paris, 1929, pp. 196–201.

these, particularly the most personal ones—those not intended for publication, and so manifesting his interior life quite simply and plainly—we are struck by the strictness of his ascetical teaching. There are few spiritual writers who seem so unremittingly concerned for perfection, whether he is engaged with uprooting the slightest sins by dint of prayer and ceaseless mortification, or with continually fostering the flame of charity, kindled at the very heart of Christ.

None the less, he insists, more strongly than any other Lutheran teacher, on the necessity of viewing the doctrine of salvation by faith in divine grace alone as the source of all the rest. This implies no contradiction; it only shows, in the most striking way, how significant is this doctrine for the Protestant life of faith. The following passage, chosen from a number of similar ones, expresses perfectly his ideas:

'If Christ's cross and his triumph are to live in us, we must live in him. If we are to have the power of following his example and keeping his word, we must follow, too, his interior voice, the voice of his Holy Spirit within us. By this Spirit Jesus calls us, reproves us, consoles us, regenerates us. This divine Spirit alone gives us true repentance, the faith that justifies, the peace that remains. He it is who unites us to Christ and teaches us to love him, not with all our strength, but with all the strength of God.' [1]

We see that, for him as for Monod, it is always grace alone that gives salvation, but grace conceived as the sole means whereby our efforts are fruitful of life, for by it alone we are reborn. They are at one, especially, in attributing salvation to the cross of Christ, not as dispensing us from the need for toil and suffering, but as giving us the power to support them. 'Suffering is the only good in this world. The cross detaches us from visible things, and turns us to the invisible. Everything must become bitter to us, even our dreams of happiness, all that on which we set our hopes of joy and repose. Only then are we ripe for heaven.' So he wrote to a former catechumen in one of the last

---

[1] *Le Devoir du Chrétien*—a sermon.

letters of his life. The passage accords perfectly with the last words of Adolphe Monod.

Similar examples could be repeated indefinitely, but a more detailed elaboration would be wearisome and useless. In all the great names of Protestantism we would meet with the same experiences asserted with equal conviction. We will conclude by referring to the case of that famous missionary, François Coillard, who based his entire spiritual life on an interior illumination he received on the meaning of St. Paul's 'My grace is sufficient for thee, for power is made perfect in infirmity.' It can be said, without the least hesitation, that this text, taken in the strictest sense, explains best the meaning that Protestants (not, perhaps, the controversialists, but the really devout, ministers and others) have always attributed to the doctrine of gratuitous salvation. In that lies the only adequate explanation of a fact that cannot be gainsaid: that Protestantism, in so far as it is a living religion, stands or falls with this doctrine.

3. *SOLA GRATIA* AND THE CATHOLIC FAITH

Although we have not been able to study the entire body of Protestant doctrine and spirituality, we have at least been able to point out its vital principle. We may even claim to have established that its heart is the Lutheran *sola gratia*, and that it is, moreover, a living heart; those who accept it as the basis of their faith view it, not negatively, but as a strongly positive assertion. Furthermore, it should be clear enough that this assertion, taken in its essence as we have sought to define it, is a genuinely Christian one, and fully in accord, of course, with Catholic tradition properly understood. This aspect of the matter is, however, too important to pass over; we cannot afford to leave it to shine by its own light. We have now to show, by the clearest evidence, that Luther's basic intuition, on which Protestantism continuously draws for its abiding vitality, so far from being hard to reconcile with Catholic tradition, or inconsistent with the teaching of the Apostles, was a return to the clearest elements of their teaching, and is in the most direct line of that tradition.

We need not insist on the importance of this fact and the

consequent need for presenting it in the fullest light. If both Protestants and Catholics could be persuaded of it, the object of the basic antagonism of Protestants to the Church would cease to exist. It would be evident that Protestantism, reduced to what Protestants themselves regard as its essence, was under no necessity to embody itself in schism and heresy. On the contrary, by the very logic of its nature, it should have initiated in the Church itself a powerful movement of regeneration, one of those returns to its own origins and rediscoveries of its own spiritual wealth which from time to time renew its vitality.

Unfortunately, that is not what happened, though the blame, in any case, does not lie exclusively with the basic principle of the Reformation. Considered in itself, and in the natural course of its development, it does not lead to division and error. These are only the accidental results of the Reformation. If we have interpreted Protestantism correctly, the schisms and heresies of the sixteenth century resulted, not from its initial impulse, but from external and adventitious factors which disturbed its development.

All the consequences of this view will be drawn out at a later stage. We allude to them here so that the reader may be persuaded of the capital importance that the basic truth we are about to treat of should be fully and absolutely demonstrated. We now set about the proof.

We have already accumulated a number of passages showing that the 'gratuitous salvation' especially dear to those Protestants who are faithful to their traditions is a positive religious reality, not a negative controversial assertion. It is clear that it must be acknowledged as definitely and basically in harmony with genuine Christian doctrine, expressed in accordance with the traditional norms of the Church. But before proceeding we have to answer a possible objection.

It may be true that the passages quoted, the evidence arrayed, the interpretation of both, leave no room for doubt. But, even granting that they lead us to the vital core of Protestantism, they do not necessarily express the whole of that religion. Certain negative formulas—that of 'extrinsic justification' (exterior to the believer), or the wholesale condemnation of good works—

are, certainly, not inventions of Catholic controversy. They are found explicitly stated by the Reformers, and repeated over and over again by their followers. If that is so, where can we find the real Reformation?

So far from being embarrassed by this objection, or trying to evade it, let us admit at once that it constitutes the central problem of this book. Its primary object is to exhibit clearly the irreducible complexity, the inescapable dualism, of the Protestantism of history. In consequence, far from trying to evade allegations of the kind, we intend to bring out their full force.

Before we do so, however, we propose to show that the main Protestant position and its basic propositions, *taken in themselves*, imply nothing of the sort. It is necessary to be quite clear ✢ about this to start with. In fact, to take account of the complexity, the irreducible complexity, of Protestantism, we must begin by proving that there is no intrinsic connection between what it affirms and what it denies. This is of the first importance for a constructive criticism of Protestantism. For, in our view, the main error of Protestantism lies in this, that it has come to associate inseparably, but quite artificially, the positive statements of the Reformation with certain negations, so that these have come to seem equally characteristic of its nature. We will try to explain how this connection, unnatural as it seems to us, has come about. But the indispensable preliminary to this, as to the rest of our conclusions, is to demonstrate, beyond all doubt, the positive character, fully Christian and Catholic, of the great affirmation of Protestantism.

Two objections may be urged against our thesis; these we will start by examining. The first is that Protestantism, as we have depicted it, contains a residue of pessimism concerning human nature which is alien both to the Gospels and to tradition. The second is that the Christian doctrine of grace, granted that it is faithfully reproduced in the Protestant *sola gratia* rightly understood, has a less considerable role in Christianity proper than is attributed to it by Protestants.

The stigma of pessimism, of Manichæism in disguise, is commonly attached to Protestantism by its Catholic opponents. In our examination of the negative aspects of Protestantism we shall find ideas and passages in abundance which lend themselves to this reproach. That makes it even more important to convince ourselves, at the outset, that the reproach is not directed upon, or at any rate does not touch, the positive aspect, whether in itself or its implications.

One point, however, may give rise to some doubt—namely, what we said above about the *sola gratia* of Luther and other Protestants; the question of the state of man left to himself, before his life is affected by Christ's saving grace. They undoubtedly imply, *even granting the most positive interpretation of sola gratia,* a radical depravation of our nature before the coming of Christ. In the view of Luther, as well as of all those faithful to his essential teaching, man without grace can, strictly speaking, do nothing of the slightest value for salvation. He can neither dispose himself for it, nor work for it in any independent fashion. Even his acceptance of grace is the work of grace. To Luther and his authentic followers, justifying faith, a subject we shall return to, is, quite certainly, the first and most fundamental grace.

Can we possibly say that this accords with ordinary Catholic teaching? We are faced here with a very real difficulty, not to be eluded, and our whole plan requires us to confront it squarely.

We admit, at the outset, that the series of statements we have just formulated would undoubtedly scandalise a large number of Catholics today. It is equally certain that they are at variance with the general tenor of contemporary Catholic writing and preaching. Catholics at the present time are usually at great pains to expound their religion in the most optimistic light, and the first instinct of their apologia is to tone down all those elements in Christian teaching which view man in an unfavourable light, or wound his susceptibilities. We have no need to stress the slurring-over of the doctrine of hell in current teaching. Nor would anyone deny that, even in ascetical writings today, we find asceticism 'spiritualised', as the phrase goes, in the highest degree. What is more, we see, to an alarming extent, a kind of hedonism put forward as the purest expression of genuine Catholic doctrine, for example, in the sphere of sexual morality.

However, we have lately been warned, by the highest authority in the Church, against the tendency to attenuate or eliminate those elements in our own tradition which militate against so evident and general an attitude of mind. We do well to bear in mind that the ordinary magisterium of the Church, the most direct source of her most authoritative teaching, is quite a different thing from the opinions most publicised, most commonplace, and, often enough, least profoundly considered. The Church's teaching is not necessarily the same as that which we chance to find in the written or spoken words uttered by Catholics at a given period.

There is a further consideration which it will be well to bear in mind. The reaction, the revulsion even, of a great number of Catholics today to the severe doctrines we allude to, would certainly be shared instinctively by the majority of Protestants. There is, therefore, nothing specifically Catholic in this refusal to admit, or reluctance and difficulty in admitting, that man can do nothing, of himself, towards his salvation, even if, in fact, such is the case with many Catholics at the present time; for their attitude is common to Protestants and to unbelievers in the twentieth century. It may well be that it is the prejudices of the twentieth century which influence Catholics, just as it is certain that such is the case with Protestants.

A serious examination of Catholic doctrine, drawn from the most authentic sources, will convince us that this explanation is, in fact, the true one.

We shall adduce nothing beyond what is incumbent on all Catholics to hold. Consequently, we shall not have recourse to theologians of the Augustinian school. True, they have never been condemned by the Church, but in the sphere of doctrine they certainly hold an extreme position. We shall restrict ourselves to what has been formally defined. Once we have set out the Church's doctrine on this unshakable foundation, we shall use the teaching of St. Thomas Aquinas to elucidate it. It is true that all parts of his teaching are not equally authoritative, but his work is, none the less, that of the 'Common Doctor', *par excellence.*

If, then, any Catholic—and there would seem to be many such these days—whose first impulse is to reject the idea that man, without grace, can do nothing towards his salvation, that he cannot even accept the grace offered except by a previous grace, that the very faith which acknowledges the need of grace is a purely gratuitous gift, he would do well to attend closely to the texts we are about to quote.

Earlier on, we alluded to the Pelagian and semi-Pelagian heresies. It is well known that, from the fifth century onwards, they sought to minimise the part of grace in man's salvation, and to exaggerate the powers of fallen man. Their definitive condemnation was pronounced by the Second Council of Orange, in 529, and confirmed by Pope Boniface II in the Bull, *Per Filium nostrum*, of the 25th of January, 531. It is equally certain that the definitions of this Council must be accepted by all as *de fide*. Now, even the most lenient interpretation of these canons, it will be easily seen, exceeds the pessimism implied in the *sola gratia* as previously expounded.

The 3rd canon runs as follows: 'If anyone says that the grace of God can be conferred in answer to man's petition, but that the petition itself is not due to the action of grace, he contradicts the Prophet Isaias and the Apostle, who both say: "I was found by them that did not seek me, I appeared openly to them that asked not after me " (Rom. X, 20; Isa. LXV, 1).'

Canon 5 is even more categorical. It rules out any beginning of faith, or inclination to faith, which is not itself an effect of grace: 'If anyone says that the increase, or even the beginning, of faith, or the inclination to believe, which leads us to faith in him who justifies the ungodly, and to regeneration by Baptism, are innate in us, and are not the effect of grace, that is, of the Holy Ghost who, by his inspirations, turns our wills from unbelief to faith, from ungodliness to piety; such a one must be held to oppose the doctrines of the Apostles.'

After this, the 6th canon rules out any possibility of acts of our own disposing us in any way at all for grace, without themselves proceeding from grace: 'If anyone says that God has mercy on us when, without his grace, we believe, will, desire, strive, work, watch, study, ask, seek, knock, and does not confess that we believe, will, and are enabled to do all this in the way we ought, by the infusion and inspiration of the Holy Spirit within us; or makes the help of grace depend on the humility or obedience of man, rather than ascribing such humility and obedience to the free gift of grace; he goes counter to the Apostle, who says, "What hast thou that thou hast not received?" and "By the grace of God I am what I am" (1 Cor. IV, 7, and XV, 10).'

It would seem difficult to go further than this; but canon 7 goes on to state, with the utmost precision, that our consent to salvation is itself the effect of grace: 'If anyone asserts that we can, by our natural powers, think as we ought, or choose any good pertaining to the salvation of eternal life, that is, consent to salvation or to the message of the Gospel, without the illumination and inspiration of the Holy Spirit, who gives to all men facility in assenting to and believing the truth; he is misled by a heretical spirit, not understanding what the voice of God says in the Gospel, "Without me you can do nothing" (John XV, 5), nor the words of the Apostle, "Not that we are sufficient to think anything of ourselves, as of ourselves, but our sufficiency is from God" (2 Cor. III, 5).'

Canon 18 is, as it were, the *résumé* of all the preceding: 'Whatever good works we do are deserving of reward, not through any merit anterior to grace; their performance, rather, is due to a prior gift of grace to which we have no claim.'

The Council of Orange did not restrict its teaching to these positive assertions on the necessity of grace. It laid down that the state of nature after the Fall was not merely one of need, but of guilt; not only weak and powerless for what concerns salvation, but depraved and prone to evil. In so saying, it goes well beyond what we have affirmed in our study of the *sola gratia*.

For instance, canon 13 tells us: 'Free will, weakened in the person of the first man, can be repaired only by the grace of Baptism, since what has been lost can be restored only by him who had the power to give it. Hence, the Truth himself tells us, "If the Son of man shall make you free, you will indeed be free" (John VIII, 36).'

Still, this could, strictly speaking, involve simply a limitation in our power to will the good, not an actual inclination of the will to evil. But canon 22 seems incapable, to say the least, of interpretation in such mild terms: 'No one possesses as his own anything but sin and deception. Whatever truth and justice man has, he derives from that source we ought to thirst after in this desert, that, bedewed, as it were, by a few drops, we may not faint in the way.'

With this view, we can appreciate the full import of the great canon 25: 'In a word, to love God is a gift of God. He, yet unloved, loves us, and gave us the power to love. While we were displeasing in his sight, he loved us, in order that we might have the power to become pleasing to him. For the *charity of God is poured forth in our hearts by the Spirit* (Rom. V, 5) of the Father and the Son, whom we love with the Father and Son. So, according to the Scriptural passages quoted above and the definitions of the early Fathers, we are obliged, in the mercy of God, to preach and believe that, through the sin of the first man, the free will is so weakened and warped, that no one thereafter can either love God as he ought, or believe in God, or do good for the sake of God, unless moved, previously, by the grace of the divine mercy. . . . Our salvation requires that we assert and believe that, in every good work we do, it is not we who have the initiative, aided, subsequently, by the mercy of God, but that he begins by inspiring faith and love towards him, without any prior merit of ours. . . .'

No laboured commentary is needed to show that the pessimistic view of fallen nature involved by the *sola gratia* is precisely that of Christian tradition. We do well to bear in mind that here is no question of ancient and venerable texts which may not be of obligation for the faith of all Catholics. They are solemn definitions of Councils, expressly confirmed by the authority of the Pope; consequently, propositions of defined faith.

Propositions of the sort are obviously irreversible; so we would be perfectly justified in letting our proof rest there. However, in view of certain extravagant theories, current nowadays, on the subject of the development of doctrine, and entertained, if not by theologians, at any rate by popular exponents of a dubious apologetic, it is as well to show that this teaching of the Council of Orange, far from being attenuated by any later decision of the Church, is, in fact, formally confirmed by her more recent definitions.

Our Protestant readers may rest assured that, in this matter as in others, what the Church taught once she teaches always. The definitions of the Council of Trent are of the greatest interest here, since they were prompted by the erroneous teaching of Protestants on the subject of justification.

Chapter 5 of the 6th session, though its purpose is to uphold the free, unforced character of our acceptance of grace, declares all the same: '. . . The beginning of justification itself in adults is to be understood as the result of the antecedent grace of God through Jesus Christ, that is, it comes from the vocation by which he calls them, without any previous merit on their part, so that those who had been turned from God by their sins, by means of his grace stirring and assisting them to turn to their own justification, in freely consenting and co-operating with this grace, are so disposed that, when God touches their hearts by the illumination of the Holy Spirit, they cannot be said to be absolutely inactive in receiving this inspiration—they could, in fact reject it—yet, without the grace of God, they could not move themselves, of their own will, to a state of justice in his sight. . . .'

It is evident that, though this text speaks of human freedom in the work of salvation, it does not, for a moment, envisage the free will as capable of the least act towards salvation, unless grace precedes and accompanies it. The first chapter had already declared that, as a result of Adam's sin, free will was not destroyed, although, in the words of the Council of Orange, weakened and warped. But the immediately preceding part of the same chapter shows that this does not imply that free will could effect anything towards salvation, without the aid of grace. What it actually says is that, neither by the powers that remain after the Fall, nor by the law of Moses, could man, without grace, 'free or raise himself' from slavery to sin, the devil and death.

The Council of Trent's insistence on the fact that man is not saved passively (we shall discuss its reasons for it later), but through his free acceptance, certainly is not to be held as implying any modification of the decrees of Orange. Its whole aim is to show that grace does not dispense us from acting ourselves, but restores to us the power to act well. This, in turn,

C

does not mean a parallel action on the part of God and man, a sort of 'synergism', where man contributes, in the work of salvation, something, however slight, independent of grace. What follows will make this clear.

First of all, the 7th chapter of the Council, which treats of the essence and causes of justification, says that 'its single formal cause is the justice of God, not that by which he himself is just, but that by which he makes us just, a gift by which we are re-newed in the spirit of our mind, and are not only accounted, but are truly called, and are, just. . . .'

Later on we shall draw out in full the implications of this pas-sage and the rest of the chapter. For the moment we will con-tent ourselves with noting that it presents justification itself as purely the gift of God.

The same is put in the clearest light by the 8th chapter, on the necessity of faith and the gratuitousness of justification: 'When the Apostle says that man is justified by faith and freely, his words are to be understood in the sense ever held and expressed by the consensus of the Catholic Church; which is, that we are said to be justified by faith, because faith is the beginning of human salvation, the foundation and root of all justification, and without it it is impossible to please God (Heb. XI, 6), and attain to the communion of his sons; yet we are said to be justi-fied freely, because nothing that precedes justification, whether faith or works, merits the grace of justification. As the Apostle says, "If it is of grace, it is not now by works, otherwise grace is no more grace" (Rom. XI, 6).'

The importance of this passage scarcely needs emphasising. Nothing could bring out more clearly that Catholic doctrine itself, as defined at Trent, does not admit salvation by faith *and* works, if by that is meant works which are not themselves the product of saving grace received by faith. On the contrary, the profound assertion of the total causality of grace in salva-tion requires that *both* the good works following on grace, *and* the faith which receives it, are its product. Our final conclusion is that the Catholic not only may, but must in virtue of his own faith, give a full and unreserved adherence to the *sola gratia*, un-derstood in the positive sense we have seen upheld by Pro-testants. The assertion that, in salvation, all is the work of grace, is neither heretical nor suspect. It is precisely what is affirmed by the genuine Catholic tradition in its witness to the doctrine of the Apostles and the early Church, of St. Augustine as of St. Paul.

The Conciliar definitions just quoted give rise to theological problems of absorbing interest, but which require delicate handling. In the whole history of the Church there have certainly been few questions so fraught with difficulty as that of the relations between grace and human freedom. How can God, in the words of St. Paul, 'create in us to will and to accomplish', without absolving us from the necessity, as he says a line or two earlier, of 'working out our salvation with fear and trembling'? [1] No other problem seems so impenetrable by reason. It would, in consequence, be most unreasonable to reproach the Church with refusing, in connection with the controversy *de auxiliis*, to condemn or to authorise any theory, since her whole aim is to respect loyally both sides of the antithesis Scripture itself propounds. It would be still more unreasonable to interpret the Church's wise liberalism on this point as a sign of her unconcern with the doctrine so strongly proclaimed by her own Councils. Without insisting on the adoption of any of the scholastic theories, either in this or in any other connection, the Church, particularly in the present age, has marked clearly enough the importance to the clergy of a knowledge and application of thomist principles. It is certainly the case that the theology of St. Thomas on grace, far from toning down the aspects of the Catholic tradition we have just been emphasising, gives them, more than any other system, their full value.

The main thesis of this theology, the keystone of its whole structure of grace, is, obviously, its doctrine of efficacious grace. This is admirably summarised by Garrigou-Lagrange, one of the most distinguished thomists of today, in the statement that 'in the work of salvation *all is from God*, including our own co-operation, in the sense that we cannot distinguish *a part as exclusively ours*, which does not come from the author of all good'. [2]

[1] Phil. II, 12–13.
[2] *Perfection chrétienne et contemplation*, t. 1, p. 88.

For St. Thomas, when grace moves the heart of man to surrender himself to God for the accomplishment of his will, if this grace is efficacious, if man believes, is regenerated, and lives accordingly in the love of God, it is by no means the free consent of man that made grace effective. On the contrary, his consent was due solely to the will of God that his grace should be efficacious in that man at that moment.[1] The great mystery lies in the fact that this consent should remain free; but the reason is that God, the Lord and Creator of all, is Lord and Creator of our very freedom. He is not just the master of our freedom in a general way, as a faculty given to us once and for all, which we can use, subsequently, in complete independence. For St. Thomas, God is the absolute master, not only of the faculty, but of its entire range of employment, and of its least acts. As such, he moves us, albeit freely, to assent to grace when we actually do so. This divine impulse it is which makes grace efficacious in us; it is not we who make it so.

Such an uncompromising assertion at once provokes the objection that it makes God equally the cause of our sins. St. Thomas rejects the parallel. Since sin is not a positive reality, but the lack of a positive good, it must be due to a defectible, or deficient cause, such as our sinful will. This is what Osee means in the passage, 'Destruction is thy own, O Israel, thy help is only in me (Osee 13, 9).' On the other hand, as soon as it is a question of the positive good of salvation, it is God, and he alone, who creates in us 'to will and to accomplish', including this radical act of will by which we simply allow grace to take hold of us. As St. Augustine says, 'Free will is a sufficient cause of evil, but for good it can do nothing unless aided by the Almighty Good.'[2]

Is anything more needed to convince Catholics that the *sola gratia*, as generally understood among Protestants, in the sense we have seen that they give it, is perfectly in accord with Catholic tradition? And those Protestants who see, in the passage we first quoted, the very heart of their faith and life as Christians,

[1] *Contra Gentiles*, III, 89; *cf. De Veritate*, qu. 22, art. 8 and 9; *Summa Theologica*, I a, II ae, q. 112, a. 3.

[2] *De Correptione et Gratia, cap.* XI. On this whole question, see Garrigou-Lagrange, *op. cit.*, pp. 88–106.

can they seriously question that the Church does justice to all
that is essential and positive in their 'protestation', once they
have read these other texts?

There remains the second objection: granted that the doctrine of *sola gratia* be considered fundamentally orthodox, to
make it the centre of all Christian devotion would be to twist
and deform the authentic structure of Christianity.

More exactly, the objection is that the *sola gratia* imprisons
the whole of Christian life and devotion within the antithesis,
sin–grace. A double simplification, it is alleged; one, reducing
Christianity to man's subjective experience; the second, narrow-
ing this to a feeling of guilt, which may easily become an obsession. In such a religion, with its interior aspect exaggerated,
and thereby narrowed to the exclusive consideration of man and
his works, where could room be found for any positive and
basic truth, such as our supernatural adoption, or, an even
broader one, our adherence to Christ for his own sake? Yet
these are, certainly, a part of real Christianity. It would seem
that the religion of *sola gratia* refuses, in principle, to see in man
anything but his sins, and in God anything but a judge, whether
he condemns or acquits.

This criticism, it must be noticed, is not confined to Catholics;
it is shared by some Protestants. However, these are generally
among the liberal Protestants; so it is no matter for surprise
that, in urging this objection, they believe themselves to be
attacking Catholicism itself, as a source of Protestantism. Or
else, if, as sometimes happens, they commend Catholicism for
its opposition, on this point, to Protestantism, the compliment
is somewhat double-edged; scrutinised closely, it amounts to
praising Catholicism for being less religious, or less Christian,
than Protestantism.

An example is P. Pfister, a psycho-analyst of Zürich, who, in
his celebrated work, *Das Christentum und die Angst*, represents
the whole history of Christian doctrine as the history of a pathological obsession. He attributes to Luther the great merit of
being the first to aim at liberation from the anxiety-complex
caused by the morbid dogma of original sin. In his view, however, the liberation attempted did not go deep enough; it is

necessary to go beyond the idea of justification by faith, and to liquidate completely the traditional notion of sin.

Schweitzer, in his book, *Die Mystik des Apostels Paulus*, takes another line. Among other things, he roundly declares that Protestant exegetes, in the importance they attach to the 7th and 8th chapters of the epistle to the Romans, are the victims of an optical illusion. This appears already in St. Augustine, and results in complete distortion of St. Paul's thought; a distortion carried over into medieval theology, though countered by other tendencies, and completed by Luther. From his time, Protestants have been, as it were, congenitally incapacitated from finding the real centre of gravity of St. Paul's teaching. Authentic 'paulinism' has to be rediscovered, and it will be found to consist in a mystical doctrine of union with Christ, with its dominant note, not that of sin and its atonement, but the prospect of our final resurrection and entrance into the kingdom, all hostile forces being conquered by the Cross.

The element of truth in this view of the great exegete will be acknowledged in our later discussion. At the moment we must insist that the reactions of both Pfister and Schweitzer are not to be accounted for by early Protestantism, or its various revivals, or, so to call it, the primitive freshness it still retains. They are aimed at a Protestantism which has steadily shrunk in the atmosphere of modern subjectivism. We might even say that the reason why Pfister extends to Catholicism the reproach first levelled against Protestantism is that he only sees in the Church the target of the earlier, and saner, reactions of Luther. This gives us our first opportunity of stating something which we will later bring out in detail. The most paradoxical and disconcerting thing about Protestantism, viewed in its historical development, is that it quickly reproduced, in exaggerated form, the very weaknesses in fifteenth-century Catholicism against which it rightfully strove in its beginning, namely, subjective humanism, extreme individualism, and the rest.

But neither Luther nor those of his followers most faithful to his original teaching considered that the *sola gratia* necessarily entailed the reduction of the whole of Christianity to the fate of the individual, and the latter to the narrow question of sin. On the contrary, whenever he sets out to expound the kernel of his teaching on justifying faith, the feature most prominent in his view of Christianity is how the antithesis, sin–grace, transcends religious individualism and mere moralism. It transcends the moralism, to which so many protagonists of the Reformation, as well as their Catholic contemporaries, fell victim; since, in fact, the antithesis, sin–grace, far from reducing grace to the function of compensating for sin, raises man from a paralysing obsession with sin to the expansive vision of a positive gift of God transforming his whole notion of his relation to God. It transcends individualism, since it makes of grace, not an abstract concept, but a vital intuition of the person of Christ, vanquishing all by the power of the Cross, and drawing us by his resurrection into his kingdom—the characteristic note, as Schweitzer justly holds, of the true Pauline doctrine.

This double affirmation finds ample justification in the central passage of Luther's *Great Commentary on the epistle to the Galatians*.[1]

'The curse, the anger of God with the whole world, is thus at enmity with the blessing, that is, with eternal grace and the mercy of God in Christ. The curse is in conflict with the blessing and would like to vanquish it, but cannot. For the blessing is divine and eternal, so the curse has to yield to it. If the blessing in Christ had to yield, God himself would have been conquered; but this is impossible. Christ, who is the divine power, blessing, grace and life, vanquishes and carries away those monsters, sin, death, and malediction. . . . When, therefore, you look on him, you see sin, death, the anger of God, hell, the devil, all evil, conquered and dead. Consequently, in so far as Christ, by his grace, rules over the hearts of the faithful, sin, death, and malediction are no more to be found; where Christ is unknown, they remain. So those who do not believe lose this blessing and this victory; for our victory, as St. John says, is our faith. This is the first article of the Christian faith, hidden in obscurity by the sophists of the past, darkened by the fanatics of the present.[2]

[1] On Gal. III, 13.
[2] In Luther's mind, the sophists are the nominalist theologians, and the fanatics are the sectaries, such as the anabaptists, who reject the traditional faith in the name of the Reformation.

Hence, we see how necessary it is to believe and confess the article on the divinity of Christ. Arius, in denying it, should have denied, too, the article on the redemption; for the conquest, unaided, of the world's sin, death, malediction, the anger of God, is the work of no created being, but of almighty God. Therefore, he who has conquered them of his own power must be, in fact, God by nature. For, to conquer such powers as sin, death and malediction, which themselves rule the world and all creation, a different and higher power had to appear; it could not be other than God. To destroy sin, lay low death, remove the curse by one's own power, communicate justice, open the way to life and give blessing, annihilate the first of these and create the latter, all this is the work of divine omnipotence alone. But, if Scripture ascribes all this to Christ, it must be that he himself is life, justice, and blessing, that is, he is God by nature and essence. Those, then, who deny the divinity of Christ are alien to the whole of Christianity, and no better than pagans and Turks. That is why, as I am always repeating, we must have an exact understanding of the article on justification. It comprises all the other articles of faith, and safeguards them all. When, then, we teach that man is justified by Christ, and that Christ is the conqueror of sin, death and eternal malediction, we testify, at the same time, that he is God by nature.'

These last words show us the wide scope of the *sola gratia*, properly understood. The entire passage reveals better than any detailed explanation what a force for the renewal of apostolic Christianity in its traditional and patristic exposition, the Lutheran insight could have been, has been, and, in fact, remains, within the best type of Protestantism. The importance of the passage can be assessed when we recall that Gustav Aulen,[1] one of the most eminent of contemporary theologians of Lutheranism, and possibly the greatest expert on Luther, views it as the key to his whole teaching.

[1] G. Aulen, *Christus Victor*, London, 1931, p. 123.

CHAPTER III

The Sovereignty of God

UP to now we have been considering the main positive principle of the Reformation, as revealed by Luther's intuition, and as the permanent source of the religious vitality of Protestantism. We have now to scrutinise its function as the root of Calvinism; otherwise, our work would be seriously defective. For while it is true that the Calvinist system has never been adopted except by a small number, its influence has been far wider. The specific contribution of Calvinism to the Reformation is a certain radicalism, a kind of logical mysticism, which permeated, at any rate as an aim and a tendency, the whole of Protestantism, and so justifies the place generally given to Calvin as second only to Luther.

What Luther asserted is, in appearance, very simple: everything in Christianity comes from grace, all is the pure gift of God, the work of God alone. Yet, looked at more closely, Lutheranism seems to contain a hidden contradiction. Everything in it comes from God; God alone, on an utterly transcendental level, is the subject of religion, in the sense that all comes from him, and him alone; yet man seems to be the sole purpose of all, all leads up to man and his salvation. The whole problem of religion reduces itself to that of the salvation of man.

The same conclusion appears even more forcibly when we come to the history of the doctrine of *sola gratia* in its subjective aspect, *sola fide*. Man's faith, the individual acceptance, utterly personal, of divine grace, came to play such a prominent part in Protestantism that its exponents sincerely believed themselves to be still faithful to the spirit of Luther, after they had left out of account the very object of this faith. This led to 'justification by faith independently of beliefs' that Eugène Ménégoz took as the definitive expression of liberal Protestantism.[1] In general, Protestantism, starting from the view that God's transcendental intervention was the sum total of Christianity, came, by this

[1] *Cf.* his *Réflexions sur l'Evangile du salut*, Paris, 1879, and his three volumes, *Publications diverses sur le fidéisme.*

road, to a humanism and religious immanentism absolutely exclusive of any element of transcendence.

However remote from Luther's such views may be, and however scandalous in his eyes, it is undeniable that they are the outcome of a certain element in his thought, though, admittedly, abstracted from what he himself held to be both a necessary counterpoise and a justification.

It was this possibility of subjectivism and preoccupation with the human, implicit in Luther, that Calvin seems to have aimed at counteracting and excluding formally. The way in which he revised and completed the principle of *sola gratia* should have sufficed to rule it out. That explains why the present Protestant revival fostered by Karl Barth and his followers is better described as neo-Calvinism than neo-Lutheranism. Hence the particular importance for us of Calvin's views on the fundamental principle of the Reformation, which we shall have to examine closely.

In the vast religious and theological synthesis of the *Institution Chrétienne*, we seem, from the very outset, to escape the impression of paradox suggested by Lutheranism, that of a religion where God is all in the order of efficient causality, but man seems to be all in the order of final causality. Calvinism, on the other hand, considered at its purest and deepest level, appears, indisputably, as a religion where God is all in the sphere of ends as well as that of means. If man's salvation still occupies the central place, it is only, as it were, in the transitional process of a creative act coming entirely from God and returning entirely to him. This reform within the Reformation was brought about by the addition to Luther's *sola gratia, sola fide* of Calvin's *Soli Deo gloria*. We may express it better and more plainly as the result of taking a more elevated view, passing beyond the idea of gratuitous salvation to that of the sovereignty of God.

As God alone is the essential agent, for Calvinism he is also the sole final end which his action could possibly envisage. If all proceeds from his grace, all tends to his glory. If it is he who does all, that is because he alone is sovereign, he who said: 'I will give my glory to none other.'

No sooner do we open the *Institution Chrétienne* than we are struck with Calvin's conviction that the fundamental error to be countered in medieval religion is idolatry. Why, as Luther was the first to say, and as he repeats—why had this religion come to water down divine grace, and to bury it under all kinds of merely human devotions? Because, he thought, man gave way to his incorrigible bias, and lost sight of the transcendence of God whose irruption into our history is what constitutes the whole of Christianity. He went so far as to seek in human 'works', in human action, or in means thought out by man and confined to this world, the salvation God alone could confer. But why, and how, did this confusion arise? Because, in the first place, thought Calvin, he had lost sight of the fact that God is unique, that he is not one being among others, lesser, no doubt, but not separated from him by an infinite gulf. By insensible degrees, man had reverted to the primordial error of idolatry. He had come to the point, within Christianity as before it, of putting the creature on the level of the Creator; that is why he expected from the creature what could be sought and found only with the Creator.

Against this error, Calvin, in language of incomparable majesty, opposes the figure of the Old Testament God, the God of the prophets. It is impossible to consider him as only one source of our life among others which we carry within ourselves, or which are provided by some institution, some human or created agency; he is clearly shown to be, not just the first among beings, but the sovereign, in a sense the only, Being. Consequently, all reality, seen from the specifically religious standpoint, can come only from him, just as, in the final analysis, it can have no other end than him. Its restoration in Christ, like its original creation, has no other meaning than the glory of God. It achieves this end precisely in attributing glory to him alone, the source and reality of all good, in demonstrating that he alone can and does all by his sovereign power.

It is certain that this magnificent conception, still more the unmistakably religious sense from which it proceeds, is not Calvin's creation, purely and simply. It derives, as we shall show, quite definitely from the Bible itself and from the purest Christian tradition, but it was through the medium of Luther that Calvin reached these sources. His idea of the sovereign

greatness of God is closely allied to Luther's strong feeling for
the element of mystery, and, in our day, has received, rightfully,
especial emphasis in the works of Barth. In this connection,
Luther's idea, that gratuitous salvation involves something
which surpasses human reason and imagination, plays a conspicuous part. To put it more exactly, the idea that there is not
merely the revealed God and the hidden God, but that God reveals himself *precisely as a hidden God*, is the germ, and more
than the germ, of Calvin's idea of God, acknowledged, before
and above all, as the Sovereign Being.[1] There, we might say,
lies the vital point in the characteristic transformation effected
by Calvin in adjusting to the Latin mind the most Germanic
element in Luther's thought, without distorting it in the least.
In fact, we have to admit that, by a stroke of genius, he succeeds,
by this transformation alone, in elucidating the most obscure
features of Luther's religious doctrine.

Undoubtedly, one of the most difficult parts of Luther's
thought is how the *Deus revelatus* can be *revelatus* precisely as
the *Deus absconditus*. None has been so much misinterpreted by
his followers, even before his opponents did so. Yet, it is quite
certain, as Barth so rightly insists, that there, and perhaps there
alone, we penetrate the ultimate depths of Luther's most original
intuitions. Once again, Calvin's genius for lucidity shows nowhere more brilliantly than in the way, quite simple after all, in
which he perceived this and conveyed it in a more intelligible
form.

The truth which, above all, is admirably elucidated in the
Institution Chrétienne, from its very beginning, is that the most
profound revelation about God in the Gospels is his utter
mysteriousness. That is to say, in the Gospel—the good news
of our salvation in Christ, of the saving love which, according
to St. Paul, is the foundation of Christianity, and, according to
St. John, is the final word about God himself—the real subject
of revelation is that God completely transcends our loftiest
thoughts, our sublimest speculations. The highest reasons

---

[1] On the importance of this idea in Luther, *cf.* R. Otto, *Le Sacré,* French
trans., Paris, 1949, pp. 136 *et seq.* See also, in Vol. 1/1 of Barth's *Dogmatik*,
the whole chapter on *Die Rede Gottes als Geheimnis Gottes*, Munich, 1932,
pp. 168 *et seq.*

philosophers may attribute to his acts, the noblest ideas they may form about his nature, are not only surpassed by his own revelation, but surpassed to the extent that it throws all human reasoning into confusion, so that nothing is left to us but to say with the Apostle: 'O the depths of the riches of the wisdom and of the knowledge of God; how incomprehensible are his judgments, and how unsearchable his ways.' (Rom. XI, 33.)

For the understanding of Calvinism, and, in general, of all that the mind of Calvin has more or less contributed to Protestantism as a whole, it is of the first importance to recover this aspect of his thought, and to be convinced that it is the basis of his system. If this system seems stern and implacable that is due to our approaching it, only too often, either by its individual features—which then seem unintelligible—or by the inevitably rigorous form of its expression. We completely fail to understand its logic, as long as we do not view it as a mystical logic; that is, the strict application of a profoundly religious insight, whose validity Catholics should find it quite impossible to dispute.

Once we are thoroughly convinced of this, the impression we receive from the work of Calvin changes entirely. It has been said that the mathematical logic of Spinoza, far from being a sign of the aridity of his religious ideas, is the expression of the deep-rooted mysticism of a man 'drunk with God'. The phrase is even more appropriate to the *Institution Chrétienne* and Calvin's whole theological system than to the *Ethics* of Spinoza. This intoxication, is without doubt, the *sobria ebrietas* characteristic of Christian mysticism since Philo, at the furthest remove from sentimentality. Provided the words are taken in their proper sense, it is absolutely certain that none of the historic forms of Christianity is, in fact, more radically mystical than Calvinism; for it is not governed by abstract ideas, whether one or many, but a genuine intuition, utterly religious in nature, of God as Sovereign, Holy, absolutely Other, who 'inhabits light inaccessible'. Now this intuition is, in the strictest sense, mystical, whatever our opinions about Calvin's temperament, and in spite of the prejudice against the word or the reality which makes Calvinists distrust the expression. There, in this intuition, is to be found the source of Calvin's thought and, likewise, of the historical religion which proceeded from it.

It is absolutely certain, as a matter of history, that the intuition of Luther, which we find to lie at the root of that of Calvin, takes us back directly to the Rhenish school of mysticism originated by Eckhardt and Tauler. If Luther had no hesitation in acknowledging his debt to the *Theologia germanica*—a work reminiscent of the pseudo-areopagite—if he went so far as to translate it into German to popularise it, that shows that he recognised it as one of the sources of his conception. The God whose very light is a 'superessential darkness' is the *Deus revelatus*, but *revelatus* as *absconditus*. That is, too, the reason why Luther was so strongly drawn to St. John Chrysostom, particularly to his treatise, *On the incomprehensibility of God*. All this indicates Luther's settled conviction that these mystical subjects, far from being due, as so many modern Protestant historians so easily conclude, to a neo-platonic infection of Christianity, are the expression, albeit in the language of neo-platonism, of that element beyond reason, that inscrutable mystery of the God of love, which is the basis of the Gospel revelation.

The effects produced by Calvinism lead us to the same conclusion as the study of its origins. The bareness, the rigorous austerity, of the forms of Calvinist worship, in France, Holland, Scotland, and New England, can be taken as a sign of religious aridity only by the uncomprehending or the prejudiced. Calvinism as a living force, as seen working in these various countries, is clearly actuated by an admirable insistence on genuineness, on sincerity with regard to God, the true, living God who has nothing in common with dumb idols. If we seek anywhere in Protestantism for a parallel to the most rigorous elements in the mysticism of the Cistercians or Carmelites, we can assert, without the least error or exaggeration, that it is to be found in Calvinism itself, or in the deepest and most lasting traces made by Calvin's great intuition even outside strict Calvinism.

If this assertion sounds like a paradox to a number of Catholics as well as Protestants, this is due entirely to a series of prejudices and misunderstandings. And if Catholics and Calvinists seem to agree in regarding Calvin as essentially anti-mystical, it is because, as a rule, Calvinists are incredibly ill-informed about Catholic mysticism, viewing it wholly on the surface, while Catholics know only the externals of Calvinism.

Rather than embark on a long discussion, we propose simply to relate a most revealing conversation we once had with the minister, Auguste Lecerf, certainly the person of our generation the most learned in Calvinism, as well as embodying in himself the highest type of strictly Calvinist spirituality. As he had said quite baldly that a mystic, in his view, was just someone who held paradise to be a place of debauchery, we read to him, without comment, some of the salient passages of the *Ascent of Mount Carmel*, of St. John of the Cross. After listening with the closest attention, he answered in perfect sincerity and without hesitation: 'If that is the real Catholic mysticism, it is precisely the religion for which Calvin fought all his life.'

Another most significant thing surely is the attitude of those Protestants who have undeniably carried to its logical conclusion the Calvinist idea of God's sovereignty, his absolute transcendence. The idea itself was always balanced, in the Calvinist system, by other elements irrelevant to us for the moment. But in sects such as the Quakers we see the outcome of these principles in their unrestricted application. Nothing is more striking, in the disciples of George Fox, than the wholeness of their acceptance and application of the typically Calvinist idea of the sovereign God, whose infinite greatness annihilates, by comparison, all else. Even those Protestants who are less radical, more faithful to Calvinism as a whole, and so do not venture to such extremes, cannot escape a feeling of nostalgia for such boldness; as if to them such radicalism constituted both a temptation difficult to resist and an attraction to something higher. If the bareness of a Calvinist church, the austerity of its worship, seem carried to excess, the Quakers do not even have churches or public worship in the strict sense. So imperious is their desire that God should be absolutely sovereign, without rival, unique, that, in their religion, he alone is there present, and, besides him, nothing. In the last resort, the only praise worthy of him seems to them to be silence.

Now, it is very remarkable that the Quakers, in throwing overboard all the impedimenta Calvinism itself despised without being able to get rid of, jettisoned also the Calvinist prejudices.

They have no difficulty in admitting that the Christians who seem to have got closest to their ideal were those in the tradition of Tauler, Ruysbroek, St. Teresa of Avila, St. John of the Cross, Brother Laurence, etc. They even go so far as to bring out new editions of their works and introduce them to Protestants. More significant still, the author of one of the most remarkable, studies of our time on the great Catholic mystics is an American Quaker, Rufus Jones.

Having considered the incidentals of Calvinism and its results, we are now in a position to rediscover in Calvin himself the essence of his doctrine, manifested both in its source and in its by-products. We have only to re-read him without prejudice to banish the idea of a God, cold, aloof from feeling, that misguided followers and hasty opponents have agreed in regarding as the God of Calvin. His Sermons, especially, make it quite plain that his austere concept of *Soli Deo gloria*, his utterly uncompromising assertion of the sovereignty of God, far from drying up the living stream of religion whose course we have followed in the genuine Lutheran tradition, have given it a greater depth and purity. That God is the sole and absolute Lord of man and of all things, that in all he does he acts ultimately for his own glory alone, signifies in Calvin's own explanation not the crushing down of man, but a liberation and expansion otherwise unattainable. He is never tired of asserting that the fact that it is God alone who, without in any way depending on us, whether for the use of means or for the pursuit of the end, works our salvation, is the only thing that can give us an assurance utterly joyful, because most sweeping and positive.

'See, then, how we ought to be so much the more strengthened in our expectation of salvation, since God concerns himself with it, and makes it his own cause. This is a point we ought to observe well. For, however much God adjures us, time and again, to be solicitous for our salvation, since we are distrustful by nature, we remain ever in doubt of achieving it. But, when it is put before us that God will maintain his right, that he will not suffer his majesty to be trampled under foot by man, here we have a doctrine that should set us in a resolute assurance. And then it is certain that God gives us this favour of associating his glory with our salvation, binding them inseparably one to the other. There is here no infallible certainty that our Lord Jesus will come and give us respite and repose; particularly as God is bound to uphold the rights of his majesty against the pride and revolt of man. Observe, then, that Jesus Christ can only maintain the glory of his Father in the measure he declares himself to be our Redeemer. The two things are inseparable. See in that the infinite love of God towards those faithful to him, uniting himself to them so closely that, as he cannot overlook the claims of his glory, he makes of it our salvation. . . .' [1]

From almost every page in the works of Calvin one could glean passages equally decisive. They, and the burning conviction they convey, can alone bring home to us the depth and scope, in Calvin's own mind, of his great assertions about the glory of God; while the dry bones of his abstractions leave us unmoved.

[1] Calvin's Sermon on the last coming. *Oeuvres de Calvin*, III, p. 266, Paris. Ed. *Je Sers*, 1936.

CHAPTER IV

Soli Deo Gloria—*a Unifying or Separating Principle?*

ON account of its wide range and its impersonal nature, the principle of *Soli Deo gloria*, to which Calvin reduced the Lutheran principle of *Sola gratia*, might seem to require an entirely different approach. There is no longer any question of an isolated theological thesis, though admittedly fundamental, nor even of an insight into the problem of salvation, however penetrating. What now concerns us is a view embracing the whole of theology and of religion too, a vision, sweeping and definitive, of the world and all that lies beyond.

If the primary intuition of Lutheranism needed first of all to be isolated in its pure and original state, precisely because of all its subsequent effects in the sphere of religion, the supreme intuition, as we may call it, of Calvinism needs rather to be linked to all its antecedents. It is in fact far less a principle, in the usual sense of a source, a spring, or a basis, a foundation, than a 'theory' in the aristotelian sense; that is, the final view in which the process of thought culminates, the goal which provides a far better explanation of it than all those fragmentary deductions reached on the way. So that, in the case of Calvin and his successors, an account of the *Soli Deo gloria*, though obscure at times and often groping, is the only way to elucidate both the ensemble and the details of a doctrine and way of life centred on the 'glory of God alone'.

In consequence, our first task in this chapter is to perceive that a number of features of Protestant thought and religion can be explained by their polarisation round this single force, apart from which they are incomprehensible. This will teach us how to distinguish between the real substance, the authentic trend, of Protestant spirituality, and its realisation at various points, with results of varying worth, but all derived ultimately from the same source, as the most clear-sighted of the Protestants themselves perceive. After that we shall be in a position to consider the verdict required by Catholic tradition on this trend and, at a deeper level, the relation between the ultimate aims of the individual Protestant and those of the Church.

1. THE *SOLI DEO GLORIA* IN CALVINISM

Authentic Lutheranism is not a theological system. It is wholly a religious movement, single and wide-ranging, which follows not always logically but vitally from a few basic intuitions, or rather from one viewed from every possible standpoint, quarried from every angle. Calvinism, on the other hand, is quite clearly a system as compact, perhaps more so, as thomism before it, or Molinism or Jansenism later. However, as a system, we repeat, its success has always been a limited one. Even in Geneva it did not survive Calvin. The French Protestants, for whom it had been originally destined, never really accepted it. Holland, which paid it a tribute of uncompromising fidelity at the synod of Dordrecht, was the scene of an irrepressible revolt in the person of Arminius and the 'remonstrants'. English Protestantism rejected, in its favour, both Catholicism and Anglicanism, but altered it profoundly in the form of Puritanism. All the same, French or Dutch Protestants, Scottish Presbyterians, English or American Congregationalists, even when they most impatiently disown strict Calvinism, all continue in their respect for Calvin. The reason for this lies in the distinction seen, with greater or less clarity, between Calvin's religious vision and the framework to which he fitted it. There is no doubt at all that even those of his spiritual descendants most firmly opposed to his ready-made system remain under the sway of the vision at its centre. We can go even further, and say that those Lutherans to whom his system is most thoroughly uncongenial, not merely in certain of its applications or effects, but as a whole, are often as loud as the 'Reformed' in their praise and gratitude for the profound vision which Calvin opened to them, a vision of the religious world in which was to be unfurled Luther's religion, so to call it, of 'instinct'.

This is due undoubtedly to the valuable testimony given by Calvin's system to this vision, accepted even by those who reject the logical structure. It is, then, highly necessary to assess, in Calvin's own doctrine, the importance of the role assigned to his

vision. The remarkable thing in this connection is Calvin's continual revision of his essential work, the *Institution Chrétienne*;
his principal aim seems to have been, at any rate the undoubted
result was, to heighten the significance of the *Soli Deo gloria*. To
show this, we will limit ourselves to the quotation and brief
explanation of one or two passages, either completely new or
newly developed in the final edition, the Latin one of 1559,
translated into French in 1560.

At the very beginning of the book, Calvin, treating of the
knowlege of God, aims at making it perfectly clear that the only
kind of knowledge that matters is what leads us to give him the
exclusive worship due to him. Knowledge of his existence, such
as Epicurus admitted, but which leaves us free, none the less,
to take refuge in indifference, is worthless. The only knowledge
that counts is what makes us recognise his sovereign power, and
so to expect all from him, and to consecrate ourselves, entirely
and exclusively, to his glory.

'What does it profit to confess, with the Epicureans, a God
who leaves the world to itself, and delights in a life of leisure?
What is the use even of knowing a God with whom we have
nothing to do? Rather should our knowledge of him first teach
us to fear and reverence him, then guide and counsel us to seek
from him all good, and acknowledge it as his gift. For, how
could the thought of God enter our minds without at the same
time the idea that, being his creation, we are rightfully assigned
and subject to his rule, that our life belongs to him, that all we
do ought to be referred to him? If this is so, it follows of necessity that our life is gravely corrupt, unless we direct it to his
service; his will must be our law of life. Again, it is impossible
to have a clear idea of God, without knowing him as the source
of all good, whence would arise the desire to cleave to him, and
to have confidence in him, were it not that man's depravity has
turned his mind from the true way. For at first the devout mind
does not dream up any kind of God, but contemplates him who
is the one true God. Nor does it imagine him according to its
own opinion, but is satisfied to accept him according to his own
revelation; it takes the greatest possible care not to be led away
by any rash folly to wander about outside the bounds of what

he has declared. Having thus come to know God, and that he governs all, it confides in his protection, and places itself entirely in his care. Because it knows him as the author of all good, as soon as it feels affliction or need, it turns to him, confident in his succour. Persuaded of his goodness and mercy, it rests on him in sure confidence, and does not doubt that for all adversities his compassion has prepared a remedy. Looking on him as Lord and Father, it judges it right to acknowledge his dominion, honour his majesty, advance his glory, obey his commands. Since it recognises in him a just judge, armed to punish sin with severity, it has his tribunal always present, whose fear restrains it from provoking his wrath. However, it is not so terrified at the thought of judgment as to wish to hide away from him, even if escape were possible; rather, it accepts him as judge of sinners as readily as rewarder of the good, for it realises that his glory is concerned equally with the chastisement of the evil and the admission of the just to eternal life. Furthermore, it does not refrain from sin solely through fear of punishment, but because it loves and reverences God as a father, it serves and worships him as Lord and Master; even were there no hell, it would have a horror of offending him. This is true, genuine religion, namely, faith united with a lively fear of God. It conjoins fear with a willing reverence, and entails the worship and service prescribed by the law of God.' [1]

We notice here the subject so forcefully developed in the sermon previously quoted: the thought of the glory to be given to God alone, to the exclusion of any other, should not crush us, but rather raise us, for he makes it his glory to do good to us, and so it ought to form the surest guarantee of the unique and absolute confidence which is the foundation of Lutheran devotion. That, however, makes it still more remarkable to find him so strongly asserting that any knowledge of God, worthy of the name, however elementary, must include the recognition of his absolute sovereignty, for without that the object of our knowledge would not really be God. If that applies to the very outset of any knowledge of God, even more should we expect it to

[1] Calvin, *Institutionis Christianae Religionis liber primus*, *cap.* XXIII.

apply to the final stage, not only of the knowledge available by reason of the Christian revelation, but of the full flowering of the life this revelation should effect in us. That is, certainly, how Calvin conceived, and summed up, the whole Christian life: '. . . the office of the faithful is to offer their bodies to God as a living, holy, and pleasing sacrifice; and . . . in this lies the reasonable service we have to give him (Rom. XII, 1). Thence follows the exhortation to the faithful not to be conformed to the fashion of this world, but to be transformed in newness of mind, and so seek to know the will of God. This is a great thing, that we are consecrated and dedicated to God, so that from now on we are not to think, speak, cogitate or act in any way but to his glory. For it is not lawful to apply a sacred thing to profane use. Now, if we belong not to ourselves, but to the Lord, it is plain what we are to do to avoid being misled, and where we are to direct all the acts of our life. We are not our own; therefore our own reason and will may not govern our intentions and deeds. We are not our own; therefore let us forget ourselves and all that is ours as much as may be. Once again, we are the Lord's; let us live and die to him; may his will and wisdom preside in all our actions. We are the Lord's; to him, then, as to its only rightful end, may our life be referred, in all its parts.' [1]

Nothing could show more convincingly that, for Calvin himself, the *Soli Deo gloria* is not only a sublime theory furnishing a base for preaching the fundamentals of Protestantism, but a magnificent religious, even mystical, vision, which ought to inspire the whole life of the Christian.

It is possibly of equal interest to discern the same motive at work in the heart of the Calvinist doctrine most bitterly controverted even by Protestants. We allude, of course, to that of predestination in its systematic exposition by Calvin. Later we shall have to discuss his system, and to distinguish in it what must be rejected in view of the primitive Christian teaching and the whole Catholic tradition. But it is important to show that Calvin and the strict Calvinists, in the degree of their adherence to his real thought, justify it solely by the desire of remaining wholly faithful to the idea, or rather vision, of the divine

[1] Calvin, *Institutionis Christianae liber tertius, cap.* VII.

sovereignty, which controls and directs their entire speculative system.

We cannot imagine anyone reading consecutively chapters 21 to 24 of the 3rd book of the *Institution Chrétienne*, on the Predestination and Vocation of the elect, without being struck by three things: first, its literally inexorable rigour of logic; second, that this very rigour is placed wholly at the service of the religious principle of the *sola gratia* of Luther, as explained; finally, that this principle, so treated, though we may be affronted by this or that detail of the structure, expands by degrees into the *Soli Deo gloria*, into which all resolves at the end.

As we follow Calvin in a line of thought which he, and Luther too, attribute, with some reason, to St. Bernard equally with St. Augustine, it becomes clear that his main preoccupation is to establish the Christian assurance of salvation on a base which no frailty or weakness, whether our own or of anything created, could possibly undermine. Now the only thing capable of giving absolute security is the pure will of God, considered in itself, whose sovereign freedom is known by his own revelation. But the argument leading to this conclusion establishes at the same time that God cannot possibly be held to depend, in the slightest degree or in any respect, on the creature, since the creature itself is in a state of total and absolute dependence on its Creator. Hence, we are driven back, more forcibly than ever, on the sublime paradox that Calvin constantly strives to illuminate; namely, that man, when he gives God alone the glory owing to him, and acknowledges the infinite greatness of this glory, far from being crushed by it, rests in an assured and stable joy and peace, since this same glory is in fact the sole, but supreme, pledge of his own salvation. We do not wonder that Calvin, in his last edition of that whole section, added the following passage; it reveals the motive-force of his entire thought.

'We shall never be properly convinced that the source of our salvation is the gratuitous mercy of God, until his eternal election becomes known to us; for this puts in a clear light the grace of God, showing he does not admit all and sundry to the grace of salvation, but contrasts his gift to some with its denial to others. It is evident that ignorance of this principle is equally detrimental to the glory of God and the genuine humility of man, for it makes us seek the cause of salvation elsewhere than in God alone. St. Paul affirms that this truth, so needful to know, would be inaccessible to us, unless God had chosen those he had decided himself to save, without the least regard to their works. In Romans XI, 5, he says: "At this present time, there is a remnant saved according to the election of grace. And if by grace, it is not now by works; otherwise, grace is no more grace." If by works, it is not by grace; otherwise, works are no more works. If we go back to the origin of election, and realise that salvation comes not elsewhere than from the sole liberality of God, those who desire to suppress this doctrine maliciously darken it as far as they can, instead of praising and exalting it with all their might; so they tear up humility by the roots. St. Paul, in ascribing the salvation of the remnant to gratuitous election, clearly witnesses to the fact that God, in his pure good pleasure, saves those whom he will; that he does not reward merit, since there is none. Those who close the door on this doctrine so as to exclude men from savouring it, do wrong no less to them than to God; for nothing is so capable of fostering in us due humility, or a heartfelt sentiment of our obligation to God. Christ himself bears witness that there is no other sure ground of confidence; to save us from all fear, and make us invincible, among so many perils, snares and mortal conflicts, he promises to save whatever the Father has given into his hand' (John X, 29).[1]

However, it is impossible to judge the work of Calvin by his theological writings alone. His personality cannot be identified with that of an academic thinker. It is much nearer the truth to say that the *Institution Chrétienne*, especially in view of its constant revision by Calvin throughout his life, is governed by his experiences in the actual working out of the task he set himself, the establishment of the Reformed Church and the city it informed. This work, it cannot be denied, was a partial failure. The preface to the *Institution Chrétienne* makes Calvin's ambitious design only too clear for us to have any doubt. What he

[1] Calvin, *Institutionis Christianae Religionis liber tertius, cap.* XXXI.

aimed at, and desired to see Francis I, to whom the book was
addressed, understand and support, was a remoulding of
Christian France, which would become the nucleus of a new
Christendom. All that he brought into being was a tiny community, very different from the pattern of his desire, Protestant
Geneva; and it was on a minority Church, the Reformed Church
of France, that he set an indelible mark, though he never succeeded in shaping it wholly to his liking. However, this work,
limited and obstructed though it was, embodied an ideal whose
influence spread far beyond those bounds. Scotland and Holland copied and surpassed those achievements. Calvin himself
was perhaps most successful where he could act only by means
of others, even if his influence was later countered by opposing
ones. Finally, in the Protestantism of the New World, he won a
posthumous, though equally partial, success, but there some
features at least of his ideal were stamped on the rebellious
material more strongly than anywhere else. His achievement
can, then, be fully assessed only if it be considered, first in the
social and religious institutions he strove to set up, next in those
established, not by him, but under his influence.

The Church he aimed at setting up in Geneva, and thereby in
the whole of Christendom, beginning with France, appears at
first sight no less repugnant in certain of its features than his
theoretical system; the same, seemingly inhuman, rigour, the
same stifling abstraction, of a framework imposed by a logic,
strict but lifeless. But we have to learn to transcend these
appearances, and to perceive the latent fervour running through
his partial successes, which alone accounts for the strange mag-
netism they exercised well beyond the Churches held to be
formally Calvinist.

Calvinist worship, in its historical setting, would seem to be
something absolutely new, without roots in the past, or rather
an artificial product, the result of uprooting practically all
traditional Christianity, and of substituting a bloodless creation
of the intellect. The cathedrals of Romansch Switzerland, where
not only the statues have disappeared, but even the altar, the
focus of the whole building, and all that goes to make up the
atmosphere of devotion and worship, seem to speak of an extreme impoverishment; one might almost look on them, not as

purified or transformed, but simply antagonistic. However, a characteristic already noted should be enough to warn us against so false an impression, at least as touching the profound significance of this transformation. The name given by French Protestants to their service is the most religious one there could be—quite simply, *le culte*, worship. And in fact it is the concern directly, I would say fiercely, implied in this word which is at the bottom of all this upheaval. This is certainly the explanation of the fact that, where the authentic spirit of Calvin has been preserved, this devastating austerity still makes such an overpoweringly religious impression. On the contrary, where it no longer exists, the well-meant efforts to rekindle Calvinist 'worship', to make it 'more liturgical', result only in grotesque absurdities utterly lacking the sublimity of true Calvinism, without recapturing that of Catholic worship. One of the most evidently sacred actions we ever witnessed was the Calvinist supper celebrated by M. Lecerf—himself the embodiment of the spirit of primitive Calvinism—without any of the traditional forms, even the customary black gown. On the other hand, it is quite certain that the spruce churches, the elaborate ceremonies, dear to some present-day Protestants, a poor imitation of a Catholicism they understand no more than their own traditions, convey the same unfortunate impression as do many modern Trappist churches, where the appurtenances of a sentimental devotion have come to smother and obscure the pure beauty of Cistercian worship.

It must be borne in mind that in Calvinist worship all that affects the senses, all that attracts the eye, is implacably excluded, in order that this very annihilation of all that is human may stress the sole presence of God, the recognition that his glory absolutely transcends all that savours of man or the world. Horror and dread of idolatry have been carried to the extreme of iconoclasm, but that is because the sense of the greatness of God, of the naked purity of a worship alone worthy of a majesty that owes nothing to the creature, has itself been carried to the point at which all symbols, all that appeals to the imagination or the senses, seem absolutely absurd.

With this element, the quintessence of Calvinism, is associated a consideration from the pastoral and pedagogic sphere. For

those who have not yet reached these heights, the Calvinist fears,
more than anything, that the means ostensibly suited to their
weakness may turn out to hinder and to screen the reality. In
the void and in nakedness, if the soul does not reach out to God,
it runs no risk of illusion and deception. It will not think that it
advances towards him, or has found him, when it is only
amusing itself, merely losing sight of itself among trifles that
have nothing in common with him. Conversely, for the soul
which truly seeks him, at however great a distance, this virile
austerity may have the most invigorating effect, sustaining its
élan, and averting the risk of its being diverted or wavering.
No intermediary between it and God, but also nothing which
divides them; only the void where real faith has to abandon
itself unreservedly, to find him, Him and no counterfeit, no
misleading image of him whom it is impossible to depict.

In this relentless void there remains one single reality, raised
up by himself precisely to make himself known to man, to
create with man the relationship that man is radically incapable
of setting up himself—namely, the Word of God. The Word of
God proclaimed to man, this is really the whole of the genuine
Calvinist worship. For nothing of human devising can raise
man to the level of the God who 'inhabits light inaccessible'.
Only his personal condescension can bring him to the level of
man. We might add that the homage man pays to the sovereign
glory of God proclaimed by his Word must itself be borrowed
from this Word; otherwise it is merely ridiculous. 'God alone
speaks adequately of God.' Calvin would have loved Pascal's
saying and would certainly have adopted it as the formula of
his mode of worship, not only as conveying a teaching, or
rather a revelation, but as implying adherence to this teaching,
and praise of the glory manifesting itself in the only way worthy
of it. That is why the authentic Calvinist worship never allows,
in its public liturgy, any other prayer than the psalms. Only the
inspired songs seem worthy to be placed with the inspired Word.
Those modern forms of the Reformed service into which, for
the last century, hymns of an individualistic, sentimental nature
have so deeply burrowed, justly arouse, among pure Calvinists,
the same nausea as the so-called Sulpician hymnody among
Catholics brought up on the traditional liturgy.

Nevertheless, the Word of God itself prescribes too clearly
the celebration of the sacramental acts of the Eucharistic
Supper and of Baptism for Calvin to think of omitting them;
the same may be said of some other rituals, like blessings, and,
in particular, the laying on of hands on ministers of the Church.
In consequence, he found room for them and even wished to
give them far more importance than they ever actually found in
the Reformed Churches. He wished every 'worship' (*culte*) to
include celebration of the 'Supper'. However, he desired this
celebration to be carried out in such a way that the Sacrament should itself become a *verbum visibile*, as bare as possible
of its human substance, as penetrable, or, better, as transparent
as possible, to the one Word of God where God alone reveals
himself in ineffable glory.

Yet, as we have already observed, the remarkable thing is
that the development of the Calvinist Churches has everywhere
inclined to the total absorption of the sacramental element in
the 'ministry of the word'. In fact, there is no Calvinist Church,
even of the strict obedience, where the celebration of the Supper
is not restricted to three or four times in the year. At the same
time, the celebration, both of Baptism and the Supper, has been
reduced to the essential sign in the most abstract form, simply a
seal placed on a 'liturgy' which is really no more than the preaching of the Word. It is remarkable, too, that even this minimum
fails to satisfy Protestants of this school. Although obedience
to the New Testament does not seem to them, any more than to
Calvin himself, to permit a complete dissolution of symbolic
ritual, it is hard to deny that they view with envy, even with an
uneasy conscience, communities more venturesome. The
Quakers, exponents of a Christianity without any liturgy whatsoever, without a ministry, without an organised Church, without
Sacrament, cannot but seem to them the ideal type of Protestant. Even while objecting that they violate the very conditions imposed by human nature in the flesh, and which Christ
himself willed to accept, they cannot prevent themselves re-
gretting that they are unable to, or may not, go so far. Here we
are in the presence of the first, and very significant, example of
the tension between what we might call the form and the matter
of the religion of the Word; we shall later find many others.

The Word of God, his final revelation as the Lord, seems
logically to lead to the duty of abolishing from his worship all
that is not, purely and simply, himself. But if this Word, as
identified with the Bible, only too clearly prescribes certain concrete 'means of grace', an unavoidable tension is bound to arise.
It will be resisted by orthodox Calvinists, whereas those for
whom Calvinism is a 'spirit', rather than a literal observance,
will yield to it with enthusiasm.

If now we pass from the sphere of worship and the Church
to the community and the social and political life Calvin desired
to build up round this centre, the subjection of this community
and the consecration of its public life to the *Soli Deo gloria* will
appear no less vividly.

Protestant historians are often at pains to reject the term theo-
cracy, applied to Calvin's Geneva, at any rate in the form he intended. They urge that Calvin, better than any medieval jurist,
defined the respective functions of the ecclesiastical authority
and the civil magistrate in such a way that the Church as such
could never, either in principle or in reality, enjoy any temporal
power. The Calvinist Church, as described in the later editions
of the *Institution Chrétienne* with increasing precision, can never,
of itself, interfere in the temporal administration. Calvin goes
on to say, in most definite terms, that it is absolutely contrary to
the vocation of his ministers to add to their ecclesiastical functions any office in the State, any judicial power.[1] The modern
rule of the separation of Church and State seems to have been
derived from him; and it is possible to see in the *Institution
Chrétienne* the root of all those democratic constitutions which,
following that of the United States, have assured the complete
autonomy of the Church (or Churches) and the civil authority.

But these principles are only sections detached from the whole
system, and to understand their application and practical effect
as Calvin intended we must turn to other elements which constitute, so to speak, the dynamic character, as opposed to the
static character, of the social organism.

In fact, the civil law, for Calvin, and the magistrate who has to
make and apply it, have no other justification than the will of

[1] On this and all that follows, consult Imbart de la Tour, *Calvin et
l'Institution Chrétienne* (Vol. IV in his *Origines de la Réforme*).

God, as contained, not only in some kind of natural law inherent in things, but in the Word of God with its exact pro-
nouncements. Consequently, the civil law, to be valid, and the
acts of political institutions, if they are to correspond to their
place in the system, must not only refrain from obstructing the
'true religion', not only forbid whatever opposes it, not only
promote it even, but may not envisage any other final end than
that supreme glory of God that man subserves in bowing to his
will and to that alone.

This amounts to saying that civil life is to be, in principle,
·entirely dominated by the Word of God, ruled by the sovereign
will it proclaims, and so tending wholly to the sole glory of the
absolute sovereign there revealed. In practice, by the very
nature of things, the whole system was bound to culminate in a
subjection of the civil to the religious order of society far more
rigorous even than Innocent III or Boniface VIII could·ever
have dreamt of. In fact, all Calvin's efforts at Geneva were
directed towards ·a radical dependence of the civil on the religious authority; and, in spite of the opposing forces which
prevented his ever realising his dream, it must be admitted that,
while refusing any other official role than that of a teacher, he
exercised an almost absolute dictatorial power.

It is indisputable that this result was due to Calvin's being one
of the most strongly authoritarian personalities to be met within
the whole of modern history. But, in considering this aspect exclusively, one would be overlooking completely what he held to
be the justification of his authoritarianism, and quite certainly
the sole aim he set himself, with absolute disinterestedness, in
exercising it. This justification, this aim, was the establishment
of a city given over entirely to the glory of God; a real heavenly
Jerusalem come down on earth, whose public law, like the wholly
interior law to be obeyed both by the individual and society,
would be solely the law of the Sovereign God expressed in his
Word.

This motive was not merely determining, but all-inclusive;·
and to understand its entire scope, we must devote some space
to another original feature in Calvin's development of Luther's
thought. Here, too, in emending his predecessor to the point
where he seems at times to contradict him, he is prompted, it

must be admitted, by a creative fidelity which continues the same trend of some of his deepest insights, but, as always, expresses itself with a lucidity and precision unattainable by Luther.

In his assertion of justification by faith alone, in the sole grace of God, independently of man's works, Luther took pains to emphasise, with undoubted sincerity, that this involved, in his view, no tendency to moral laxity. On the contrary, as he constantly insisted, good works ought to flow spontaneously from the person justified by faith, as fruit grows from a sound tree. But Calvin does not stop there. For him, justification, if genuine, is prolonged into a sanctification which is effective externally. He goes on to show that the soul of this sanctification is obedience, just as faith is the soul of justification. Even this parallel is inadequate; it is necessary to add that obedience is but the prolongation of real faith into the whole of life, so much so that sanctification in the end is nothing but justification expanded and expressed in act. On this point, the *Institution Chrétienne* and the whole preaching of Calvin are as categorical as could be desired.

'We confess that, when God reconciles us to himself by means of the justice of Christ, and, by the free remission of our sins, reputes us to be just, he joins to this mercy a further benefit, namely, he dwells in us by his holy Spirit, by whose virtue the lusts of our flesh are daily more and more mortified, and we are ourselves sanctified, that is, consecrated to God in true purity of life, our hearts once moulded to the obedience of the Law; so that the principal aim of our will may be to serve his will, and to advance his glory alone in every way.' [1]

By sanctification, then, so closely bound up with justification, the entire life of man, organised according to the will of God, has to be directed to his glory.

A few pages further on, Calvin demonstrates the intimate and essential connection between this sanctification and justification, and how obedience is the prolongation of faith. He does

---

[1] Calvin, *Institutionis Christianae Religionis liber tertius, cap.* XIV.

so by showing that the good works of the Christian are not a partial, or in any way independent, cause of justification, something added to the pure gift of God, but that they all have their source in this gift itself. If then, he goes on to say, Scripture sometimes considers works as the cause of the blessings of God, 'this must be understood in such a way that all that we said above still holds good; namely, the origin and effecting of our salvation is the love of the heavenly Father, the matter and substance is the obedience of Christ, the instrument, is the illumination of the Holy Spirit, that is, faith; its end is that the goodness of God may be glorified.' [1]

All this is summed up in this salient passage, which not only accords justification by faith alone with the necessity of good works, and declares them illusory apart from sanctification, but affirms the profound unity of both in Christ, with a vigour unequalled by other theologians of the Reformation.

'We do not dream of a faith empty of good works, or a justification existing apart from them; the point is that, in maintaining that faith and good works are necessarily bound up together, we attribute justification, not to works, but to faith. The reason for this is easily seen, if we turn to Christ, to whom faith is directed, and from whom it draws its whole force. How is it we are justified by faith? Because by faith we take hold of the justice of Christ, which alone reconciles us to God. But we cannot take hold of this, without taking hold, at the same time, of sanctification. For he is given to us as our justice, wisdom, sanctification, redemption (1 Cor. I, 30). Therefore, Christ justifies no one without also sanctifying him. For these benefits are joined by an eternal bond, so that whom he enlightens by his wisdom he redeems, whom he redeems he justifies, whom he justifies he sanctifies. But, since the whole question only touches justice and sanctification, we will confine ourselves to them. Though we may distinguish one from the other, Christ contains them both without division. Do you, then, desire to obtain justice in Christ? You must first possess Christ. But you cannot possess him, without participating in his sanctification, for he cannot be torn apart. Since, therefore, the Lord never

[1] Calvin, *Institutionis Christianae Religionis liber tertius, cap.* XIV.

gives us the enjoyment of these benefits without giving us himself, he gives us both at the same time; never one without the other. Thus we see how true it is that we are not justified without works, but yet not by works, since our participation in Christ by which we are justified includes sanctification as well as justice.' [1]

Only in thinking over passages like this, setting them alongside the crucial sentence of the text previously quoted, which sums up the Christian life in the words, 'from henceforth we are not to think, speak, meditate, act in any way, except for his glory', can we come to appreciate Calvin's immense effort of reconstruction in the ecclesiastical and political spheres. Not only the Church within the City, but the city in its entirety has to be built up, in his view, by and for the progressive sanctification of man justified, so that, in the words of the apostle, 'in all things God may be glorified'.

2. THE *SOLI DEO GLORIA* IN THE LIFE OF PROTESTANTISM

It was extremely important to give this aspect of the thought of Calvin, not only particular attention, but a detailed exposition. For it is precisely this aspect of Calvinism that had the greatest success and gained him most followers. The Puritanism of Cromwell and his Roundheads, of New England with John Cotton and Thomas Hooker, the undoubted fathers of the peculiar Christianity of modern America, all arise from the same source. There lies the explanation of the apparent paradox that a religion which started with the condemnation of 'works' should have culminated in a moralism unknown to any of the Catholic countries.

It is, moreover, from this feature of Calvinism that its moralism derives its real significance, its genuinely religious meaning. The Puritan ideal is that of a society in which the collective life, as well as the personal life of its members, is entirely consecrated to the 'sanctification' spoken of by Calvin, and so, in effect, centred on the *Soli Deo gloria* ... If we confine our

[1] Calvin, *Institutionis Christianae Religionis liber tertius, cap.* XVI; *cf. cap.* I on faith and repentance.

D

attention to the severe moral prescriptions, public as well as private, to the minutely detailed rules for applying them, the compulsion and even tyranny, of the political organism created to enforce them, we shall overlook what gives meaning to the whole; namely, the will, rooted in faith, to make the whole life of man, and the world organised in function of it, an act of homage to the sovereign God. The beauty and nobility of this ideal, at once moral and political, endow Puritanism with a soul which, rightly understood, might excuse all its narrowness and pettiness.

It is not surprising that the present followers of Karl Barth, remote though they are from Puritanism, in their desire to re-vivify Protestantism by returning to its sources, have a distinct preference for Calvin to Luther, precisely on account of the doctrine of 'sanctification', with its application both to the individual and to society. In face of a world which denies God, they consider with some reason that Lutheranism, taken literally with its almost entirely negative conception of 'works', runs the risk of surrender without conflict, and is in danger of taking convenient refuge in a wholly interior religion. In contrast, they see, rightly, an indestructible basis for uncompromising witness to God in the developed Calvinist teaching, with its ethic of obedience to him alone, and its concept of society radically opposed to the virtual idolatry of modern totalitarianism. More precisely, they are justified in finding in Calvinism the only legitimate totalitarianism, which brings back everything to the one true God, and is consequently irreconcilably opposed to every kind of 'humanist' totalitarianism, whether it claims to be 'materialist' or 'spiritualist'.

However, the Barthian neo-Protestant, while adhering firmly to this particular aspect of Calvinism, acknowledges enthusi-astically its dependence on more fundamental ones. Barth, we may say, not content with recovering the full implications of the Calvinist *Soli Deo gloria*, has carried it to an extreme of con-scious, deliberate purity, unattained possibly even by Calvin himself.

We shall notice later the very rich contribution of Barthian thought to the theology of the Word of God. Certainly, as we have already observed in connection with Calvinist worship, there is a direct link between a revival of the Calvinist idea of the Word and a deep penetration into the Calvinist doctrine of the sovereignty of God. But the real essence of Barthism is undoubtedly its rediscovery of the idea of the divine glory, not merely a return to Calvin, but an extension of his thought, though along the same lines.

The entire thought, the whole spiritual movement of Barth, are, as it were, penetrated by this rediscovery. In this, Barth is opposed to the worldly, even materialist, humanism of today, and still more so to the Protestantism developed from the 'liberalism' and the 'social Christianity' in which he had received his first formation. Often enough, Catholics misunderstand this primary aspect of Barthism; they see clearly that it is a reaction, without perceiving precisely what it reacts against. This consists, in fact, of the very deformation which threatens Lutheranism and to which we drew attention in our last chapter, one which could bring it from the most radical theoretical transcendentalism to an utter immanentism in fact. Barth reacted against this degenerate Protestantism which sees in God merely a 'spiritual energy' domesticated by man, rather like physical energy in modern civilisation, and restored the Calvinist vision. But in his restoration, we repeat, Barth goes much further than Calvin; he brings back the sole glory of God as the ultimate meaning of things, but he refuses to associate it as closely as Calvin with the salvation of man. With him, the idea of the glory of God so invades all that it cannot let anything subsist, even apparently, on the same level as itself. Calvin, though reducing all to the divine glory and to that alone, left intact the personal assurance of salvation with which, as we shall see in greater detail, Luther had identified faith in grace. Barth rejects this, and on this point, strangely enough, finds himself in agreement with Catholic doctrine, while at the same time he diverges, far more than the Reformers had ever done, from the traditional teaching of the Middle Ages on justification.

Barth, in fact, holds that faith excludes any self-regarding attitude of mind. On the contrary, it withdraws man completely from himself, and excludes any possibility of reversion, substituting for a religion divided between the interests of God and man something he will not even call by the name of 'religion', for it rules out any supposition of two comparable terms. For him, God alone is the subject of religion, in an extreme sense undreamt of by Calvin; the subject, not the object, for he cannot be in the least dependent on our apprehension, but He alone affirms himself in his Word as the sole agent, the sole reality, and not merely the sole end. The first *cri de cœur* of the Barthian faith comes in the commentary on the epistle to the Romans, uttered there with an intensity and purity never afterwards repeated; it is the principle, *Finitum non capax infiniti*, the finite is not 'capable' of the infinite. Later, Barth found this sounded too philosophical and substituted the formula, more Scriptural in its terms, *Homo peccator non capax justitiæ Dei*, sinful man is not 'capable' of the justice of God. The first formula, in its direct abruptness and its uncompromising antithesis, may, however, be thought to express more exactly his intuition. The way in which Biblical phrases like 'Thou art on the earth, and God is in heaven', or 'I will give my glory to no other', recur in Barth's writings is a perpetual warning or reminder of the absolute character of the divine glory, admitting no conceivable limitation.

Barth, too, never tires of recalling that God is 'the Lord', and that that ultimately is the whole message of his Word. But to say that, in regard to his unique dominion, our duty is to acknowledge that we are slaves does not go far enough; it is our nothingness we must admit. Not only any comparison, but any possibility even, of a real relation between God and his creature, is excluded. Creation, far from being such, and redemption, further still, affirm its impossibility, its complete meaninglessness. That is why Barth denies that Christianity is properly speaking a 'religion', and the Gospel in his eyes, far from conveying anything of the sort, ought to make the possibility unthinkable. In a world ceaselessly attracted by the illusion of reducing God to its own measure, the divine Word is God's protest, putting back everything in its proper place through Christ; that is to say, it exalts God above every measure imaginable, literally annihilating all that is not He, and, first of all, the pretensions of man.

The impression conveyed by Calvinist worship, still more by the Calvinist logic, of a kind of desert, is here carried beyond

all bounds. Yet here more than anywhere, in the wild exultation
of this apparent nihilism, it ought to be impossible not to recognise an understanding, rarely equalled, of the sacred majesty
of God. In a world, in a 'civilised' Christianity, where even the
religion of the Gospel seems now to tend only to the exaltation
of man, we ought certainly to recognise that Barthism exacts,
before and above all, a return to the Biblical and Christian idea
of God whose genuine nobility no believing Christian should
hesitate to respect. Never, perhaps, has anyone so forcefully
grasped and expressed the unknowable, the inexpressible—that
God, if he be truly God and not an idol constructed by us for
our use, escapes our grasp absolutely, not only the grasp of our
mind and will, but that of our 'religion', in so far as even that is,
in a sense, ours, and not the avowal of our nothingness in the
presence of his Word.

The most important fact about Barthism in the sphere of
present-day religious thought, like the Puritanism of yesterday
in that of the Christian civilisation so mercilessly criticised by
Barthism, is that the main value of both lies in their different
ways of expressing the same 'sense of God', intimately felt by
all genuine Protestants, however remote from Cromwell or
Barth. There can be no understanding of the most enduring,
as well as the most immediate, reactions of the Protestant mentality, unless this is borne in mind. We have already drawn
attention to the strange paradox, mostly due to misunderstandings, which considers Calvinists hostile to all 'mysticism',
though, in fact, of all the Protestants they are the most 'mystical'
in inspiration, provided the terms are understood in their true
historical sense. Similarly, though Barth has delivered himself
of a stern criticism of the concept of 'religion', it must be admitted that the Barthians are the most 'religious' of Protestants,
if 'religion' is used in the traditional meaning of theology, as
when we speak of the 'virtue of religion'. No others have carried
to a higher pitch their intense reverence for God, nor placed in
such a clear light the ultimate source of the strength of Protestantism as a religious movement. Perhaps the most difficult
thing for Catholics to understand, the Protestant repugnance to
so many modes of thinking, speaking and acting that to

Catholics raise no difficulty, derives entirely, or at any rate basically, from the same source. All the anthropomorphisms used by the devout in speaking of God, the expressions used equally in relation to God and the saints, even to his representatives on earth—all these matters to which Catholics often pay such slight attention that they cannot even imagine them in the light of problems to be solved, are to Protestants so many intolerable blasphemies. For them, all that is 'idolatry', since it seems tantamount to admitting that God may be set on the same plane as the creature, or at any rate a comparable one.

For the same reason, any confidence placed in ascetic practices, in 'religious experiences', mystical or otherwise, in 'merits', or even in rites or prayers, sacraments or liturgy, they consider 'magic'. For in all this it seems to them that man attributes to himself, or to some empirical procedure, what pertains exclusively to the sovereign action of the Word of God. 'Idolatry', 'magic', the two charges continually levelled by Protestants against Catholicism, seem so absurd to Catholics, and are taken so seriously by Protestants, solely because they are seen to be necessarily prompted by a sense of the majesty and holiness of God, whose utter genuineness Catholics rarely come to understand, misled, as they are, by externals to which they are unaccustomed. In a Protestant church, Catholics will be struck by the apparent lack of anything sacred: but they fail to recognise that the Protestant soul, whose reactions are often so difficult for an outsider to penetrate, possesses a very lofty, absolutely Scriptural and Christian sense of the sacred. The true Protestant is a man so caught up by God, his majesty, his holiness (in the primary sense of the word, implying infinite elevation, absolute religious transcendence), that all the rest seems absurd in comparison. That is why, with someone whose reaction is different, the Protestant is irresistibly drawn to suspect the absence of this sense, that God is not recognised, but that some idol or other is worshipped in his place, and that, while the pretence is made of serving and worshipping him, he is in fact dishonoured and made subservient to procedures, consciously or unconsciously magical.

There lies, without doubt, the most tragic and deepest-rooted misunderstanding between Protestantism and Catholicism. Yet, if Catholics desire at all to help their separated brethren to overcome it in time, they must first realise the root cause of the Protestant attitude.

3. THE *SOLI DEO GLORIA* AND THE CATHOLIC FAITH

Granted that the pre-eminent characteristic of the most clear-sighted and self-conscious Protestantism is its intimate sense of God, what should be the response of a Catholic? Here, without any doubt, we enter on territory where prejudice and misconceptions on both sides have played a much more extended and serious part than in the *sola gratia*. Yet it seems that here equally (perhaps even more) the Catholic should have no hesitation in acknowledging the true Christian character of the Protestant assertion, provided it is reduced to what is primary and essential in it. This sense of God, so finely expressed by Calvin, which Barth raised perhaps to a still higher plane, and which makes every Protestant, true to the best in his religion, recognise his affinity to them, however remote he be from entire agreement—this sense of God so distinctive of Protestantism is, in certain of its aspects, undoubtedly part of the content of Scripture, and so cannot be called in question; nor can we dispute that it is in fact something supreme and final. Moreover, this sense of the sacred is found expressed in Catholic tradition, as we have already indicated, in a form as complete and undisguised as could be wished, though we shall have to return to a fuller and more exact analysis of it later. Indeed, as we have also observed, it is sometimes these aspects of Catholicism that have become the most incomprehensible to Protestants, though they could find in them the very assertion they have most at heart, and ought to recognise it. They would do so, without doubt, if they were not prevented by prejudices which are far from being entirely their fault. To dissolve such prejudices, together with those which Catholics for their part may still entertain, even after what we have written above, on the real motive force of Protestants, is the task to which we now address ourselves.

Whoever compares the great principle of Protestantism, if we have succeeded in transcribing it accurately, with the sublime

conceptions of the Bible itself, will have no difficulty in recognising their agreement. Our account of Calvin and his various
followers cannot be fully understood, except by those who
recognise in their teaching a true echo of the revelation of Moses,
of the great Hebrew prophets, and, in no less degree, of the
Gospels.

It should be clear to anyone that the God of Calvin is,
primarily, the God of Sinai, the God who makes himself manifest in a splendour and majesty inaccessible to man. The
divine glory, on which Calvin insisted so strongly, is precisely—we use the word in its Biblical sense—that unbearable
splendour of the divine majesty as revealed in the Mosaic theo-
phanies. Nor is it doubtful that the equation set up between
the recognition of this glory, which admits of no analogy, and
the rejection, not only of idols, but of any attempt at represent-
ing it adequately by anything created, is the first and most insistent statement in the decalogue. 'Thou shalt not have
strange gods before me. Thou shalt not make to thyself a
graven thing, nor the likeness of any thing that is in heaven
above, or in the earth beneath, nor of those things that are in
the waters under the earth. Thou shalt not adore them nor
serve them. I am the Lord thy God, mighty, jealous, visiting
the iniquity of the fathers on the children, unto the third and
fourth generations of them that hate me, and showing mercy to
thousands of them that love me, and keep my commandments.
Thou shalt not take the name of the Lord, thy God, in vain; for
the Lord will not hold him guiltless that shall take the name of
the Lord his God in vain.' (Exodus, XX, 3–7.)

It cannot be disputed that these words are at the basis of the
whole of revelation. That, above all, is what the whole of Calvinism and the whole of Barthism aim at safeguarding; and, in
so far as they actually do so, under the noblest and purest impulse of Protestantism, the Catholic can only agree with them
entirely. But the Protestant affirmation is perhaps even closer
to the great prophets, particularly in what we have singled out
as most characteristic of Calvinism and of Barth, who in turn
laboured to emphasise it still more strongly than Calvin. The
divine sovereignty, the omnipotence of God which is a super-
eminent dignity and sublimity, is precisely the divine holiness

that Isaias has described in incomparable language, in terms to which Calvin and Barth are constantly recurring. Further, the assertion, so typical of Calvin, that faith in this God insists remorselessly on standing alone, to the exclusion of any faith in man or this world, is precisely the central assertion of Isaias. And what we have stressed as the great advance of Calvin's thought on Luther's, the admirable way he re-establishes continuity between faith and obedience, is, once more, the most distinctive feature of Isaias's concept of faith.

Consequently, if there is one point where the Protestant Reformation, in its basic impulse, is absolutely faithful to the Bible, it would seem to be here. Besides, the ceaseless denunciation of all forms, open or veiled, of idolatry, which seemed to Calvin and his successors an indispensable counterpart of their fidelity to the true God, is no less characteristic of the religion of Isaias. Barth's own distrust of the term 'religion' itself proceeds obviously from the same solicitude which impelled the prophets to make it absolutely clear that Yahve's alliance with his people had nothing in common with the imaginary alliance of other peoples with other gods. There is no room here for any magic bond, any reciprocity on an equal level between Creator and creature; the alliance to which God consents is a pure grace; it asserts rather than rejects his sovereign liberty. After it Yahve remains, as before, 'the God who dwelleth not in a house made by hands', that is, he does not let himself be taken over by man. Far from his being made, by the alliance, the possession of his people, it is the people that no longer belongs to itself, but is totally made over to him. All the great themes of Calvinism and Barthism must be recognised for what they certainly are—scriptural themes, and especially the central themes of the great prophets.

At the same time, it would be vain to try to get rid of them, in the too facile manner of many a Catholic apologist, by discarding them along with much in the Old Testament that is merely preparatory. On the contrary, if the Old Testament contains anything at all of ultimate validity, these have the very first claim. If the martyrs of the New Testament were really such, that is precisely because of their refusal to sacrifice to idols, even in the most harmless forms. It is in the epistle to the

Hebrews that we find the words: 'It is a terrible thing to fall into the hands of the living God'; and again: 'Our God is a consuming fire.' We are told in the first epistle to Timothy that God 'inhabiteth light inaccessible'. Christ himself said: 'Why callest thou me good? One only is good, that is God.' In general, the constant theme of the numerous doxologies of the New Testament, notably of St. Paul, is that ultimately all glory is to be returned to God alone through Christ. When the seer of the Apocalypse is tempted to adore the angel who reveals to him the divine secrets, the angel tells him, in words that practically summarise the whole teaching of the New Testament: 'See thou do it not [adore me]. For I am thy fellow servant, and of thy brethren the prophets and of them that keep the words of the prophecy of this book. Adore God.' (Apoc. XXII, 9.) The truth is, the formula of Barth is the exact echo of the final teachings of the New Testament; all that the divine Word wished not only to tell us, but to accomplish in us at the same time, is that God, and he alone, in Christ, is the Lord.

Actually, it would be absurd to waste time in bringing forward more proofs. The more familiar we are with the Word of God, the more clearly we see that this sums up its message. It is much more important to agree unreservedly with the Protestants that, if there is one error Christians must guard against more than any other, it is idolatry. For, there is no error capable of vitiating Christianity more thoroughly, not only in its teaching, but in its life, than to put the Creator and the creature on the same plane. No single error, in consequence, demands so much precaution, since there is none more inveterate in our sinful nature; none into which, in spite of so many warnings and safeguards, it tends so strongly to fall back, once it is left, however slightly, to its own inclinations.

At the same time, there is no error, and it is most necessary for Protestants to recognise this, that the traditional teaching of Catholic theology, ascetical and mystical, pursues with greater insistence and perspicacity. The fact is, it is utterly inconceivable how many Protestants could persist in viewing Catholic asceticism as 'magic', and Catholic mysticism as 'idolatry'. If this error receives frequent support from the infidelities, the inconsequence, the clumsiness, of Catholics, it still remains so gross that its root, too, must lie in a misunderstanding for which Protestantism is itself responsible, one we shall later have to denounce. But, before coming to that, it is better to show how an unbiased acquaintance with the mystical teaching most characteristic of Catholicism, and most closely and explicitly bound up with its ascetical doctrine, annihilates these accusations of magic and idolatry. If the Catholic Church, at the very period when Protestantism came into conflict with it, acknowledged the teaching of one writer in particular as the purest account of her spiritual doctrine, it is the teaching of St. John of the Cross, proclaimed by the Popes the doctor *par excellence* of ascetical and mystical theology. Now the most striking thing about St. John of the Cross is that he draws his teaching from exactly the same Biblical sources as Calvin and his successors, and that the dominant themes of his whole life and thought are just those which govern what we do not shrink from the apparent paradox of calling 'Calvinist mysticism' and 'Barthian religion'.

What, then, is the basic doctrine expressed in St. John's great themes (quite obviously Biblical in inspiration) of the dark night of the soul and the ascent of Mount Carmel? Essentially, it is the divine summons to pass beyond and renounce all that is not God in his absolute transcendence, as dimly perceived in his own Word. For St. John, no less than for Calvin and Barth, the radical error and vice is idolatry. For him, asceticism has no other end than to prevent us from confusing with God, not only any 'earthly good', but even any earthly image, even the most religious. He goes still further, since even our most spiritual ideas of the divinity have to be abandoned in the 'night of the spirit'. With all the greater reason does he insist on our going beyond the 'practices' themselves, and even that is not enough; he even denounces our pernicious tendency to make a last idol of our 'religious experiences' in so far as they still pertain to our senses, our imagination, or our intellect. Nor does he stop there; he goes to the extreme of warning us that even those mystical experiences, the most authentically divine in origin we could possibly have, become the last and most pernicious of idols if we confuse them ever so slightly with God himself, if we do not allow his grace to carry us beyond them. Thus, for him, true mysticism, that which is a real foretaste of the heavenly vision, consists solely in total abandonment to the night of faith; abandonment, he is careful to point out, which can in no way be attained so long as we see in it, or tend, however slightly, even unconsciously, to see in it, our own 'work'; it can only be the work of God in us.

The principle behind all this is given by St. John in a passage Calvin himself would not have disowned, for it embodies just the themes so familiar to him. It runs: 'The Lord is a God too jealous to allow another to share the same altar with him. . . . The only desire the Lord allows the soul to have along with him, is that of keeping perfectly the divine law, and of carrying the cross of Christ.' [1]

And, as regards the means at man's disposal for this ideal, the following passage, though it makes use of a different terminology from that of Calvin or Barth, surely aims at conveying precisely what they had most at heart; namely, renunciation of all that comes from self, docility without reserve to the gift of God. 'The disposition required for union with God does not consist in understanding, tasting, feeling, or imagining God; it consists solely of purity and love, that is, of *complete submission of the will and absolute detachment from all for the sake of God alone.'* [2]

Once more, St. John of the Cross is as categorical as the most clear-sighted and exacting of Protestants could wish on the fact that the 'union with God' he speaks of is nothing else than a gift of faith which, coming entirely from God, by reason of its very fulness empties us of all that, coming from us, would hinder it. He says: 'God is darkness for our understanding; faith blinds and dazzles it. Faith is, therefore, the only means whereby God manifests himself to the soul in his divine light, which surpasses all understanding. Consequently, the richer the soul is in faith, the more it is united to God.' [3]

Finally, we must point out that St. John of the Cross, though he expresses himself with a quite original strictness and power in conveying the aim of Catholic asceticism and mysticism, is far from being an innovator. He simply provides the whole prior

---

[1] *Ascent of Mount Carmel*, I, ch. 13, 7–8.
[2] Our italics. *Ibid.*, II, ch. 4, 6.
[3] *Ibid.*, II, ch. 8, 1.

tradition with its definitive and complete expression; he translates into the abstract terms of psychology and theology the
driving force of the great ascetical movement of Cîteaux, at the
height of the Middle Ages. Calvin and Luther were certainly
not mistaken, when they sought in the pages of St. Bernard the
confirmation of their highest intuitions. Already we find the
'God alone', his glory alone, impossible to confuse with anything created, by the sole force of his sovereign grace, likewise
set absolutely apart from any human or worldly agency, as
the explanation of the fierce iconoclasm of the Cistercian ascetic
teaching. Doubtless, this tradition is not without its rivals in
Catholic spirituality. But the existence of other legitimate
traditions neither precludes nor in any way attenuates the fact
that Cîteaux expresses the most ancient and profound element
in the Catholic ascetic and mystical theology of the interior life,
and that it was perfectly summarised by St. John of the Cross
in his rigorous exclusion of any alternative but God or nothing.

At the same time it may be well to emphasise that this absolutism of the God of the Bible and of Christ is not confined to
the mystical and ascetical aspects of Catholicism, particularly in
modern times. It is perhaps as much a feature of its active side.
For, if we consider Calvinistic Protestantism in its 'moralist'
and 'political' aspects (we use the words in their best sense),
historically the most significant, we see that Catholicism offers a
striking parallel in the ideals of St. Ignatius. The Jesuit State
of Paraguay, at least as much as the Puritan State of New
England, resembles, almost to the point of identity, the Geneva
of Calvin, above all the Geneva of Calvin's dreams rather than
the actual one. In both cases, the ideal aimed at was a society
where all was directed to the glory of God through a perfect
correspondence of its laws with the law of God, channelling the
whole life of the individual within the obedience of faith. Apart
from this individual instance, the whole organisation of the
Society of Jesus, centred on this obedience, the heart of both
the ethic and the city of Calvin, has for its direct and exclusive
aim the *Ad majorem Deo gloriam*, just as the other had the *Soli
Deo gloria*. In both cases, the seeming rigour of an unbounded
authoritarianism is but the homage paid to the sovereignty
of God, a homage entire and practical, actuating a religious

determination of the will, itself illumined solely by faith in the God of Christ.

It would be hard to find a more impressive subject of reflection on the unity existing, almost in spite of them, between Catholics and Protestants at the deepest level, even at the time and place where they seemed most at enmity. The two 'cities of God', that the friends turned foes vainly strove to build over against each other, not only shared a common aim, but ultimately employed for its attainment the same means.

CHAPTER V

Justification by Faith and Personal Religion

ALTHOUGH we have now compassed practically all the aspects of the great principle of the Reformation systematically treated by the Reformers themselves, there remains one more to be elucidated: the question of personal religion. It is not the first time that a creative genius has been little aware of the extent of his innovation and its momentous significance for the future. In point of fact, the Reformers, though desirous of accentuating the divine, transcendent, aspect of Christianity, promoted more than anyone else the development of humanism and, in particular, the religious individualism of modern times.

Doubtless, this aspect of their work, whose importance they themselves failed to gauge, contains many negative elements. Among these might be included, in some senses, what before long was to hamper and stifle in their descendants the positive assertions to which they themselves attached such importance. But to insist on this unduly would lead us to overlook a final positive contribution that is perhaps not the least of their achievements, one in whose absence all the rest would lack proportion and completeness.

It would not really be quite just to stress overmuch the relatively secondary and unconscious character, in the minds of the early Protestants, of the element we are about to examine. It is more accurate to say that for them it has always been closely allied to what we have already discussed at length. However, it is also true that its dependence on the rest is, in their eyes, so intimate that they have never done full justice to this side of their achievement.

Luther, in his constant insistence on the *sola gratia, sola fide,* aimed always at turning the mind entirely from the human side of salvation, to make it rest absolutely in God. The same applies, even more strongly, to Calvin and the *Sola Dei gloria.* None the less, the emphasis on grace which gives all, with its corollary, faith which receives it, entailed a conscious personal

97

attitude at the very centre of all Protestant religion. This stands
out clearly, if we consider what the discovery of this 'faith' meant
for Luther; it was essentially the act of an isolated individual,
in contrast to all ideas simply received from others.

In his early writings on the Reformation, Luther expressed
this element of his experience in terms which were to have a
considerable success in later Protestantism. Hence arose what
is called the dialectic of the interior and the exterior. The religion of faith came to be contrasted with the religion of works,
as a personal, interior religion, engaging the deepest level of the
soul, to a religion of social attitudes, liable to degenerate into
pure conformity. However, it must be admitted that the antithesis was not a new one; it was but the recapture of a theme
already common in medieval spirituality, and mainly due to St.
Augustine; and it is far from doing justice to all the positive
values resulting from this renewed insight into the subjective
aspect of Christianity. To reduce that insight to a formula of
the kind would be to fall victim to an error no less serious than
to take the whole, or chief part, of the *sola gratia* to be 'extrinsic
justification'.

What is present in the case of Luther, and indeed in all
Protestants—it is even the characteristic note of the Protestant
mind—is a conviction, which need not necessarily be stated explicitly, whether by the master or his followers, to be active
and even decisive. It is best expressed by Dean Inge, in an
unpretentious, empirical phrase: 'One cannot be religious by
proxy.' [1]

Kierkegaard was perhaps the first to draw out all the implications of this; that is what makes his work of such importance, however disconcerting we may find it in so many ways.
He himself was never conscious of being an innovator, but considered himself simply to be bringing out a prominent element
in Luther's own teaching. Yet, if we grant him this, we must
also hold that he expressed it much better than Luther himself.

However, we must not be confused by this way of speaking of
subjectivity. If it is, as we maintain, quite other than subjectivism, the difference lies chiefly in this—it is not merely unthink-

[1] *Cf.* his *Outspoken Essays.*

able apart from its relation to the object (grace, or the Word), but it is entirely directed towards, even determined by, the intrinsic properties of this object.

In fact, once grace is seen to occupy the central place, and especially when grace, as in Luther's case, stands directly in the strictest relation with the Word, the believer is necessarily drawn personally to the very heart of the essential thing in Christianity. Grace in itself, and still more in its close bond with the Word, is a gift offered to an individual, not to a thing, not even to a group of persons collectively, in the same way as we speak to a particular person to whom the words are addressed, by whose needs they are shaped. To think of salvation as a matter of uniform practices, common rites, beliefs accepted *en bloc*, would leave the individual, if not out of the question altogether, at least not directly involved, as such, by religion. On the other hand, to conceive salvation as grace, as a grace received through the divine Word by faith, implies, not only a personal decision on the part of each, but, as occasioning this decision, a previous attention to the individual, a divine interest, so to speak, which considers him and, in a certain way, distinguishes him from everyone else.

Once this is pointed out, it will be realised that, as we maintain, such an 'individualism', in its root, has nothing in common with the cramped and negative outlook so often indicated by the term. It implies, on the contrary, a real and fundamental awareness of something over and above him, a positive attitude based on a vivid appreciation of this relationship. That is exactly what Kierkegaard, with his concept of the 'individual', brought out so clearly that the other kind of individualism, patronised by the contemporary existentialist philosophy, which tried to promote it under his auspices, is seen to be the absolute opposite of his through a too easy misuse of the word.

This individualism, not merely consistent with the divine transcendence, but based upon it, is already present in Luther, a fact made strikingly clear by his treatises *On Christian Liberty* and *On the Babylonish Captivity*, if we pay them a little attention. This is particularly significant, as in them the dialectic of the interior and exterior is most prominent, giving considerable scope to the other kind of individualism. Yet the latter, by its undoubted presence, only serves to bring out more clearly the concomitance of that individualism we are at pains to distinguish, for, so far from the two being confused, it is obvious that they are contrasted, even where Luther does his best to enlist the support of both.

The sole, fundamental aim of the *De Captivitate Babylonica* is to separate the individual soul, in its living relation with God, from all the complexities of an ecclesiastical organism which would stifle it, once the means of grace were either misdirected or made an end in themselves. Similarly, the *De Libertate Christiana* aims at freeing the Christian from all the practices of a legalist ethic or ascetical system which, by a kind of ossification, had changed from a support to a hindrance. In both works the main concern is to re-establish contact between the soul and Christ, by ignoring the intermediaries which had become screens. There is no doubt that the attempt goes too far or, rather, that it frequently diverges from its aim. To secure freedom from an externalised Church, it tends to dissolve the entire Church; in rejecting the burden of a fossilised ethical and ascetical system, it runs the grave risk of depriving the Christian life of its scaffolding. But a careful reading of these works reveals his real aim. What is really striking is that Luther's primary motive was his desire, not to set up the individual as a king in the midst of a desert, but to recall him effectually to a direct dependence on Christ, which ought to be the very basis of his life. Hence, faith is opposed both to a purely collective religion and to a religion reduced to externals; it implies a religion whose whole principle is the opening of the heart of man to the heart of God, man's gratitude for what the heart of God feels for him. Only this can make us understand how the Luther who wrote these treatises was moved to do so by the same impulse as would later impel him to write the admirable commentary on the second article of the Creed that we have already quoted: 'I believe that Jesus Christ is not only truly God, born of the Father from all eternity, but also truly man, born of the Virgin Mary; that he is my Lord, and has redeemed and delivered me from all my sins, from death and slavery to the devil, when I was lost and damned. He has truly bought and won me, not with silver and gold, but with his precious blood, his sufferings and innocent death, that I may be his entirely, and, living under his dominion, may serve him in eternal justice, innocence and happiness, who, risen from the dead, lives and reigns for ever and ever. That is my firm belief.'

This is the text to which anyone seeking the real heart of Lutheranism must constantly return. What should impress us, at the present stage, is that the individualism it affirms has quite certainly nothing to do with the emancipation or autonomy of the individual, but asserts on the contrary his joyful and loving dependence. Equally certainly, it implies, at the core of faith, the recognition that God takes a personal interest in each believer; it is this that involves each one, individually, in his faith. Grace is not indiscriminate, nor is the Word anonymous. We are given grace precisely as individuals, and for each the Word has its special message. Hence the impossibility of accepting either except by an entirely personal response to its call and its prompting.

This is the meaning of the passage in Kierkegaard's journal where he says that 'faith can never be detached from the person; the aim of science is to disengage the object from the person, that of faith to preserve the person with and within its object'.[1] In other words, the religion of salvation by faith in the sole grace of God implies our recognition that we are personally involved by the gift of God, and this recognition, in detaching us radically from ourselves, is at the same time the most personal act we could perform.

All this could be summed up by saying that, for Luther and his disciples, our religion is quite unreal as long as we ourselves are not personally committed; and by 'ourselves' is not meant our superficial or assumed character, but our most profound recesses of consciousness. However, they mean, too, the personality, not considered in isolation, but aware of itself in its awareness of being loved by God, and so abandoning itself to that love.

The most valuable result of contemporary research on Luther has undoubtedly been the demonstration that here lies the vital sense in which he uses the word 'faith' most of the time. This

---

[1] *Papirer*, III, 89 A, 216, 1840.

explains why those who fail to grasp this are completely at sea in their interpretation of the Lutheran teaching on justification. As Anders Nygren in particular has so clearly shown, 'faith', in Luther's sense, is, properly, response to the love of God. That is, it is the response to that unique love which is the great revelation of the Gospel, love which consists in giving, not desiring; love that gives, and is given. And what more exactly specifies this divine love is that it loves, not because of any previous merit of ours, but in spite of our actual demerit. Thus, 'faith', in discovering the divine love, discovers, with it, its own unworthiness. However, in so doing, it discovers it as overcome by the divine initiative alone, and to this it abandons itself without reserve. Once more, in this very act, it recognises that its abandonment is not its own work, but the working in it of the love which seeks and has found.[1] Thus, the soul itself finds the principle of its new life in an act that, far from being an affirmation of its own autonomy, is the most complete renunciation of it conceivable.

In this sense, there should be no hesitation in asserting—though here, certainly, Nygren himself is not bold enough, embarrassed as he is by preconceived ideas—that 'faith', in Luther's meaning, implies love in a high degree. But it is a love that feels and knows itself as not only a pure response to the love which loved first, in a way beyond comprehension, but as itself created entirely by this very love. We must not be misled on this point by Luther's later assertions opposed to the *fides caritate formata*. His object in disowning this formula was to reject the idea that faith justified man only if there were added to it a love proceeding from a natural disposition, not coming as a gift of God, the whole being the gift of God. But it cannot be questioned that justifying 'faith', as he understood it, leads of itself, in its natural course, above all in virtue of the grace it accepts, to a total self-commitment to God, if we read once again the commentary on the 2nd article of the Creed, quoted above. This is made clear, also, in the central part of the treatise on Christian liberty, where Luther, after he has extolled the preach-

[1] *Cf.* Anders Nygren, *Eros et Agape*, French translation, especially t. I (Paris, 1948), chapter on St. Paul, and t. III (Paris, 1951), chapter on Luther.

ing of the Gospel as a means of arousing faith in the heart of
man, concludes with these words: 'How could the soul, hearing
such things, fail to tremble at them? How could so perfect a
grace fail to enkindle its love for Christ? Is there any law, any
work, that could bring about such love? . . .' [1]

The same idea shines forth in the most explicit language of
paragraph 17 of the sermon on *Good Works*, where Luther
strives to give, not an abstract definition, but a living description, of his 'faith': 'If you ask me how to attain to faith and confidence, you recall me to what we need to know most of all.
There is no doubt at all that confident faith is not the effect of
our works or merits, but comes from Christ, and is promised and
given freely, as St. Paul says (Rom. V, 8): "God commendeth
his charity towards us; because, when as yet we were sinners
according to the time, Christ died for us." God means by that:
"Does not this give you unshakable confidence in me, that, before you asked, or had any concern, for your salvation, while
still living in your sins, Christ died for you?" You see, you must
picture to yourself and understand how God offers you his
mercy in Christ before you had done anything to deserve it.
This image of the divine grace will arouse in your heart faith
and the certainty of forgiveness . . . As you contemplate in
Christ and his sacrifice the immensity of God's gift to you, your
heart will be vanquished by love, carried up to God, and confidence will be born in this atmosphere of mutual love, of God's
love for you and your love for God.' [2]

Kierkegaard, again, simply draws out, with great accuracy,
these implications of Luther's 'faith', when he writes: 'Christ
said, To him who loves me, I will make myself known. That
applies universally. It is to him who loves that the revelation is
made. One naturally looks on the recipient as passive, and on
him who reveals as communicating himself to him; but the relation consists in this—he who receives is he who loves, and it is
for that reason that the loved one is revealed to him. For he
transforms himself into a resemblance with the one loved, and
to become what one knows is the only way to know. We see,

---

[1] P. 44 in French translation.
[2] French translation of H. Strohl, *La substance de l'Evangile selon Luther*,
Paris, 1934, pp. 105–106.

moreover, from this that loving and knowing are one and the same thing, and, since to love means that the other is revealed, for the same reason it means that one reveals oneself.' [1]

We have quoted this passage particularly for the last sentence, '. . . since to love means that the other is revealed, for the same reason it means that one reveals oneself'. For these words put in a clear light the positive individualism conveyed by the Lutheran 'justification by faith'. Yet, with all their subjective import, they themselves draw their life from the objective nature of the *sola gratia*, and would be meaningless if severed from the branch which bears them, and from the sap it alone can provide.

The importance of all this for an understanding of Protestant spirituality cannot be exaggerated. It profoundly affects the nature of that religious training we have already noticed so often and characterised as one of the consistent and revealing features of Protestantism. Nothing could be more repellent to Protestants in general than an education, particularly one claiming to be religious, that tended to stifle, rather than to stimulate, the personality. For them it would be a real *corruptio pessima*. The absurd and ridiculous prejudices they so generally and obstinately nurse on the subject of Catholic schools and convents would not be so long-lived unless they were backed by a fear and horror of moral constraint, particularly when exercised in the formative years, the time when a person ought to learn to be himself.

Even more than authoritarianism in excess, Protestants mistrust those educational systems which, though based on a wise psychology, tend so effectively to mould the personality to a given type, particularly when they are discreetly applied.

This fear and mistrust may seem rather naïve; in fact, we see there, and also in the methods of Rousseau and their extraordinary popularity in Swiss education, a humanist optimism completely at variance with the original Augustinian outlook of Protestantism. But it would be a serious mistake to overlook the profound reality which is quite independent of these accidentals. Protestants least suspect of belief in 'man naturally good' are stirred by indignation and disgust, as spontaneously

[1] *Papirer*, IX A. 438, quoted by Haecker, p. 429.

as Rousseau would be, against any tendency to contract the
person to a fixed mould, still more so against all those contriv-
ances, machiavellian in their eyes, which aim at shaping him,
imperceptibly but infallibly, in a desired direction.

That explains why Protestants are so easily aroused, even to
a fanatical degree, by what seems to them religious constraint;
and this, in spite of the paradox of history by which Protestant
countries have often been as intolerant as those that remained
Catholic, have even continued to maintain, in the religious
sphere, oppressive laws, long after most of the Catholic nations
have abandoned them. For them, a religious act, if ever so little
compelled, is always worse than all the blasphemies a lawless
licence might permit. That alone counts in the sight of God,
they consider, which is a personal act, conscious and deliberate, wrought in the most perfect freedom, interior and exterior. Consequently, anything which, aiming at any sort of
religious assent or at a correct mode of conduct, violates this
liberty of conscience, far from having any value, only under-
mines the very possibility of the sole religion acceptable to God,
that of a man who gives himself freely. 'Liberty of conscience'
and 'worship in spirit and truth'—not only are these the two
watchwords sure of an immediate response among all Protestants; they must be recognised, too, as, in practice, equivalent.

We can see why so many Protestants in all periods feel uneasy
about infant Baptism. It is for the same reason that they always attach such importance to a ceremony performed on the
threshold of adult life. Before that time, they consider, the
child cannot really belong to God and Christ, for belonging
means nothing if it is not personal. From this point of view, the
contrary tendency of Catholics to lower the age for Confirmation and first Communion seems to them absurd, even if they
do not simply discern in it a purely magical idea of Sacraments
acting as a lucky charm.

The counterpart of this insistence, too exclusive though it be,
on the personal character of every genuine religious act, is a
quite remarkable development of the sense of responsibility.
Since all gregarious activity appears valueless to the Protestant,
he feels himself in no way dispensed from personal action by any
form of mass-movement or collective acquiescence. Thus it is

that Protestant individualism does not prevent Protestants from having a civic sense—quite the contrary, in fact; in general, they have a practical respect for the law much greater than a number of non-Protestant Christians. In most of the Latin countries putting anything 'under the protection of the public' is tantamount to delivering it over to the vandalism of each and all. In countries where Protestantism has left its stamp, it constitutes an appeal to all much more likely to be effective than any command enforceable by penalties. The temptations offered by a casuistry which, under the impulses of egoism, tends to become more and more elastic, are unavailing, as experience shows, for those who are convinced that ultimately they must obey their own law. Hence too, in education, those so-called libertarian methods, which non-Protestants are always tempted to interpret as tacit invitations to licence, but which, in a Protestant context, are seen to be extremely exacting. The idea that one will do one's duty, or do it well, only if practically compelled, at least to some degree, is not only false but shocking to the Protestant. On the other hand, self-imposed discipline, that which results from a moral condition created by suitable training, seems to him obviously the strictest conceivable, in fact, the only kind impossible to evade. He considers that the person who has not arrived at this point, or who does not aim at it, does not even know in what the idea of duty really consists.

At the opposite extreme, all methods of education, and, besides, all political organisations, which, with their constant scrutinising, are based on a process of minute supervision, if not on espionage and detection, seem a negation of true education and a perversion of the life of society. Everyone ought to aim, in virtue of his education, if it is worthy of the name, to look on God as his only real judge, and so to judge himself more severely than anyone else could. For the constant background, and the only explanation, of this attitude is the living conviction that each of us, every moment, is under the eye of God, each is called to account to him for all his acts, even the most hidden, and that at every instant God is present and makes of each circumstance of life a personal appeal to which we must respond.

To many Catholics, the assertion of Protestants that they do

not confess to man but to God is only a euphemistic way of saying that they do not confess at all. This judgment, in the eyes of
fervent or merely serious Protestants, is a naïve admission of an
appalling lack of faith; to them, the duty of confessing to God
or, rather, of a constant awareness that God sees us and tests us,
is the most severe and inescapable of all the obligations that religion or ethics could impose.

The same reasons lie behind another conviction characteristic
of Protestantism: that the only prayer worthy of the name is
personal prayer, where each one speaks from his own heart and,
therefore, only says what he intimately feels. The almost inescapable Protestant mistrust of all set prayers, even sometimes
of the Our Father, is accounted for by this, and this alone. Prayer
exists or not, according as it is, or fails to be, an absolutely
personal impulse of the soul towards God, where no one can
replace the individual, nor draw him without his entire consent.
In the use of set prayers, the Protestant is always inclined to suspect insincerity, words used without meaning, exemption, more
or less consciously sought, from personal decision by assuming a
collective attitude with no real individual commitment.

Hence also in so many, often the best, Protestant communities, the insistence on 'conversion', that is, on a personal act,
fully deliberate, even recorded in time and place. It is looked
upon as the source of the religious life of the individual, much
more so than a ceremony, sacramental or otherwise, in which he
might be merely an onlooker or, at the most, a passive participant. When Baptism is given, when one takes part in a 'confirmation' or 'reception of catechumens', they always insist that
none of it has any real value if there is not, in the deepest part of
the soul, a corresponding attitude, free and spontaneous, which
nothing can dispense from, and for which no one can replace
the person professing to be a Christian. In all this we see the
same thing at work, the idea of being personally concerned in
all one does, that only the person concerned can act for himself,
and in doing so is involved far more seriously than he could be
by any external or collective agency. Hence, the distrust, always
felt, of the ready-made gesture, the uniform ritual, all that
savours of an attitude imposed from without, to which at best a
person may adapt himself, but without necessarily having ever

in his life freely and consciously experienced what it is all meant
to express.

An objection easily suggests itself when we compare this with
what we said before about the Calvinist system and its basic
authoritarianism. As a matter of history, both the rigorism of
the Puritans and the sergeant-major approach of Prussian
'Evangelism' appear as the opposite extreme to all this. Protestants themselves would undoubtedly admit the possibility of
conflict between certain principles equally native to Protestantism. It was to counteract what he considered too extreme in the
first generation of Protestantism that Calvin developed his own
system; and, in the name of a truer Protestantism, others, in his
lifetime or later, criticised him more sharply than anyone. Still,
even admitting this, we must acknowledge that Calvin's
authoritarianism was not an end in itself. It was simply a means
to confront man with his obligations as a Christian; in Calvin's
own view, its only purpose was to bring each one to realise the
necessity to apply to himself those obligations once admitted.
On its side, the authoritarianism of the Calvinist city should result in the free acceptance of his responsibility by each of its
members; but, once arrived at this, each has the duty to apply
to himself the law of God more stringently than any external
force could do. Actually, we have to admit, that is exactly the
course of development taken by the Puritan communities of the
Anglo-Saxon world, those of New England in particular. From
an organisation apparently resulting from a real theocratic dic-
tatorship, they passed insensibly to the most liberal forms of
democracy. Meanwhile, among those members still faithful to
the earlier religious ideal, the sense of their obligations, as it
became more interior, was felt more imperiously. That is
perhaps the characteristic of the final stage of Protestant rigorism at its purest; a compulsion, implacable at the beginning,
gradually disappears from social institutions, may even vanish
entirely from customs and from all that makes up the unwritten
law of the community as such; but, in so doing, it remains existing in a more spiritual and intangible form than ever, in the
conscience of the individual. It is, too, this complete interiorisa-
tion of the sense of duty that, far from mitigating it, comes to
make it obsessive, and gives it the form of a taboo which may be

systematically violated, but which cannot be escaped, however much one might wish to do so—a final reaction, typical of the various forms of Protestant 'immoralism' from Gide to Lawrence and Miller, which remains so profoundly strange and perplexing to those who have never known Protestant education.

Having said all this, and without dreaming for an instant of concealing all the deformations which constantly threaten the ideal, from religious and moral anarchy to the most pernicious kinds of repression and the reactions that follow, what should be the judgment of a Catholic on this ideal of personal religion? How does it fit into the authentic and complete framework of the Christian tradition?

Once again, we think it impossible to deny the fully Christian nature of the basic intuition. Here, more than ever, we need the balance of complementary truths; we have already alluded to them, and also shown to what extent they were present in early Protestantism. Yet, in spite of this reservation, or rather definition, it must be admitted that this positive individualism, as distinct from the negative kind which we shall meet in a moment, is fundamentally a very pure expression of what may be called the individualism of the great prophets, of Christ himself, and so of all the most orthodox among the great spiritual writers.

The utterance of Ezechiel is surely decisive; it expresses the central point of all spirituality based on the Word of God: 'The soul that sinneth, the same shall die; the son shall not bear the iniquity of the father, and the father shall not bear the iniquity of the son. The justice of the just shall be upon him, and the wickedness of the wicked shall be upon him.' (Ez. XVIII, 20.)

That does not deny the very real solidarity, both religious and moral, of the human race. It insists, however, most rigorously, that no one can transfer to another his obligations to God, rid himself in that way of his responsibilities. The same prophet says again: 'Son of man, when a land shall sin against me, so as to transgress grievously, I will stretch forth my hand upon it, and will break the staff of the bread thereof; and I will send famine upon it, and will destroy man and beast out of it. And if these three men, Noe, Daniel and Job, shall be in it, they shall deliver their own souls by their justice, saith the Lord of hosts.' (Ez. XIV, 13–14.)

However, it is only in the Gospel that we find the positive religious significance of this individualism, when Christ says: 'You do not believe, because you are not of my sheep. My sheep hear my voice, and I know them and they follow me. I give them eternal life, and they shall not perish for ever, and no one will pluck them out of my hand. That which my Father has given me is greater than all, and no one can snatch them from the hand of my Father.' (John X, 26–29.)

What lies behind these words is in fact what gives to the religion of personal commitment and the ethics of individual responsibility their infinite depth of meaning; it is the certainty that God knows and loves each human being uniquely, giving him an eternal value, in a sense an infinite one, and promises him a destiny equally eternal and infinite; but the only possible ground for this is that, in the judgments of conscience and decisions of the will, no one can take the place of another.

This Biblical character is not confined to the principle, the soul, of religious individualism; it extends to the consequences or offshoots emphasised, with characteristic force, by Protestants. This refers not only to the impossibility for the individual to hide behind the group, as emphasised by Ezechiel, but also the mistrust of even sacred rites, as soon as they become, or are in danger of becoming, a pretext, more or less conscious, for avoiding personal decisions—a mistrust which implies what we must unhesitatingly call religious moralism.

Never have the 'protestations' of the Reformers, at their most daring, surpassed in vehemence the language of Amos or Isaias. 'I hate and have rejected your festivities; and I will not receive the odour of your assemblies. And if you offer me holocausts and your gifts, I will not receive them; neither will I regard the vows of your fat beasts. Take away from me the tumult of thy songs; and I will not hear the canticles of thy harp. But judgment shall be revealed as water, and justice as a mighty torrent.' (Amos, V, 21–24.)

Isaias is perhaps even more brutal: 'To what purpose do you offer me the multitude of your victims, saith the Lord? I am full, I desire not the holocausts of rams and fat of fatlings and blood of calves and lambs and buck-goats. When you came to appear before me, who required these things at your hands, that you should walk in my courts? Offer sacrifice no more in vain; incense is an abomination to me. The new moons and the sabbaths and other festivals I will not abide; your assemblies are wicked. My soul hateth your new moons and your solemnities; they are become troublesome to me. I am weary of bearing them. And when you stretch forth your hands, I will turn away my eyes from you; and when you multiply prayer I will not hear. For your hands are full of blood. Wash yourselves, be clean. Take away the evil of your devices from my eyes. Cease to do perversely. Learn to do well. Seek judgment. Relieve the oppressed. Judge for the fatherless. Defend the widow.' (Isa. I, 11–17.)

The most decisive passage in this connection is that of Osee, repeated by Christ himself: 'For I desired mercy and not sacrifice, and the knowledge of God more than holocausts.' (Osee, VI, 6; *cf.* Matt. IX, 13.) One could say that the point of Christ's opposition to the Pharisees was to eradicate an entirely ritualistic religion and a wholly legalistic idea of justice, and substitute a religion in which the very heart of man is committed to God, and where his whole life translates this gift into action. In prayer, in almsgiving, in fasting, Christ always opposes to the formal and visible act the necessarily hidden reality of a gift of self unwitnessed save by the God who receives it. The condition of true prayer is the silence of recollection unseen by others, the solitude of intimate intercourse undisturbed by any alien presence, the filial converse not dependent on set phrases. Likewise, almsdeeds and fasting, to be acceptable to God, must be a real and spontaneous gift of self, without ulterior motive, both to the brother one sees and to the God unseen, following the formula expressed by St. John, but evidently taken from the Master himself (*cf.* Matt. VI and 1 John IV, 20).

St. Paul simply adds a final word to the teaching of the Gospel, when he makes each man's justice or injustice before God consist in fidelity to his own conscience, whatever may be the conscience of his neighbour. 'Why is my liberty judged by another man's conscience? If I partake with thanksgiving, why am I evil spoken of for that for which I give thanks? Therefore, whether you eat or drink, or whatsoever else you do, do all to the glory of God' (1 Cor. X, 29–31). And, after he has explained the whole difference between the Old and New Testaments as that between justification by the works of the law and justification by faith, he proceeds to apply the word 'faith' in the special sense of fidelity to conscience, and so lays down as a final principle, 'Whatsoever is not of *faith* is sin' (Rom. XIV, 22).

Broadly speaking, the whole Gospel, from this standpoint, amounts to proclaiming the liberty of the believer, as opposed to all systems which would subject him either to the exterior prescriptions of a particular group, a closed society, or to the restraints of some system of law or ritual. This is the sense of Christ's declaration in St. Matthew that 'the sons are free' (Matt. XVII, 26), in regard to the laws of men; while in St. John he says more definitely, 'when the Son has made you free, you will be free indeed' (John VIII, 36). Did not he say, even of the divine law of the sabbath, 'the sabbath was made for man, not man for the sabbath'? (Mark II, 27). On this point, too, St. Paul speaks conclusively: 'Owe no man anything but to love one another, for he who loveth his neighbour hath fulfilled the law. . . . Brethren, you have been called in liberty, only make not liberty an occasion for the flesh, but by charity of the spirit serve one another; for all the law is contained in one word, Thou shalt love thy neighbour as thyself.'

There is, surely, no need to argue at length in order to show how the whole Catholic tradition has always been firmly attached to these affirmations. The guiding principle of Catholic ascetical teaching has always been the necessity of a personal effort from each individual—from which no person or thing can absolve him—to appropriate the spiritual riches of faith and the sacraments. There lies the whole point of the constantly renewed teachings and exhortations of spiritual authors and saints; to persuade us ever anew that neither adherence to the faith of the Church, nor the sharing in its rites and sacraments, are of the least value to us apart from an effort no one can make in our stead, the effort to carry our faith into our lives, to make the grace of the sacraments fecundate our lives. Without this interior response, authentic and personal, so we are assured by the whole Catholic tradition, the most scrupulous observance of the externals of religion, the most verbally correct profession of the faith of the Church will, in effect, be quite useless to us and will serve to our own condemnation.

At the same time, this tradition is equally unanimous on the worthlessness before God of any religious act not freely performed (particularly of the fundamental act of faith by which we make our adherence to Christianity) and, moreover, of the strict obligation of each to follow his own conscience, even when in fact erroneous. All this is not just one among other permissible opinions in modern and medieval theology; it has always been received unanimously by theologians.

What is more, it is certainly true that the 'protestation' of the Reformers on this point, whenever it has been made, besides conforming, as we have seen, to the strictest orthodoxy, has been no less amply justified by the circumstances. For a religion that had come to be identified with the observances of a community and which was in so advanced a state of religious and moral decay as was the Christian community at the end of the Middle Ages, nothing was more urgent than to insist on the inescapable necessity for a personal and, as we say now, 'engaged' response to what God exacts. At that period there was no more serious threat to the survival of real Christianity than man's acquiescence in a façade of religion, and his being satisfied with a respect, often wholly external, for the religious framework acknowledged by society. We may add that, in the changing world of today, where the revival of the communal aspect of life, so beneficial in some ways, appears, in others, as a special danger to real Christian 'personalism', the same reminder is no less opportune than in the sixteenth century. Christians so hypnotised by mass-movements, class-consciousness, racism and all sorts of collectivism, need more than ever to be reminded that the religious problem is one which ultimately confronts each person individually, and that each has to solve it for himself. The salvation of souls, without any doubt, implies the salvation of bodies, and so of the whole social body of mankind supernaturally incorporated in the Church. But the Church, unlike most modern associations, is not a crucible for the fusion of souls into a single mass. It is a society where they must flourish, each and all, in that freedom of love so admirably described by St. Paul.

We are far from denying that the association in time of the positive individualism we have been dealing with and the negative kind that remains to be examined, may have made Catholics of the Counter-Reformation reluctant to accept the theses we have just argued. Yet it is significant that, none the less, these were given an important place at the centre of the spiritual creations most characteristic of that same Counter-Reformation.

Already, we have alluded to the paradox of the close similarity between the Calvinist idea of Christian society and that of the Jesuits in its authoritarianism. Now, to conclude this chapter, we have to mark the point to which, in spite of appearances, the Ignatian idea of the spiritual life approximates to Protestant individualism. It would be a gross misinterpretation of the *Spiritual Exercises* to view them as merely a process for bringing those making a retreat under the obedience of a director. As the commentators who approach the *Exercises* historically have no difficulty in showing, their aim, properly understood, is to rouse the individual to the most personal 'realisation' of his beliefs as a Christian. The entire fundamental meditation on the two standards has no other purpose than to drive home the necessity of a conscious and deliberate decision, not only for the Augustinian 'city of God' as opposed to the city of the devil, but for Christ, to whom every Christian, the Jesuit in particular, ought to come to feel bound in a wholly free and personal manner.'

In more general terms, as the example of Père Léonce de Grandmaison shows so clearly, the placing of oneself under the direction of a superior, the practice equally in accord with the modern Jesuit ideal at its best and the ancient doctrine of the Fathers of the desert—the acknowledged source of the inspiration of Ignatius—has for its sole aim the preparation for perfect docility to the interior Master, the Spirit, which touches and moves each soul individually, without further need of any created medium.[1]

---

[1] See the volumes of spiritual notes by P. de Grandmaison, posthumously published by Beauchesne.

Thus, it is not surprising to find such frequent and close analogies between methods of spirituality worked out simultaneously in the Protestant Reformation and the Catholic Counter-Reformation—the same psychological teaching on each side, the same emphasis on the will and on conduct, the same constant appeal to personal decision, to interior 'conversion', and thence to continuous militant activity. A fine example of this agreement between separated brethren, not only surviving their division, but strengthened by it, we may find in the work of Angelus Silesius. Those of his poems which seem to the hasty critic most characteristic of the Catholicism he came to embrace, and of his adherence to the Counter-Reformation, are, often enough, those where he simply puts into verse passages from Luther.

E

CHAPTER VI

The Sovereign Authority of Scripture

WITH this chapter we come to a new aspect of Protestant-ism, the complement of those we have studied up to now. More precisely, we are about to develop the theme of Protestant 'personalism' that gives it that basically positive character we have been at pains to emphasise. All that we asserted in the last chapter should find in the present one the elucidation and the substructure it demands. The same applies equally, though not with the same evidence, to all we have written up to this point. To adopt the formula of Melancthon, if justification by faith is the material cause of Protestantism, its formal cause is the supreme authority of the Bible. We were obliged none the less, it will be remembered, to begin our account with justification by faith, for, in Luther's experience which set the pattern for the whole of Protestantism, the Biblical principle came to be adopted reflexively; his primary discovery was the *sola gratia, sola fide*, to which he was impelled by his reading of the epistle to the Romans. In other words, what first struck him was his insight into a great truth of re-ligion; then, subsequently, the means whereby this truth struck him became clear to him, and so compelled him to assign it a place of fundamental significance.

It would be a decided exaggeration to say, though it has been said even by Protestants, that the authority of the Bible was impressed upon Luther simply because the Bible seemed to him to certify the truth of what he took as the basis of all. Yet it is certain that the process of his thought, whatever its quasi-scholastic exposition by Melancthon might lead us to think, did not by any means originate in some general theory on authority in matters of faith, and lead up to particular conclusions about salvation. On the contrary, it was a living intuition of salvation that crystallised his view of the Bible and continues to do so for Protestants who, in this respect, share Luther's view of the Scriptures. To say this does not imply that Protestantism is bound up in subjectivism; rather, it is to affirm that the

Protestant conception of the Bible and its authority is no abstraction, but a vital understanding. Actually, there is no need to fix the two principles of the Reformation in their order of importance or time. It would be better to say that there is but one enduring principle, namely, the discovery of gratuitous salvation in the recognition of the Bible as the Word of God, or, what comes to the same, the recognition of the Bible as the Word of God taking concrete shape in an assertion that appears straightway as the very heart of its content: salvation by grace.

Once it is granted that such was Luther's original view, and that it remains the permanently animating principle of Protestantism, we are enabled to understand the basically positive character in the feature we are about to examine, as of those we have previously discussed at length. That this view was, as a matter of history, that of Protestantism in its origin and in all its exponents who have kept and renewed its first fervour, is easy enough to show.

In the first place, there is no doubt that Luther's insistence on the Bible and its supreme authority did not, in the first instance, signify to him or the Protestants in general a denial of tradition or the authority of the Church; it was in fact a spiritual rediscovery immensely rich in results. This is conclusively shown when we consider that Protestantism, in equating the Bible with the Word of God and the Word of God with the Bible, did so originally not in opposition to Catholicism, but to sectarian movements like Anabaptism. In other words, what moved the Reformers to define the Word of God, with increasing insistence, in an exclusive, and therefore negative, sense, and thus raise it up above every other authority, was not their conflict with ecclesiastical authority, but with those who declined to accept any authority other than themselves. Doubtless, Luther's primary intuition, in its application to the Bible, renewed his sense of the transcendence of Scripture. But here, at the initial stage, it is purely affirmative; when it begins to strengthen itself with negations, its target is the illuminati of Münster rather than any traditional authority.

What Luther believed himself to have really discovered, or rediscovered, in his 'experience in the tower', is that God has spoken to man, for each individual, more clearly than any human speaker, and that he has done so precisely in the great promise of the 'Gospel', the 'good news' of gratuitous salvation in Christ, offered to all who should have faith in him. The 'preaching of the Word of God', with all the biblicism of Protestantism in its first stage, does not constitute a religion of the book (like another Islam) so much as a rejection of traditional religion. Far from being a religion of the book, it is a religion of the Word; the religion of the God who speaks, who utters the Word of life. The importance it gives to the Bible, however great, proceeds entirely from this, and from the fact that the Bible contains this living Word which, starting from the heart of God, reaches and touches the heart of man. Criticism of other authorities comes only in the second or third place, according as it is deemed useful or necessary to set off the importance of the Bible as recognised (rather than defined). And this criticism itself remains secondary to the opposition to the illuminism of the sects, which substitutes for the authentic Word of God, in its full transcendence, an illusory message, a fantasy created by the heart of man shut up in itself.

Indeed, throughout the history of Protestantism, the preaching of the Word of God remains, in its essence, the proclamation of a living 'good news', which ultimately is always identified with Christ, considered as living and acting within us. It involves the exaltation of the Bible, in so far as it is seen to incorporate or incarnate permanently this living Word. The controversy of Bible against tradition appears only as a derivative. Very often, if not most of the time, this controversy is not aimed so much at Catholicism as at the ultra-individualistic illuminism which, claiming to free the Christian from every hindrance, shuts him up in a solipsism, obviously fatal.

The first intuition, the one which governs all that follows, we find expressed in the best possible way in a paragraph of the *Treatise on Christian Liberty*; so important did it appear to Luther that he used it again, in the same form, in the first of his Wittenberg sermons in 1522:

'If you ask me what is this Word that gives so great grace and how we are to make use of it, I answer that it is no other than the preaching of Christ as contained in the Gospel. It is such that in it you hear the God who speaks to you, and who says to you that all your life and works are nothing before God, but can only bring you to eternal perdition. If you truly feel how guilty you are, you can only despair of yourself and acknowledge the truth of the word of Osee: "Thy perdition is from thee, O Israel, thy help is only in me." But that you may be able to liberate yourself and escape perdition, God sets before you his beloved Son, Jesus Christ, and makes him say, in his living and consoling word, that you are to give yourself to him with a firm faith, and trust yourself entirely to him. In virtue of this faith, all your sins will be forgiven, and all the evil which is in you, conquered. You will become just, truthful, peaceful, devout; all the commandments will be fulfilled, and you will be free in all things.' [1]

In this passage, the supreme Word is seen as a Word that is living, concrete, always actual, inseparable from what it contains, from the 'good news' of the salvation freely given in Christ. That is decidedly its fundamental aspect. But there is a still older passage from one of Luther's first writings that sets this aspect within a complete survey of the Word of God that distinguishes its three different, though inseparable, modalities. The *Dictata super Psalterium*, which date from the years 1513 to 1516, tell us in effect *quod verbum Dei triplici modo dicitur.* The first mode is *per verbum externum et linguam ad aures hominum*, and Luther includes in it all preaching from the prophets to the Fathers of the Church. The second is that *verbum consummans et abbreviatum* which is identical with the Incarnate Son of God, as made known to us on this earth by the Spirit. The third is the revelation of himself that God will give finally to his saints in eternal glory *cum nobis verbum suum ipse sine ullo medio revelabit.* [2]

Here we find the germ, or summary, of a singularly rich doctrine, since the Word, while centred always on the living knowledge of Christ given by the Spirit, extends, on the one hand, to the entire Scriptures and even the great witnesses of

[1] See H. Strohl, *La substance de l'Evangile selon Luther*, Paris, 1934, pp. 66–67.
[2] In Ps. XLV, v. 2 (Weimar edition, Vol. 3, p. 262, §5).

ecclesiastical tradition, and, on the other, is seen to embrace these only as a preparation for direct knowledge, face to face.

In a third passage, written by Luther towards the end of his life, we find him proclaiming the exclusive authority of the Word of God. What, however, he intends is, not so much the rejection of any authority but that of the Bible, as the affirmation of the transcendence of the Word of God, above any that does not proceed from him as its author. At the beginning of the second part of the *Treatise on civil authority* we read the following: 'Wherever a human law requires the soul to conform, in religious matters, to the opinions of men, it is certainly not the authority of the Word of God which speaks. . . . God wills that our faith be based uniquely on his divine Word. It is, then, pure madness to command belief in the Church, the Fathers, the Councils, when their opinion is not supported by the Word of God. . . . It is even more senseless to exact of a people conformity to the opinion of its king or ruler. We are not baptised in the name of a king, a ruler or a majority, but in the name of Christ and of God himself. . . . No one ought to, or can, lay down laws for the soul, if he does not know how to point out the way to heaven. No man is capable of so doing; God alone can. Therefore, in all that concerns the salvation of the soul, nothing must be taught and heard but the Word of God.' [1]

This passage is all the more interesting by its very ambiguities. In it we see the germ of a possible opposition between the Bible and tradition or the teaching authority, on the supposition of a conflict between the Church and the Word of God. But what is more noteworthy is to see the context bring out so clearly that the basic problem is to safeguard the Word of God in all its purity, that it may be also preserved in its divine fulness. It is because the Bible and the Word of God seem to be perfectly equivalent expressions, by reason of the doctrine (itself entirely traditional) of the divine inspiration of Scripture, that the latter is so highly exalted. Luther's motive in setting aside, or putting in the second place, all other authorities, whatever they may be, is only subsidiary and dependent on what remains from beginning to end his first aim: to recognise the divine Word

[1] Quoted by Strohl, *op. cit.* pp. 358–9.

as the living, supreme Word which brings us the gift of God in Christ.

It can already be seen how later Protestantism came to be exposed to two opposite dangers. One is that of illuminism which, while preserving the idea of the Word of God as a living reality, refused to admit any objective criterion, and so fell into the error of admitting individual inspiration, incapable of being verified. The Anabaptists of Münster were followed along this way by the disciples of Schwenckfeld and the Quakers under George Fox. It was a way which might lead to an uncontrolled mysticism, but also—as appears with the Cambridge Platonists, who developed from the theosophy of Henry More to latitudinarianism, pure and simple—to an ultimate rationalism with little trace of mysticism. The other danger, prompted by a reaction against the first, was that of 'fundamentalism', a Protestant doctrine which restricted all communication from God to man to the letter of the Scriptures, so hardening the religion of the Word into a religion of the book. Thus it happened that a reactionary theology came to build up a theory of Biblical inspiration which detached it completely from its living roots in the community of the people of God. This new kind of orthodoxy, without example in the old Catholic tradition, is quite remote from Luther's own thought, even in its most conservative elements. Had he not said in a passage, substantially in full accord with tradition: 'The Word of God cannot exist apart from the people of God. In the same way, the people of God cannot exist without the Word of God. Who would preach it or hear it, if not the people of God? And how would the people of God arrive at faith, if the Word of God were not preached to them?' [1]

What is most surprising is that these theories about inspiration, which made of the Scriptural writings a kind of meteor fallen out of the sky, unrelated to the life of the Church, came during the nineteenth century to carve their way even into certain manuals of Catholic theology.

However, neither of these errors is really characteristic of Protestant spirituality in its most direct and living branch.

[1] *On Councils and Churches* (1539), beginning of 3rd part (quoted in Strohl, *op. cit.*, p. 178).

Rather, it could be said that the Calvinist theology of the Word of God, asserting the agreement of the 'interior witness of the Holy Spirit' with the inspired words of Scripture, is the expression of the best Protestant experience. This theory, rightly understood, does not necessarily mean that every isolated Christian is capable, apart from the Church, both of recognising what are the inspired Scriptures and of giving them an authentic interpretation. What it asserts is, first, that the most personal illumination given by the Spirit finds only in the inspired words the formulas it needs, and, next, that these formulas are continually shown to be the gift of God by their unique power to nourish in each believer the life of the Spirit.

Thus, it must be recognised that, in spite of all its possible defects, Protestantism has lived by, and handed down, an authentic life, constantly renewed, precisely in the degree in which it has handed down the Bible and, with this, a living practice of recourse to it, of drawing nourishment from it as from a source of life, of finding in it personal contact with Christ, while interior experience is constantly referred to it as to the highest ideal.

Here we touch upon the greatest and richest element in Protestant living, that which has always kept it above all the narrownesses which threatened it, but also the most difficult to appreciate without personal experience. For the objection often made, that Protestantism tends to replace a living religion with the religion of a lifeless book, misunderstands the very essence of Protestantism; a collective experience, ever sought after and renewed, of a life discovered and maintained by familiarity with the Bible, is the very opposite of a bookish devotion.

The first thing that should help even the stranger to Protestantism to obtain some grasp of this is the exact care that Protestants have taken in their translations of the Bible, and in their efforts to popularise them. Doubtless they have not all had the same success; but it is highly significant that the two great Protestant peoples are those with translations of the Bible which have never been excelled. Luther's Bible and the Authorised Version are both literary and religious monuments whose exceptional importance we must try to understand. In this we are helped greatly by Luther's prefaces; they show us, above all, the care he took to make of the Word of Scripture a Word, living and actual for his people. He succeeded to such a point that his version, both in style and content, fashioned the language itself and, with it, the spirit of the nation. In this way, the Bible became, for Germans, not only a classic in the formal sense of the word, but a spiritual universe, a common reservoir of thought, imagination, moral and spiritual reactions, which has given to the people as well as to the élite a rich soil, an atmosphere and a light, on which the living depths, both of mind and heart, can draw without ceasing. The same may be said of the English Bible, and even more, since, not being the work of a single man, though a genius, the range of its influence was to prove still wider.

Having said this, we have now to observe in Protestant communities, families and individuals, the life which the book, thus reinvigorated in its form, and restored to its primitive state as an outpouring of the 'Word', has, as it were, relived in fostering it in the consciences of so many. It is not read merely as a moral code or a statement of doctrine, nor even as the record of an unforgettable history, but as the 'Word', always living, in its unbounded richness and its personal unity, centred, as it was recognised to be, on Him who speaks in Christ, and addressed to an ever-living audience. For this is really what has made the Book a continual source of life in Protestantism, namely, the active conviction of its readers that it was written for them, that it spoke to them and of them, while speaking always of Christ and his Church, of the Lord God and his people. This certainty may at times have found expression in forms which arouse annoyance or contempt in those who do not share it, as in the case of the character in Hardy, reading the heading in an old English edition of the Song of Songs: 'Praise addressed by the Lord to the spiritual beauty of his Church.' The same applies to the habit, particularly among Puritans, of expressing everything that happens in words and phrases borrowed from the Bible. It has even degenerated into superstitions as low as those found among backward or degraded Catholic peoples—the practice, for example, dear to the peasants of Scotland and the Cevennes, also to the Moravians, of 'consulting the book', opening the Bible at random to decide something. Behind all that, what is permanent is a life of faith and prayer, in which the world of revelation is the world simply and solely in which belief is not an idea but a history affecting oneself and where one takes part; in which God is no abstraction but the living God by whom we live; in which, finally, the Church is recognised as the people he sought out for himself, whom he formed for himself, whom he does not cease to call and fashion, breathing into it the breath of his mouth.

So in Protestant education the Word of God is the native environment of a spiritual life which, at its source, is life with God who lives and converses familiarly with his people. In it the great Christian truths are shown as saving realities, as intimate experiences, and as governing the whole of life. It is these which are incarnated in the persons of the Bible, sung by the psalmists, and inculcated by the prophets and apostles, not by instruction, but by exhortations which speak to the heart.

In Protestant worship this same Word ceaselessly recalls to itself the people of God, arouses it, inspires its response in prayer, as in an intercourse, tireless and unending, of God with man, where God himself draws man's trust, helps him to express his needs, and anticipates in his reply the questions man is conscious of, but does not know how to express. The most interior life is but the constant renewal of this dialogue, and enriched always by the most intimately personal experience, because fed inexhaustibly by the Word, and so making ever fresh discoveries. 'Thy word is a lamp to my feet, and a light to my paths'; this verse of the 118th psalm may be considered the main theme of the spiritual experience which, more than anything else, contributes to the undying fecundity of Protestantism and to its power to attach so many fervent souls, in spite of all the weaknesses they meet there. The extraordinary interior concentration, the richness, both compacted and expansive, of a Protestant art whose highest expression is the painting of Rembrandt and the music of Bach, are but the ultimate fruit of this experience.

This is conclusive proof that the so-called 'religion of the Book' is far more than the religion of a book, however great—a fact already plain from the passages we have quoted from Luther on the Word of God. But we have had to wait for a contemporary theologian, Karl Barth, to give an account which does full justice to what the 'Word of God' means to the Protestantism of which it is the very life. He expresses undoubtedly the most positive and enduring element of the contemporary Protestant revival, whose weaknesses we shall point out after treating of its true greatness.

In the judgment of Barth, to say that the supreme authority of Scripture is the formal principle of the Reformation, while gratuitous salvation is its material principle, is to view the matter very superficially. The Word of God is not important simply because its authority guarantees, or puts forward, a doctrine. If we are to continue to look on it as the formal principle, we have to say that it shows itself as a form which creates its own matter, or as being itself its own content.

Barth does not overlook that 'word', in its full sense, implies the idea of thought and, therefore, has an intellectual, even rational, significance (*cf.* the Greek λόγος). The divine Word, then, like the human word, is discourse, *Rede*. Thus, the product of the Word is, in regard to us, a revelation.[1] But this aspect, particularly in regard to the divine Word, does not exhaust the whole reality. If it is unduly emphasised, it could bring us to overlook the essential nature of the word in general, and especially of the divine Word. This narrow conception is ruled out for us by the passage of St. John: 'In the beginning was the Word, and the Word was with God, and the Word was God.' That is, the Word must be understood as living, as belonging not to the sphere of things, but as a person; and this person is not any person at all, but divine.[2]

What does this mean? The Word is not primarily, still less exclusively, what is said, thoughts which are communicated to us, but the living act by which God comes to us in person. It is thus creative and, still more, all-powerful. In its omnipotence it is the manifestation of the highest freedom: that of God. Finally, it cannot be conceived as distinct from the living person of Christ; wherever the Word of God is authentically present, Christ must necessarily be there in person.

We will consider each of these assertions in turn.

[1] Barth, *Kirchliche Dogmatik*, Vol. 1/1, p. 140.
[2] *Ibid.*, Vol. 1, pp. 141–2.

In every utterance certainly, man expresses his intention to communicate himself. He tends, or claims, to give himself in some degree. But he may fail to realise this intention. If in the end it is to be realised, it is not enough that the word is uttered and the meaning expressed. There is needed, besides, a laborious effort, distinct from the word itself, for the promise to be fulfilled. That supposes, too, that the word is sincere. But, often enough, human utterance is not so and, even when it aims at being sincere, it succeeds only in part.

The Word of God, on the other hand, is truth itself and reality itself. When God says that he wishes something, we cannot doubt that he actually does so; with him there is no disparity between thought and expression. At the same time, for a thing to be done, it is enough for him to express his will by his Word; no disparity, again, between intention and execution. What he says is done, by the sole fact that it is he who says it.

The Word of God is, then, essentially creative, and its creative power knows no other limitation than the power of the God who speaks. Whatever he says is done by the mere fact that he says it. Not only is this so, but there is ultimately nothing that happens otherwise. Not only is the divine Word, immediately and unrestrictedly, the source of being, but it is the only source of being there is. Once again, St. John tells us: 'All things were made by him, and without him was made nothing that was made.' [1]

In particular, the Word which announces our election, our forgiveness, our new birth, is not a simple invitation, in the moral order, to realise all this; itself, by itself alone, effects it. Human words have never more than a moral, indirect causality; that of the divine Word is always physical, immediate, absolute. [2]

In the second place, the Word of God is free; with the supreme liberty of the sovereign God, who is not conditioned by anything, but who himself creates the conditions of all things. This means that the divine Word is at once determinant and decision (*Entscheidung*), in the sense that God commits himself in what he says and, at the same time, his Word cannot be determined by anything else, so that when it intervenes in history it is by no

[1] John I, 3. *Cf. Kirchliche Dogmatik*, Vol. 1/1, pp. 148–9.
[2] *Cf. Kirchliche Dogmatik*, Vol. 1/1, p. 138; also pp. 155–8.

means subject to the accomplished fact, any more than it is in any way a product of the past, but is the unforeseeable event that renews all. In this consists properly the revelation that 'the Spirit breathes where he will'.[1]

Finally, and this is the essential, the Word of God, in its aspect of *Rede*, thing said, cannot be absolutely isolated from its aspect of *Wort*, the act of saying. God, in speaking, utters himself; it is enough to note this for us to understand that no other than God can utter the Word of God, without its ceasing to merit the title. The Word of God can only be authentically proclaimed if God himself is present in Christ proclaiming it, and always actively present. It cannot become something ready-made, an independent reality, that man may handle, use as he pleases, separating it from Him who has said it, from his act, always actual, of saying it. Whenever we think we do so, what we really manipulate is absolutely no longer 'the Word of God', even if they are the words, the ideas, conveyed by the divine Word. It can only belong to him, it cannot become the property of another without ceasing to be.[2] Thence comes the importance Barth attributes to the idea of 'contemporaneousness' which he borrows from Kierkegaard. The Word of God can never be considered and treated as a thing of the past, delivered over to the historian or to any process of human exploitation of the divine datum in general. Conversely, the divine Word in its authentic nature takes hold of us as something that happens, by which God takes hold of us; nor does he condescend to our level so much as raise us to his, and place us directly in his presence.[3]

This being the doctrine of Barth, a question naturally arises, one which Barth himself is quite prepared to face: how does the Word of God so described, in its full actuality, its personal presence and life, stand in relation to the Bible?

The answer to this question, as formulated by Barth, contains essentially the answer to this other one: what is the relation between the Word of God and this or that defined dogma?

[1] John III, 8. *Cf. Kirchliche Dogmatik*, Vol. 1/1, pp. 163–4.
[2] *Kirchliche Dogmatik*, Vol. 1/1, pp. 141–3.
[3] *Ibid.*, 150–5. On all these aspects of the Word, a *materially* excellent account is given by Père J. Hamer, O.P., in *Karl Barth*, Paris, 1925, pp. 25 *et seq.* His complete lack of sympathy for this magnificent doctrine is all the more surprising.

It goes without saying that the letter of Scripture, and the
dogmas recognised in it by the Church, are always in one aspect
human productions, and so of this world. They are therefore
determined by historical events, in which they are distinct from
the divine Word in itself and, in a way, opaque in its regard.
God is not, then, bound to them, in the sense that he cannot be
limited or hemmed in by any of these restrictions, any more than
he is by the individual human nature of the Logos incarnate.
But it is we who are bound to them, for the Bible, with the truths
it proclaims, is the way God has chosen to come to us, to make
himself known to us; and it is only by our obedience to this
decision of his that we can hope to be touched by the Word itself.
However, this by no means implies that the Word of God is
committed and, as it were, abandoned to us in Scripture. We
may never take hold of it, make it something of ours, build it
into our systems, and so on. On the contrary, it is only in the
degree in which the Word itself, by the power of the Spirit ever
in union with it, takes hold of us, that the Bible as a whole, and
in each of the truths discerned there by the Church for us, will
be illumined by the active and living presence of the Word.
Otherwise they will be always for us a dead letter, however much
we apply to them all the resources of human learning.[1]

These latter statements, however clearly enunciated by Barth,
are inseparably bound up in his exposition with certain negations. This also applies, though less strongly, to some of the
preceding statements. These negations, as we shall shortly see,
are particularly disastrous; they are, too, less defensible perhaps than any of the other negative assertions of Protestantism,
in the face of the New Testament and of the traditional Christian
teaching. We have to admit also that the affirmations we have
just presented receive in Barth a vigour and range hard to re-
produce, and to which our account renders scant justice.

What should be our final verdict on this impressive wealth of
doctrine on the Word of God and its supreme authority,
handed down in the living experience of Protestantism from
Luther to Barth, presented in its most engaging aspect?

If there is any sphere where both Scripture, in its correct in-

[1] *Cf. Parole de Dieu et parole humaine*, French translation, Paris, 1936.

terpretation, and the entire Catholic tradition seem readily to corroborate what Protestantism affirms, it is this, without any doubt.

For in the first place it is undeniable that the whole of Old Testament religion is a religion of the Word; the divine Word addressed to the patriarchs, from Abraham onwards, guiding their whole life, directing their hope; the divine Word addressed by the prophets to the descendants of Abraham, and meditated by all the faithful in the inspired writings, as shown, for example, in the 119th psalm (118th in the Vulgate). So obvious is this that it would be a waste of time to prove it in detail. Similarly, in the New Testament this Word is seen to be focused and illuminated in the life and person of Jesus of Nazareth, to the point, as all contemporary exegetes agree, that the Word and the Gospel are made one, the Gospel being the 'good news' of Christ, of his message, of his acts, of what he was in our midst and remains for ever.

On the other hand, it is certain that an exclusive and narrow identification of the Bible with the Word of God is not required by the Bible itself, any more than by the ancient ecclesiastical tradition. However, as we have already insisted, this view has always been restricted to certain stereotyped forms of Protestant orthodoxy, late in time; they are certainly not part of the present doctrinal renascence inspired by Barth in particular.

With this in mind, it is right to insist that this narrow 'biblicism' is by no means to be confused with the affirmation that the Bible, and in one sense the Bible alone, is the 'Word of God' more directly and fully than any of its other expressions, since it alone is so inspired by God as to have him for its author. In making their own this assertion, and giving it the vigour and emphasis so characteristic of their doctrine, the Protestant reformers did not go beyond the unanimous verdict of Judaism on the Old Testament, once constituted, and of the Fathers and theologians on the Bible as a whole. The cautious reservations introduced by modern Catholic writers, as a result of the controversies of the sixteenth century, cannot disguise the fact that the Protestants, in the positive statements we refer to, say no more than the unanimous ecclesiastical tradition.

St. Augustine may be said to have given definitive expression to this in a passage of his 19th letter to St. Jerome, repeated so often by writers in the Middle Ages: 'To those books of Scripture alone that are now known as canonical I have learned to pay the honour and respect of believing firmly that none of their authors made any mistake in what they wrote.' [1] St. Thomas, far from moderating this expression, brings out its doctrine most precisely in the beginning of the *Summa Theologica*. The scriptural books alone, in and by themselves, enjoy absolute authority, since the Christian faith rests entirely on the revelation made by God to the apostles, and before them to the prophets; it is handed down to us with the direct authority of God only in the canonical books. All other writers, including the doctors of the Church, can by themselves only be the basis of probable arguments. Arguments drawn from Scripture are alone by themselves conclusive. Therefore, the Bible alone provides the real foundations for sacred science. [2]

Duns Scotus is no less trenchant. According to him, Scripture alone is necessary and sufficient to make known to man the truths of salvation. That does not mean that all other kinds of writings, within and even outside the Church, may not be useful in this respect; but they cannot do more than throw additional light on our understanding of Scripture. Likewise, all the work of theologians and doctors only serves to bring out the content of Scripture. [3]

Can we believe that the Church in modern times would disown these assertions of tradition? No doubt the negations Protestants added to them, which we will point out, have led theologians since the Council of Trent to introduce certain distinctions. They have come to insist, not more strongly than in the past but more explicitly, on the necessity of tradition for the understanding of Scripture. It is none the less true that no Catholic theologian worthy of the name, today any more than in the Middle Ages, would place any doctrinal authority on the level of Scripture. If the authority of the Church be declared necessary to judge between the different interpretations of theo-

---

[1] *Cap.* I (his 82nd letter in modern editions).
[2] *Summa Theol.* I, q. 1, arts. 8, 9, and 10. *Cf. Contra Gentes,* IV, 1; *Quodlibet,* VII, q. 6, arts. 1, 2, and 3.
[3] *Scriptum Oxoniense,* all the beginning (fol. 1 to 4 in Paris edition, 1519).

logians, it is by no means because she claims for herself an authority superior to that of the Bible, but because her magisterium is necessary for our submission to Scripture, as well as hers, to be real as well as intended. The Church in her magisterium is the first to recognise that she is subject to the Word of God as contained in the Bible; she claims no more than to assure, by the ways chosen by God, the constant submission of the whole Church to this Word.

For, if the definition of Councils, the teaching of the magisterium and of theologians, have, since the sixteenth century, brought into sharper relief the traditional doctrine, the aim has not been to heighten the authority of the Church at the expense of that of Scripture, but to bring out clearly their respective positions, and so to emphasise the unique excellence of the inspired writings. This process of development has established once and for all the distinction between the inspiration of Scripture and the supernatural assistance granted to the magisterium in its various forms. Consequently, it is now absolutely clear, not only that Scripture is inspired, but that there is no other ecclesiastical document of which the same may be said, even a solemn definition of Pope or Council. Thus, in the Catholic teaching of today, the truth appears more clear-cut than ever that the Bible *alone* can be said to have God for its author. In fact, to it alone the Council of Trent, in the same decree in which it affirms the authority of tradition, reserves this distinctive phrase: *Omnes libros tam Veteris quam Novi Testamenti, cum utriusque Deus sit auctor.* . . .[1] The Vatican Council is even more explicit, and proclaims, in words which leave no loophole, that 'the Church holds [these books] as sacred and canonical, not because, composed by unaided human effort, they have been approved by her authority; nor solely because they contain revelation unmixed with error; but because, being written under the inspiration of the Holy Spirit, they have God for author and, as such, have been delivered to the Church.'[2]

---

[1] *Decretum de canonicis Scripturis, Sessio,* IV (8 April 1547): Denzinger-Bannwart, no. 783.

[2] *Constitutio de Fide Catholica, cap.* 2, *De revelatione, Sessio* III (24 April 1870); Denzinger-Bannwart, no. 1787.

It is not possible to improve upon these texts to show how the very thing that Protestants affirm about the supreme authority, unique of its kind, of Scripture, is likewise affirmed by the Church of today, as always without reserve and with unequalled precision.

What, then, shall we say about that Biblical piety which we have described as typical of Protestant spirituality? It would be useless to deny that modern Catholics have often viewed it with distrust. In Spain, for example, it was even forbidden for a long period to own or use any translation of the Bible in the vernacular. Elsewhere, without going so far, a devotion, wholly or mainly scriptural, has been certainly viewed with reserve. However, in this we see the inevitable reaction following upon the rupture between Protestants and the Church, after they had made a kind of speciality of a return to Scripture; the mistrust was not of Scripture itself, but of the aptitude of the mass of Catholics of those days to profit from it. In an environment partly dechristianised, where the Bible had become an occasion of attacks to which theologians alone could reply with relevance, though they did not always manage to, it was natural to hesitate to leave the faithful alone in the presence of Scripture where probably hostile propaganda would insinuate itself. For several generations, it cannot be denied, Catholics have felt a kind of uneasiness or insecurity in the presence of a Biblical piety. Neither theologians nor authority have ever seriously considered the Bible to be harmful in itself, but many have thought it safer, in the circumstances brought about by controversy, to guide the faithful to an indirect presentation of the truths conveyed by the Word of God. It was thought preferable, to avoid misunderstanding, to set before the mass of the faithful, at any rate, only the most modern, the most easily understood, expressions of Christian truth, so formulated as to avoid whatever might seem to lend itself to interpretations condemned by the Church. It must nevertheless be emphasised that this policy has never been universal in the Church, nor approved without reserve by the highest authorities.

In fact, it would have been difficult to adopt it without running counter to the most authentically Catholic tradition. The Fathers of the Church, St. Augustine above all, themselves practised that devotion derived from Scripture, whose ideal the Protestants steadily upheld; they hardly knew any other. No doubt they were much more careful than many Protestants not to isolate the Word of God in its settled form of Scripture from its living form in the Church, particularly in the liturgy. But, this reserve apart—to which many Protestants, without acknowledging the principle, have in practice adhered—they were no less enthusiastic, or insistent, or formal, in recommending this use of Scripture and in actually promoting it. Particularly from St. John Chrysostom, one might assemble exhortations and injunctions couched in the most forcible terms; they have often been recalled by those Protestants, from the sixteenth century onwards, the best grounded in Christian antiquity. It would be impossible to find, even among Protestants, statements more sweeping than those in which St. Jerome abounds; *Ignoratio scripturarum, ignoratio Christi* is doubtless the most lapidary, but not necessarily the most explicit.

What is more, in this case just as when the authority of Scripture is viewed as the foundation of theology, the constant practice of the Church, in the Middle Ages as well as in patristic times, is a more eloquent witness than all the doctors. In the same way that Popes, Councils, theologians, always resorted to the scriptural argument as the really fundamental one, the practice of the great spiritual writers of every epoch attests the fully traditional character of a devotion based on the Bible. Writers as eminent and influential as Origen in the East and Augustine in the West equally prove the truth of this. Their entire spirituality in both cases is but an immense meditation on Scripture. The same is true of the great teachers of the Middle Ages, who often enough are disciples of both, as was St. Bernard. We can apply to them all that we said of the best of Protestant spirituality: not only did they know the Bible and make abundant use of it, but they moved in it as in a spiritual world that formed the habitual universe of all their thoughts and sentiments. For them, it was not simply one source among others, but the source *par excellence*, in a sense the only one.

The best proof that this was no exceptional thing, proper only to a few great geniuses, is what may be called the method of prayer of the whole of Christian antiquity, popularised by monastic practice from the time of St. Benedict at least, and in vogue all through the Middle Ages. The twelfth century in particular witnesses to it, and to its wonderful reflorescence at the time, with the schools of Cluny and Cîteaux. The recent works of Dom Jean Leclercq and Dom J-M. Déchanet abound in texts and information in support of this.

What in fact was for so many monks the most important of their personal religious practices, the one which virtually contained all the others? It was what the Benedictine rule, which only codified in this the practice of the sixth century, called the *lectio divina*. This *lectio*, which turned directly on Scripture, illuminated by the writings of the Fathers and the liturgy, was both contemplative meditation and personal prayer, engaging every side of one's being. It was nourished exclusively on the Bible, the Bible conceived as the Word of God actually addressed to the soul, rousing and creating the response in which the soul surrenders itself, as it recognises the voice of the love who loved it first.

Moreover, though the circumstances we mentioned forced for a time into the background of Catholicism this practice, always deeply centred in tradition, its restoration is one of the most remarkable features in Catholicism today. Not only with the approval of the hierarchy but by the positive and emphatic insistence of the Pope himself, there has come about a general return to the close study of Scripture, which has been restored, not only as the base, but as the source, of all teaching of theology. At the same time, and under the same impulse, the text of the Bible has been widely spread among the people, and proposed for their meditation as the most excellent source of the spiritual life and the truths of religion.

In the light of all this, how should we judge that theology of the Word of God which we have seen worked out by Barth, which undoubtedly in its essentials is but a magnificent expression of the best kind of Protestant and Biblical spirituality up to his time? The Catholic theologian could wish to see it completed and elucidated at certain points, notably in all that concerns the difficult problem of the relations between the Word of God and Holy Scripture. But it seems to us, if we confine our attention to those aspects of his thought which appear the most fundamental, that none of these additions or clarifications could alter anything of his real doctrine. In the whole account we have given of his theology, mostly in his own words, there is nothing that does not follow directly from what the Word of God itself affirms. To this the Catholic theologian must add that Barth, in his selection of these principal subjects from the Bible, is evidently guided by the most ancient and persistent current in the great patristic tradition, from Origen to St. Augustine. We will return to all this when we come to examine critically the negative elements by whose introduction Protestantism so early adulterated its own principles. At present, there is only one conclusion to be drawn from this chapter: the supreme authority of Scripture, taken in its positive sense, as gradually drawn out and systematised by Protestants themselves, far from setting the Church and Protestantism in opposition, should be the best possible warrant for their return to understanding and unity.

CHAPTER VII

The Negative Elements of the Reformation

WE have now come to the decisive turning-point in our study. All we have seen of Protestantism up to now, and we have seen the essential, suggests one question: how could a religious movement, starting from such principles, create a schism, turn aside from the Catholic tradition, set up over against the Church a multiplicity of 'Churches', very often as hostile to one another as to Catholicism? From all we have said, it might have seemed that the Lutheran movement, with its development by Calvin and Barth, was destined to become a great, positive factor of expansion, to restore the central and fundamental elements of tradition, to renew the Church itself from within. In its main lines, it seemed to bring in an incalculable wealth of constructive power; even to constitute a rediscovery and application of what was capital and permanent in Christianity.

The first answer that suggests itself is that, had there been no more in Protestantism than what we have singled out, the schism, still more the heresies accompanying it, would be inexplicable. On the other hand, we must insist that our investigation has gone straight to the essential, and we may even claim that it is, in a sense, exhaustive. The principles we have examined are considered by Protestants themselves as necessary and sufficient for the Reform. Moreover, we have studied them, both as they sprang forth at the outset, and as they gained in significance, in the development of their essential scope and aim. Always we have confirmed the evidence of the sources with their actual results in the religion as lived throughout the whole of its history, not merely as confined within the bounds of an abstract exposition. Obviously this only makes the question more urgent: how did a movement which seemed and still seems to bear within itself the power to rejuvenate and restore traditional Christianity, the Church of all time, come in fact to set up a Christianity disrupted from tradition, and to injure and attack of set purpose the Church it had wished to renew?

136

Those Protestant readers who have followed us to this point will naturally react with the objection: 'Surely the real question is: why did the Church reject the Reformation along with the Reformers?'

This, however, has already been answered in advance: in so far as the Reformers simply desired all the points we have developed, their movement was never rejected by the Church. On the contrary—we think we have now made it evident—in all the essentials it upheld exactly what the Reformers strove for. In spite of all the misconceptions created by modern controversy, it may be said to continue to maintain it today more exactly than it has done since the sixteenth century, in view of all the facts and quotations to which we have alluded. If none the less the Protestant Reformers were undeniably expelled from communion with the Church, it was obviously not on account of their positive principles. There is no alternative but to admit that with these principles were associated others that the Church could not accept. That is what we hope now to show; at the same time making it clear that this 'something else', so far from following from the principles already examined, or from being necessarily implied by them, or even useful or expedient, has only succeeded in stifling them within Protestantism itself.

We will begin by summarising what has been said up to now. It should be quite evident that the principles of Protestantism, in their positive sense—that most consonant with the spirit of the Reformation—are not only valid and acceptable, but must be held to be true and necessary *in virtue of Catholic tradition itself*, in virtue of what makes up the authority of the Church both of today and of all time. Salvation as the pure gift of God in Christ, communicated by faith alone, in the sense that no other way can be thought of apart from faith or even along with faith; justification by faith in its subjective aspect, which means that there is no real religion where it is not living and personal; the absolute sovereignty of God, more particularly of his Word as contained in the inspired writings—all these principles are the heart of Protestantism as a reforming movement. Yet, if we go to the root of them all, to what the Reformers considered most essential, to what is retained by living Protestantism, today and always, we are bound to say that they are all corroborated by Catholic tradition, and maintained absolutely by what is authoritative, in the present, for all Catholics.

That is why we have to insist that the real question is not: 'Why did the Church disown the Reformation, which proceeded from such principles?'—but: 'What was present in the Reformation, so bound up with these principles, that the Church had to reject the Reformation in spite of them?'

The answer to this demands an inquiry exactly the reverse of that pursued up to now. In the first part of our study, we have worked out an analysis of Protestantism in all its complexity; we have striven to go behind appearances, the most various and at times the most misleading, to reach its unifying principle, one, moreover, which constitutes its essence in the opinion, if not of all, at least of those most faithful to its original spirit. Now we are to undertake the opposite process, a much easier one. We have to view Protestantism as a whole, take the statements it has itself developed and systematised in its disputes both with Catholicism and with scholastic theology, and then, most important of all, those it has affirmed in the course of its development; this has often taken it far from its origins, but it brings out a complexity unsuspected by the first Reformers themselves.

No sooner do we adopt this standpoint than one thing strikes us forcibly. It is not that other principles appear side by side with those which we have already stated and developed in all their positive implications; it is that within Protestantism these very principles seem drawn by a mysterious fatality to adopt a negative significance. This stands out from the very first when Protestant enunciations were made in reaction against Catholicism, against certain of its degenerate forms in the sixteenth century, but which very soon became hostile to Catholicism in its essence. This tendency becomes prominent in the systems constructed by Protestants, which take on the character of an elaborated anti-Catholicism, though using considerable parts of Catholicism itself. The same tendency is fully explicit in the generation almost immediately following this Protestant scholasticism, which it disowned and refuted in its turn by the very same arguments which make it reject Catholicism.

Let us examine this more in detail. The reader cannot fail to be impressed, even astonished, at seeing how strictly the historical reality unfolds in that sequence, no matter what the principle in question.

The further Luther advanced in his conflict with other theologians, then with Rome, then with the whole of contemporary Catholicism and finally with the Catholicism of every age, the more closely we see him identifying his affirmation about *sola gratia* with a particular theory, known as extrinsic justification. That is to say, he himself unites two statements so closely that they become inseparable—one an affirmation, grace alone saves us; the second a negation, it changes nothing in us in so doing. To recall a simile he himself popularised, the grace of God envelops us as in a cloak, but this leaves us exactly as we were. The sinner, after receiving grace and so saved, is no less a sinner than before.

This is far removed from the other affirmations of Luther that we have seen, those he returns to whenever he lays stress on his inner experience at its source, or as soon as he speaks as a religious guide or educator, anxious simply to give Christians, learned and unlearned alike, a statement of living Christianity as conceived and realised by himself. But, as soon as he engages in controversy, it is this that comes to the fore, displays itself, and becomes more and more involved; and it is this that is seized upon by the theoreticians in their efforts to fix the new doctrine in a logical framework. So they came to say that grace saves us independently of any change effected in us, that no change is effected, that it could not be effected, that it ought not to be effected, that the contrary assertion is scandalous, destructive of all true Christianity, and so forth.

At the same time, the affirmation of *sola fide* is not content with excluding works in the Jewish sense, or works done before faith is received, or works done by the believer apart from the agency of faith in grace, or even apart from this as the unique means giving man power to do good works. The Catholic faith could not do otherwise than take all these exclusions as its own, and ratify them. Luther, and after him the Protestantism that aimed at reducing to a system its opposition to Catholicism, did not stop there. He declared that, not only works antecedent to faith or in some way more or less independent of faith, are

useless for salvation, even harmful, but that all possible and
imaginable works are harmful, that faith itself has not to produce them for salvation, cannot, should not, do so. He made it
quite plain that he was not excluding just exterior works, but
even the most intimate sentiments of the soul, even what is
strongest of all, the love of God. He went so far as to focus his
attacks on the scholastic idea of faith 'informed' by charity, contrasted with faith without charity as living faith to dead; he
declared that such a doctrine was the ruin of all he set out to
preach. Even in our own day, one of the most eminent of
Lutheran theologians wrote a work to show that this rejection
of a justification which should include any kind of love of God
on the part of man is the highest point of Lutheran teaching.

On the other hand, in spite of the conservatism Luther and
Lutheranism have always shown in the matter of the liturgy
and the sacraments, it is beyond doubt that Luther closely
linked the subjective side of justification by faith, personal religion in fact, with denial of the objective value of the sacraments and of all the other means of grace. Once faith is present,
there is salvation, but there is nothing in the sphere of salvation
existing apart from faith itself, and faith in its turn has no
transcendental object, no content outside itself. All this can be
supported by the most categorical passages from Luther; it was
to be systematised little by little down to its ultimate consequences by Protestant writers, although the early scholastics of
Lutheranism saw the dangers of this position and eluded its
logic. This view in fact reduces the sacraments, the Church,
defined dogma, to the status of mere signs, easily dispensable,
lacking even any content of their own. They are made into mere
psychological stimulants or supports of a wavering faith, which
a clear and firm faith can do without. At the same time, faith
is not so much belief in an objective salvation, or in Him who
grants it, as, in an immediate sense, faith in one's own individual
salvation. Once withdrawn from the need for any support outside itself, since it is immediately felt, it tends naturally to
eliminate, as a useless encumbrance, all rites, the whole visible
Church, and even all definite doctrine.

By a similar process, the sovereignty of God comes to mean
the crushing down of man, the uselessness, the non-existence, the

impossibility, the total undesirability, of any activity on his part which might claim any religious value, constitute 'merit', in whatever way that may be understood. Thus, in the view of Barth which is simply an extension of certain aspects of Calvinism, brought out more strongly than Calvin ever dared, the existence of saints in the Church, far from being a homage to the divine holiness, can only be an intolerable offence, a personal affront, to the all-holiness of God.

Finally, if we turn to the doctrine of the supreme authority of Scripture, we notice, at the very outset of Protestantism, the tendency to equate it with an absolute denial of the authority of the Church, whether manifested in tradition or in particular decisions of her magisterium. The positive principle of the sovereignty of God speaking by his Word, even at the time of the first Reformers, of Luther himself, but more systematically later on, became in fact identified with the denial of any authoritative value both to tradition and to decisions of Popes or Councils progressively defining the deposit of tradition.

What is to be thought of all these negations? There is no doubt whatever that, either in detail or in principle, they were formulated from the time of the first generation of Protestants. It is equally certain that from the outset they were directed against the Catholic Church. The first statements identifying extrinsic justification with the *sola gratia, sole fide* are found in Luther's commentaries on the epistle to the Galatians; perhaps earlier still, in his commentary on Romans. The exclusion from the sphere of justification, not only of works in general, but even of the love of God in 'faith informed by charity', is one of the most conspicuous traits of strictly Lutheran theology, as expounded by the most capable interpreters. Luther's own radical criticism of the sacraments, the organised Church, and of its definitions of the object of faith, is already formulated in his treatises *On the Babylonish Captivity* and *On Christian Liberty* in terms to be taken up and systematised at a later date, by him or by others, but never surpassed in their force.

Similarly, the whole of Barth's teaching, in his strictly controversial aspect, is directed against Catholicism, whether in itself or what remains of it in Protestantism, and reiterates incessantly the absolute denial to man of any possible religious value before God. Barth himself has shown, better than anyone else could, that in this he follows a line of thought which goes back to the origins of the Reformation.

Finally, the identification of absolute submission to Scripture with rejection of the Church, of the authority of tradition and of the existing hierarchy, was Luther's own reason for refusing to accept his condemnation, and of the persistent refusal of Protestants, even the most conservative, to return to the Church that condemned him. It would be a waste of time to prove points of this sort, on which all are agreed: the evidence is plain and indisputable.

What, however, are we to think of the association, or rather confusion, wrought by Protestantism from the outset, between the positive assertions we have dwelt on at length and the negations that now confront us? The least that may be said is that they have no necessary connection. What is more, the New Testament and the whole of Christian antiquity, which certainly corroborate the positive assertions, not only do not support, but seem to reject, more or less clearly, all the negations that have been mixed up with them.

However strongly the New Testament affirms the impossibility of any positive contribution on the part of man towards his salvation, whether before, apart from, or side by side with grace, it is as emphatic as possible on the fruitfulness, the necessary fruitfulness, of grace acting within man for his salvation. The commentaries of Luther, and his disciples up to Barth, on the epistle to the Romans are an involuntary witness to this by the pains they take in vain to hide it. No modern exegete with any degree of objectivity, whether Protestant, Catholic or free-thinker, fails to recognise that the thought of St. Paul on justification, in all its complexity, exacts equal attention to the 7th chapter of the epistle to the Romans, in its description of fallen man, and the 8th, which describes the action of the Holy Spirit in man raised up by grace. Against this, it is impossible not to be struck, in reading what Luther, still more what Barth, wrote on this epistle, by the way in which, *a priori*, the 7th chapter is put forward as presenting St. Paul's complete and final view of man. All that they deduce from it seems to have no other purpose than to attenuate, or rather excuse, the affirmations of chapter 8. Once this has been pointed out, it is easy to appreciate the sally of Albert Schweitzer, one of the greatest Protestant exegetes of St. Paul, that justification by faith is not nearly so important to St. Paul as to Luther, but has been forcibly crammed by the latter into texts which in fact do not mention it. This assertion is obviously indefensible if taken strictly, but if by 'justification by faith', we understand the whole negative structure Luther and his 'orthodox' followers built upon the doctrine, the exaggeration is easily comprehensible. Without the least doubt, grace, for St. Paul, however freely given, involves what he calls 'the new creation', the appearance in us of a 'new man', created in justice and holiness. So far from suppressing the efforts of man, or making them a matter of indifference, or at least irrelevant to salvation, he himself tells us to 'work out your salvation with fear and trembling', at the very moment when he affirms that '. . . knowing that it is God who works in you both to will and to accomplish'. These two expressions say better than any other that all is grace in our salvation, but at the same time grace is not opposed to human acts and endeavour in order to attain salvation, but arouses them and exacts their performance.

Luther was the first to have to recognise that all the writers of the New Testament, other than St. Paul, deal a crushing blow to the theological structure he tried to build on the latter. He had to rid himself of the express teaching of the epistle of St. James by treating it as an 'epistle of straw'—strangely inconsequential in one who claimed to restore the Scriptures to their place of supreme authority. Blinded as he was by the so-called Pauline character of the structure he had erected on a few texts taken apart from their context, he did not see that St. Paul contradicted his system no less formally than St. James. After three centuries, all serious exegetes are obliged by the evidence to accept this fact; there is not a single Protestant author whose works are of scientific value who disputes it. Extrinsic justification, a justification independent of any interior change, of any new capability given to man to perform acts pleasing of themselves to God, is so far from being a Pauline doctrine that it is quite irreconcilable with the whole body of his teaching.

Calvin, as we have seen, was quite conscious of this, and

applied himself with some success to correcting Luther on this point. None the less, the clear-cut distinction he tried to draw between justification and sanctification, while willingly admitting that they are inseparable in fact, cannot be maintained in a scientific exegesis. Scripture, even St. Paul alone, apart from the evidence of the four Gospels, sweeps aside the last dialectical device for safeguarding the theory of extrinsic justification.

If this is the case with the opposition set up between grace and a justification intrinsic to man, or inclusive of some element in man, what are we to say to the opposition defined by Luther, the controversialist and systematiser, against the idea that the love of God (having God for its object) pertains in some way to justification—whether the connection is expressed by the formula of faith 'informed' by charity, or in some other way? It would seem hard to deny that this is the least defensible of Luther's negations that Lutheranism has striven to justify. The recent book of Anders Nygren, *Eros et Agape*, in spite of the extreme ingenuity, and even forcefulness of some of its analyses, unintentionally makes this fact brilliantly clear. Nygren guides his whole inquiry on the Christian doctrine of love towards Luther's paradoxical negation, contrasting faith with the love of God, and making their opposition the basis of that between Protestantism and Catholicism. Nygren attempts to show that it is at this point that Protestantism alone has shown itself faithful to the new creation proclaimed in the Gospel. But the price that has to be paid for this demonstration is, he admits, so heavy that one wonders if it is not the best refutation of the whole system. He finds himself obliged to reject the whole body, the heart in particular, of the thought of St. John, as already infected with the 'Catholic error' *par excellence*. Further, he is driven to the necessity of denying the fundamental importance, even the bare truth, of the summary of the law as given in the Synoptics: 'Thou shalt love the Lord thy God with thy whole heart, and with thy whole soul, and with thy whole mind; that is the first and the great commandment. And the second is like to this: Thou shalt love thy neighbour as thyself.' The fact that he had to go to such an extreme in order to maintain the Lutheran position which turns on its opposition to the *fides caritate formata*, or else admit its invalidity, constitutes, we believe, the most tragic but the clearest admission possible that Protestantism was led, in the elaboration of its own principles, to a crisis which it cannot resolve.

Here we will make an observation we shall often have to repeat. Even the most extreme of the negations adopted by Protestantism always have their counterpart of truth. The same, of course, is true of every heresy. In the present instance, it is certain—St. Augustine had already pointed it out—that St. Paul speaks ordinarily of love, ἀγάπη, as having man for its object, just as faith, πίστις, has man for its subject. But does that mean, in his view, that man has not to love God? Or that this love has only to do with the interior state of the one justified, as such? Pseudo-logic of this kind is a monstrosity. The real truth is that the love by which God loves is the cause of everything in justification considered objectively, whereas 'faith' is its only principle in the subjective aspect. But 'faith', in St. Paul's sense, being the fruit of 'the charity of God poured forth into our hearts by the Holy Spirit', supposes the total abandonment of man to the gift of God. For this reason, as Luther himself says in a passage we have quoted, one where he forgets his controversial system, either the 'faith' which justifies is wholly penetrated with charity, or else it is the source of the charity restored, in our hearts, both to God and to everything he loves. To suppose, on the other hand, that the person justified by faith, who calls to God, in the Spirit, 'Abba, Father', does not love God, or has not to love him in order to be justified, is certainly to maintain, not only a false deduction from a premise absurd in itself, but one not even conceivable, apart from supposing, what goes against the whole of St. Paul, that grace passes through man without affecting him at all, without changing his heart, without creating in him a new human nature in the image of that of the Son of God.

This brings us to the strangely ambiguous doctrine of the sovereignty of God, and to some of its aspects developed by Calvin, and particularly attractive to Barth and his disciples.

In the light of numerous Protestant accounts, from the sixteenth century to the present day, it may be summed up by saying that it is impossible to affirm and uphold the sovereignty of God without a corresponding annihilation of the creature, especially man. To recognise any worth at all in man, whether in his external acts, in the innermost workings of his mind, even in his being, while maintaining his close dependence on God, would seem an infringement of the divine majesty, by the very fact of this dependence. In particular, to suppose that man as the result of God's grace has the power to do acts good in themselves, even granted his total dependence on God, would be to destroy the gratuitousness of grace, and so to deny the sovereign freedom of God's action. And to say that man, as the recipient of saving grace, could be himself pleasing to God, is to be guilty of blasphemy. Finally, it would be a relapse into idolatry to suppose that man, even when regenerated and recreated, in St. Paul's words, in holiness and justice, could possess any value, and still worse to attribute to him the power to 'merit' anything, in any sense of the word. Affirmations of this sort occur frequently in Luther, and even more in Calvin. As for Barth, his entire system turns on them.

It is tempting at this stage to analyse this axiom, or rather postulate, since it is evidently the extreme to which the 'protest' against the Church arrives, when it seeks ultimate vindication. Before doing so, however, it is as well to see what the New Testament, and the Bible as a whole, not to mention early Christianity, have to say about a supposition of this sort.

On the one hand, it is clear that the Bible is always on the watch against an inveterate tendency of sinful man, the Christian included, to ascribe to himself what belongs to God, to take himself, or the world of which he is a part, as the ultimate source of the gifts of God, and so to appropriate the honour which ought to be given to the Creator. On this matter, undoubtedly the famous sentence of Isaias, 'I will give my glory to no other', is of universal application, and the New Testament insists on it no less than the Old.

However, this only sets out in stronger relief the plain scriptural assertion of the reality of the gifts of God, of his first creation and, no less, of his new creation. None of what has been said above, true as it always is, seems to have made the scriptural writers at all hesitant in asserting this other aspect.

It would clearly be useless to try to find in them any pessimism regarding the actual reality of divine grace. On the contrary, the Bible refutes in advance, more strongly than any Catholic disputant could, the false axiom that God is great only in the degree in which the creature is little, that he is only sovereign if the creature is pure nothingness.

Certainly, Isaias says that 'all our justifications are like a soiled garment', and Job, that God 'finds fault even among the angels'. Nothing could express more strongly the reality of sin, not only as a transient act, but as a permanent state, causing a radical privation of justice in sinful man before God. The second of these texts means, too, that even a creature untouched by sin is at an infinite distance from the holiness which is God's and his alone. Yet none of this prevents the Bible from insisting with equal force on the 'goodness' inherent in every creature that comes from the hands of God, and that goodness which it recovers after sin, when moved and taken up by grace. No doubt Christ himself declared: 'God alone is good', but, just as explicitly enjoins, 'Be ye perfect as your heavenly Father is perfect'; the supposition that he could have called men to this without giving them the means to respond is not worth considering.

The very condition of existence of the 'new creature' is the loving recognition of his actual and necessary dependence for everything upon God. But this, all the New Testament goes to show, does not mean that he has to remain in the state where sin has placed him, but that he must bear the image of the heavenly Adam as he did that of the earthly one; this amounts to saying that God reveals himself as Sovereign and alone Holy, not by leaving sinners to their powerlessness and sinfulness, but by rescuing them from it. The cry of faith, then, is not simply a perpetual contrasting of the holiness and greatness of God with the misery and sinfulness of man, but it is equally what St. Paul means when he says: 'By the grace of God I am what I am, and his grace in me has not been void' (1 Cor. XV, 10). That this is not a casual utterance, but indicates something actually existing and, in some degree at least, capable of being estimated, appears from a passage which itself occurs in a context contrasting utterly the weakness of man, his radical impotence, with

F

the omnipotence of God: 'We labour, whether absent or present, to please him. For we must all be manifested before the judgment-seat of Christ, that everyone may receive according as he hath done, whether good or evil, while still in the body.'[1]

The uneasiness felt by Protestant systems opposed to Catholicism is nowhere so evident than in the long controversy on the meaning in St. Paul of the word δικαιοῦν, to justify. All Protestant exegetes, anxious to safeguard the expressions used by Luther and Calvin, set out to show that it can only mean 'to declare just', not 'to make just'; that is, it applies merely to extrinsic justice, which has nothing real to correspond with it in the person justified. Nevertheless, modern scientific exegesis unanimously acknowledges that the word can only mean 'to declare officially just someone who is so in reality'. Even the idea of the Word of God creating what he says by the act of saying it—so well drawn out by Barth from the entire Bible— would be enough to show that God makes just whom he 'declares just', even if he were not so beforehand, by the very fact of his declaration, so the opposition set up is without meaning.

To sum up the question, if the Bible sets God's holiness, his sovereign greatness, in an 'inaccessible light', it does not at all intend to deny him the act of creating, or recreating, anything real or of value outside himself. Rather, it does so to emphasise how much the first creation, still more the second, attest by their intrinsic reality and goodness the incomparable reality and goodness of him they manifest. The God of Calvinism and Barthism, it seems, keeps all his greatness only if his creatures return to nothingness. The God of the Bible, on the contrary, shows his greatness in snatching them from it, not only, as St. John says, 'that we are *called*, but really *are*, the sons of God.'[2]

This alone throws a great deal of light on the points which remain for discussion. The reality of the gifts of God, witnessing to the sovereign greatness of the giver, is what, even in the Bible, refutes completely the sophism which would oppose 'justifica-

---

[1] We keep the minimist version of τὰ διὰ τοῦ σώματος, given in Protestant translations, though it is hard to deny that the Douay version, 'the proper things of the body', is more in accord with the context: 2 Cor. V, 10.
[2] John III, 1.

tion by faith' to sacraments that are not just empty signs, to
defined dogma, to an objective Church. In fact, contemporary
exegesis, and Protestant scholarship in particular, has shown
with the utmost clarity how the New Testament, especially St.
Paul, requires and explicitly teaches a doctrine of the sacraments
which attributes to them all the characteristics which distinguish Catholic from Protestant sacrament, such as transub-
stantiation and the principle of *opus operatum*—instances given
by Maurice Goguel in his *Eucharistie des origines à Justin
Martyr*. The Church in question is seen to be a Church
formally defined by certain 'ministries' whose institution is
attributed to Christ; by a settled doctrine, the apostolic κήρυγμα,
and the preaching of the Gospel in terms very early defined; a
common celebration of traditional rites effecting union with
Christ, and so on.[1]

Faith, in fact, though directly orientated to God and him
alone, is none the less determined, as to its objective content,
by an event recorded in history. This content, in its ultimate
object, surpasses any human expression; the historical event, too,
is transcendent. But, just as this event is not thereby rendered
evanescent, but rather supremely real, so this content is to be
accepted by us, by our intellect enlightened by the divine Word,
in the formulas given from above, which make up precisely the
κήρυγμα, the 'proclamation' assigned to the heralds of God.
To deny and reject this, far from attesting the sovereignty of
God, would be nothing less than to reject his authority which
affirms its supremacy, through Christ, in human history.

This leads us to the fictitious opposition set up between the
authority of the Word of God in Scripture and that of the
Church in its tradition and magisterium. The Church described
in the New Testament is one which speaks with authority in the
person of its leaders, which appeals to the Word of God spoken
by Christ as the source of this authority, one for whom the
Gospel, the 'good news' of salvation, is the message entrusted
to it, the message whose servant it acknowledges itself to be.
The New Testament, the Gospels especially, are never anything
but the final form of this κήρυγμα that the Church, in the

[1] *Cf.* the passages from contemporary exegetes collected by Père Braun
in *Aspects nouveaux du problème de l'Eglise.*

beginning, carried within itself, and proclaimed with the authority that the Word made flesh had given with its mission: 'He who heareth you heareth me, he that despiseth you despiseth me, and he that despiseth me despiseth him that sent me.'

In the light of this, the opposition alleged to exist between the authority of the divine Word in Scripture and that of the Church is reduced to an absurdity, as soon as it is examined closely. Contrary to the supposition, not so much of Luther as of his disciples, who wished to follow out systematically his line of opposition to Catholicism, the Church did not come into existence after the Word had been set in writing, simply in order to apply it as from the outside. Scripture itself testifies that it was the Church that drew up, collected, and declared the authenticity of Scripture in its final form, so giving fixed shape to what it had from the beginning carried within itself.

The ambiguity in the view held by Barth, more evident in his case than with any other Protestant theologian, of a Word of God held to be sovereign and yet forbidden *a priori* to say anything capable of definition, can only be maintained in the abstract. As soon as it is brought to the test of Scripture, it must either yield to the weight of its explicit affirmations, or else the 'sovereign authority', attributed in principle to the Word, dissolves into nothing. One cannot at one and the same time proclaim that, when God speaks, man has only to be silent and obey, and forbid God to make his voice heard whenever it threatens the system one has built up. Now, it appears that the Word of God contained in Scripture is as little favourable as possible to the general Protestant attitude on grace that saves man without changing him, on a 'justification by faith' that would make useless and impossible any enduring alliance with grace, any sacrament having objective reality, any authoritative teaching of the Church—in short, all that would form the content of faith instead of letting it receive it from itself. None the less, it is these that Barth undertook to restore, setting up a radical opposition between the sovereignty of God and the whole of creation, in virtue of the principle, *finitum non capax infiniti*, or, *homo peccator non capax justitiae Dei*; so spurning in practice the Word on which he had theorised so splendidly.

So, in this supremely revealing case of a theology of the Word

of God desirous of carrying to their ultimate consequences the
principles of the Reformers, in their own formulas and systems,
we see undisguised, not merely the absence of any real bond, but
the implicit opposition between the positive content of these
principles and the negative import assigned to them. Either
this magnificent theology of the Word of God, that we have
followed in the steps of Barth, culminates in admitting that the
Christianity incumbent on the Church, as being that of the New
Testament, is substantially that which the Church has upheld
against the Protestant negations; or else, the whole fine system
is but a *flatus vocis*. If anyone persists in maintaining a grace
devoid of real content, ineffectual, sacraments that are signs
without substance, a Church not invested with the authority,
in a sense, of Christ himself, a faith elusive of definition, truth
compels us to say that to that extent, he forgets all he has said
about the Word of God, or else has made himself incapable of
obeying it by his *a priori* refusal to hear it on certain points.

This typical example, following on all that we have established in this chapter, forces us to the conclusion that the
negative elements, so soon apparent in the formulation of the
positive principles of the Reformation, are not organically
bound up with them, but come from some other source than
that which the Reformation exalted above all others, the Word
of God. Hence arises a new question: what was the origin of
these negations?

Whether it concerns the *sola gratia, sola fide*, in one or other
of its aspects or the *Soli Deo gloria*, or the supreme authority of
Scripture, the negative element arising out of the polemical use
of the positive principles seems invariably the same. It was
apparently impossible for Protestant theology, as elaborated, to
agree that God could put something in man that became in fact
his own, and that at the same time the gift remained the possession of the giver. Or else, what comes to the same thing, that
even after the intervention of grace man could ever belong to
God; it would seem as if man could only belong to him in
ceasing to have a distinct existence, in being annihilated. That
amounts to saying that there can be no real relation between
God and man. Barth repeats incessantly that according to the

Gospel there is no way that leads from man to God. The Catholic theologian, contrary to expectation, finds it easy to agree with him in this. His objection to Barth, and to the whole of Protestantism as represented by him, is that he in fact disallows that God can himself come to man. It may be granted that there is no way from man to God that is not illusory. But the Gospel is the way of God to man; and the charge against Protestantism, as a system directed against Catholicism, is that, whatever its intention, it does in fact bar this way. If the grace of God is such, only on condition that it gives nothing real; if man who believes, by saving faith, is in no way changed from what he was before believing; if justification by faith has to empty of all supernatural reality the Church, her sacraments, her dogmas; if God can only be affirmed by silencing his creature, if he acts only in annihilating it, if his very Word is doomed to be never really heard—what is condemned is not man's presumptuous way to God, but God's way of mercy to man.

This, and this alone, is the ultimate reproach which the Church levels at the Protestant system. This she refuses to allow, and in fact has no right to allow in virtue of the divine Word whose sovereign authority is so much invoked. For it is clearly declared false by this Word, not in rare and obscure expressions, but on every page; in terms, too, more clearly elucidated than ever by modern exegesis and relevant to each of the points mentioned, which all derive from the same initial error. The Word of God categorically proclaims a grace that is a real gift; a justification by faith that makes man really just; a faith that does not give itself, but receives, its content, proclaimed by the κήρυγμα of the apostolic Church, in the celebration of the Eucharist; a God who puts his greatness in giving, giving himself, by a fully effective gift, where there is no question of docetism or legalism, for his Incarnation is no more a pretence or a legal fiction than was the creation—he is the living God who gives life.

What, then, is the source of the element in Protestant theology of a God forbidden to communicate himself to his creature, of man unable, even by the divine omnipotence, to be torn from his own solitude, from the autonomy of his so arro-

gant humility, of a world and a God inexorably condemned to
the most utter 'extrinsicism'? To the historian, the reply is
obvious. The Reformers no more invented this strange and
despairing universe than they found it in Scripture. It is simply
the universe of the philosophy they had been brought up in,
scholasticism in its decadence. If the Reformers unintentionally
became heretics, the fault does not consist in the radical nature
of their reform, but in its hesitation, its timidity, its imperfect
vision. The structure they raised on their own principles is
inacceptable only because they used uncritically material drawn
from that decaying Catholicism they desired to elude, but whose
prisoners they remained to a degree they never suspected. No
phrase reveals so clearly the hidden evil that was to spoil the
fruit of the Reformation than Luther's saying that Occam was
the only scholastic who was any good. The truth is that Luther,
brought up on his system, was never able to think outside the
framework it imposed, while this, it is only too evident, makes
the mystery that lies at the root of Christian teaching either inconceivable or absurd.

What, in fact, is the essential characteristic of Occam's
thought, and of nominalism in general, but a radical empiricism,
reducing all being to what is perceived, which empties out, with
the idea of substance, all possibility of real relations between
beings, as well as the stable subsistence of any of them, and
ends by denying to the real any intelligibility, conceiving God
himself only as a Protean figure impossible to apprehend? [1]

In these circumstances, a grace which produces a real change
in us, while remaining purely the grace of God, becomes inconceivable. If some change is effected in us, then it comes from
us, and to suppose it could come also and primarily from God
amounts to confusing God with the creature. In fact, this consequence is inevitable, once we admit that we are identical with
our experience. If being is reduced to action, and action to what
takes place in us, our experience is closed to anything transcendental; or else, on the assumption that the transcendental
could intervene, it could only do so by reducing itself to becoming a part of ourselves.

[1] *Cf.* Etienne Gilson, *La philosophie au moyen-âge*, Paris, 1944, pp. 638
et seq.

Similarly, and as radically, it follows that grace, to remain such, that is the pure gift of God—must always be absolutely extrinsic to us; also, faith, to remain ours, so as not to fall into that externalism that would deprive man of all that is real in religion, must remain shut up within us. For to suppose that dogmas defined by some external authority, that rites whose content surpasses in any way our personal experience, could be essential to our faith, would be to alienate us from ourselves, to place our life in something that does not, cannot, concern us, condemned, as it is, to be not only external but totally foreign to us. In such a system, every being is doomed to remain a monad impenetrable by any other, or else becomes a prey to confusion, to the dissolution, pure and simple, of its individuality.

Inside such a framework, the sovereignty of God is no more than a total independence of all that could be considered as laws of reality, whether the moral law, or the logical principles indispensable to thought. To say that God is all-powerful would amount to saying that he could make good evil and *vice versa*, making a being other than it is; otherwise, it means nothing at all. For if being is no more than a word without content, infinite being cannot be other than the indefinite, pure and simple. In such conditions, it seems quite natural that God may 'declare just' the sinner, leaving him as much a sinner as before, that he may predestine some to damnation, just as he predestines others to salvation. If he did not do so, nothing would distinguish him from us, his transcendent sovereignty would disappear. Doubtless he could remain greater than us, but within the same order. He would no longer be sovereign.

From the same standpoint, we can easily see how the Word of God can remain such, only if entirely external to us. This does not only mean that its transcendence excludes any immanence of it in a tradition, an ecclesiastical authority, or even in mystical experience. It means, besides, that the Word can be given to man only through a complete emptying of his own mind; it becomes a dictamen from above, in face of which the human instrument has not even a passive part, but must be entirely effaced. The counterpart of this is that the Word is totally inexpressible in human ideas and language. Man can only receive it blindly, just as it can only speak by his mouth in making him dumb.

All these negative statements may seem so many aberrations, but they form part of the inexorable logic of nominalism in its application to the religious principles of Protestantism. Conversely, if we make use of Occam's razor, in other words, if we apply his criticism of any metaphysic at all realist, to suppose a grace that intervenes in us is to suppose that grace is only a word to designate something that is in reality part of us, or of the same nature as we are, and so capable of being made ours purely and simply. To suppose, on the other hand, a faith dependent on something outside us, still more one drawing us towards it, would be tantamount to asking us to be no longer ourselves, to destroy our own personality, to alienate us from ourselves. To suppose a God who makes us really act and have being, is to suppose one who lessens himself correspondingly. To suppose a Word which could be assimilated by us, minted, without complete degradation, in the form of commands or promises not purely symbolical, provisional, liable to be instantly reversed, is to suppose a Word which has ceased to be of God, has become no more than one human word among others.

The whole tragedy of Protestantism can only be grasped when it is borne in mind that the first Catholics to attempt its refutation, being themselves confined in the same framework of ideas as the Reformers, could not oppose them without rejecting the truth contained in what they affirmed. There was no escape from these dilemmas: either a grace which saves us by itself, and so saves us without affecting us, or a grace which saves us with our independent collaboration, so that properly speaking it is we who have to save ourselves; either a faith which is faith in our faith, in our direct experience, and ultimately in it alone, or a faith which is but a pure and simple withdrawal from ourselves; either a God who is all, while man and the world are literally nothing, or man and a world having real powers and value, though limited, and a God who is no more than the first in a series, a creature magnified, but not the creator; either a Word that is always completely foreign to us, that man can only traduce, not translate, and which has no possible meaning for him, or a word which ultimately is only his, in which he makes demands and replies to them, and dares to attribute to God what is merely his own lucubration.

The debate between Luther and Erasmus is one of the first and most remarkable examples of this *impasse*. It shows up clearly the inability of Catholic thinkers contemporary with the Reformers, both prisoners of a vitiated philosophy, to admit what was positive in the Reformation, and to lay bare the root of its errors. Hence there arose among Protestants the conviction of the solidity of their system and of the necessity to accept it with all its consequences, to safeguard the positive intuitions to which they were so attached, and with every reason.

Even the title of the treatise of Erasmus against the Lutheran theory of justification is a warning that the problem is to be passed by unnoticed—it is called *De libero arbitrio*. The title of Luther's reply illustrates excellently the irremediable gravity of the misunderstanding that resulted; he called it *De servo arbitrio*.

Erasmus saw perfectly that Luther diverges, not only from the tradition of the Church, but from the Gospel and St. Paul himself, in creating the chimera of a salvation which should save us, without drawing us in the least from the state of sin. But, a prisoner, like Luther, of the nominalist categories, he was incapable of formulating clearly the true answer: that grace is grace, a pure gift of God, not in giving us nothing real, but in giving us, in so far as we remain dependent on it, the reality we are incapable of acquiring by ourselves. Far from seeing this, he tried to salvage the free-will of man without recourse to grace. His whole treatise aims at showing, not how grace regenerates nature, but that nature is not so deeply impaired that it cannot do something efficacious for salvation. It betrays, implicitly, a view of things as remote from the *De gratia et libero arbitrio* of St. Bernard, for example, as is that of Luther. Moreover, it is exactly the same as Luther's, except that it chooses the opposite horn of the dilemma. For both Erasmus and Luther, to say that God and man act together in justification must mean that their joint action is analogous to that of two men drawing the same load. Consequently, the more one does, the less the other; whence, for Luther, realising anew that grace does everything in salvation, it follows of necessity that man does nothing. But Erasmus desired to uphold the other aspect of tradition; that salvation is truly ours implies that we are ourselves active; it is far from covering us with a cloak that would leave us unchanged and merely passive. Hence the necessity that God does not do all, that his grace is simply an aid from outside, not the source of the saving action which must come from us.

On the other hand, for St. Bernard and the whole authentic tradition, in one sense God does all, and in another man must do all, for he has to make everything his own; but he cannot—he can do absolutely nothing valid for salvation, except in complete dependence on grace. This view, we may say, must have appeared absolutely unimaginable to both Erasmus and Luther. It is so, in fact, so long as one cannot conceive a world other than that of nominalism, as was the case for them both. In these circumstances, the way in which Erasmus himself so evidently destroyed the true Christian doctrine of grace enormously strengthened Luther's conviction that it could only be recovered by means of the negations he had embraced. These, we may judge from the *De servo arbitrio*, reach the confines of lunacy; but it has to be acknowledged that they follow strictly from the argument that Erasmus, far from curbing, did everything to further.

The true theological position, wholly consonant with revelation, is that man is himself only as he recognises his radical dependence on the Creator; but this does not mean that creation is a fiction, legal or otherwise, but the most authentic of all realities. Man saved is therefore man restored by faith to the consciousness of that absolute dependence, and so recovering his life at the very source. It may seem strange, but it is undeniable that in the whole course of this unhappy controversy this view does not seem to have occurred to either of the protagonists. There lies the whole tragedy of Protestantism.

As to the extreme subjectivism implicit in Luther's formularies of belief, his own conservatism, very early aroused by the mad freaks of the Anabaptists of Münster, acted first as a counterbalance. But, at the most, it could only check it from the outside, and postpone an evolution bound to follow from the terms of the problem. That faith in salvation, to be certain, must be—

as is clear in Luther, and endorsed by Calvin—immediate and undoubted faith in 'my' salvation, is once more a consequence of a mental climate where the spirit is enclosed in itself, and so cannot have any real certitude beyond the immediate field of its psychological experience. But this initial confusion between the personal character of our acceptance of grace and a despairing philosophical attitude was certainly carried to the extreme by what it saw opposed to it, a view equally derived from the same identification of a wholly positive personalism with a wholly negative individualism. Though this cannot be verified in the same detail as the controversy over free will, it is only too certain that the Counter-Reformation, in reply to the unrestrained subjectivism of the Reformation, adopted the easy course of an untempered authoritarianism. Nothing could more firmly and unhappily strengthen Protestants in their conviction that all personal religion must be fiercely individualistic. To exalt authority without counterbalance, to make blind submission the touchstone of orthodoxy, that could be, and was, an effective means of defending Catholics against any Protestant trend. But it was, also, one of the most effective of the negative arguments to persuade Protestants, however wrongly, that they could save one of their most cherished and rightful convictions only by rejecting, not simply authoritarianism, but the principle of authority, to the point of replacing it in practice by free thought.

The same factors are more clearly evident in the dispute over the sovereignty of God. While the whole Catholic tradition, first in Augustinianism then in thomism, was occupied in breaking down the fallacious parallelism, so tempting to the human mind, which would make God equally the author of good and bad acts, Calvinism brought it to the point of identification. Thus, he made the doctrine of predestination inacceptable, making God the author of the damnation of the wicked as well as of the salvation of the just. Nowhere else is it so clear that the framework of nominalism is responsible for either the rejection of the mystery or its reduction to absurdity. As soon as infinite being becomes confused with pure indetermination, either God is in no way, strictly speaking, the cause of our salvation, or else he is no less the cause of our damnation, since good and evil are distinguished, not by anything intrinsic, but by an arbitrary decision of the Almighty.

However, the Catholic controversialists of the time were so little able to detect the fallacy at the base of this identification that they had no other recourse than to abandon in practice the doctrine of predestination. The Dominican, Peter de Soto, one of the first to promote a renascence of thomism, has vividly described this collapse of the traditional teaching in the face of Protestantism.[1] This inevitably caused the Calvinist reaction, which had much in common with that of the Jansenists in the following century. For, if Catholics no longer thought themselves able to defend predestination, so clearly affirmed by St. Paul, St. John, St. Augustine, and the Councils which condemned the Pelagians, without yielding entirely to Calvinism, how could one fail to believe that Calvinism, with its implacable line of reasoning, was the only possible way to salvage this essential doctrine? But all this obviously presupposes that both sides were unable to conceive the kingship of God in other than human terms. Obviously, wherever we meet with finite authorities, purely empirical, one can be absolute only in so far as the others are nullified. If man is to possess any real value, any effective power, there is so much the less for God. But here more than anywhere else, it must be obvious that the suppositions behind the theory of the sovereignty of God prove an initial inability to conceive it aright. The concepts of a purely empirical system, such as nominalism, since they rule out any idea of a being not subject to the categories of our own experience, exclude utterly even the possibility of anything transcendental. Hence comes the adoption of various substitutes, whose inherent contradictions, carried to an excess of absurdity, only reveal their radical sterility. For it must be admitted, a God who remains God only so long as he creates nothing real, but only deceptive appearances, is as far from being really God as one could imagine. To set him up in a metaphysical wilderness, annihilating, in principle, all other beings, is to grant him an entirely illusory sovereignty, since it can only subsist if exercised over absolute nonentity.

[1] See his *Epistolae duae*, published as an appendix to Reginaldo's *De mente Concilii Tridentini*, Antwerp, 1706.

To pass to the theology of the Word, the persistence with which Karl Barth attacks the thomist principle of the *analogia entis* is particularly revealing, both of the blindness at the base of the entire polemical structure of Protestantism, and that of Catholics in the sixteenth century, which contributed to make it incorrigible.

For Barth, to speak of an 'analogy of being', and to make it the principle of the whole of theology, is to admit that the words of man and the Word of God belong to the same order, that human thought and the data of revelation are capable of harmonisation as components on the same level; thus to admit the possibility of constructing a dogmatic synthesis in which the thought of man and the revelation of God would be so closely fused that the human element would simply assimilate to itself the 'revealed data'.[1]

But whoever understands the real meaning and scope of analogy in the thomist system, can see at once that this interpretation confuses it with one of the two possible errors it was precisely designed to avoid. At the same time, anyone who knows the history of scholastic nominalism, which persisted all through the 16th century in its claim to be the heir of the great medieval tradition of theology, whereas it was in fact its destroyer, realises thereby the sole apparent justification for Barth's extraordinary misconception. Catholic writers are certainly to be blamed for it, but only through their subservience to fallacies that Protestants did not dream of criticising, Barth least of all.

The analogy of being is only a philosophical theory which enables us to deny both that the Word of God is the same in nature with the human word, and so reducible to it, and also that it is without any relation with the human word, and so completely inassimilable by it, totally unable to bring about any real interchange. The theologian who has thoroughly grasped the thomist doctrine (which in fact does no more than systematise accurately the practice of the Church since the prophets and apostles) will not imagine that he can understand and manipulate any enunciation of the divine Word as he could those of his own mind. Nor will he conclude that the Word of God has to

[1] *Kirchliche Dogmatik*, 1/1, pp. 40, 123, 175, etc.

remain an unresolved enigma, a symbol impossible to decipher. Knowing that God made all things as a reflection of his own thoughts, and the human mind as a reflection of his own word, he will strive, his mind illumined by faith, to open himself to the mysteries God reveals, not confining them in the framework of his own ideas, but transposing and enlarging these, not destroying their value in their own order, but transcending the limits of mere reason—a real elevation, not a collapse into the subrational. Thus, the supernatural is received by the mind enlightened and elevated by faith, not as darkening its natural lights, but by the acquiescence of the human mind in its invasion by the Spirit of God; in this unique experience, it recognises both that it is rapt from itself and taken back by Him who had made it for Himself, in His own image.

All the same, nothing has contributed more—and still does so today—to confirm Protestants like Barth in the conviction that the analogy of being is really only a univocity which reduces the divine Word to the level of the human and binds it up in the human word, than the practical nominalism of so many Catholic theologians, even if thomist in principle. Any theological system which aims, not at admitting the mystery, setting it in place, pointing out its demands on human thought, but, albeit unconsciously, at reducing it, dissolving it, digesting it, as it were, into the ready-made categories supposed to be adequate for it, can only corroborate the assurance of Protestants that there is no alternative other than a divine Word, inexpressible, wholly incapable of assimilation, and a Word immersed in the human, acceptable only as reduced to the measure of man and conformed to his categories.

All this does not exhaust the matter. We have ascertained that the Reformation did not derive any of the negative and unacceptable aspects of any of its principles from any necessity inherent in its positive principles, considered strictly in their religious content; further, that the cause lies in the uncritical application by the Reformers of the barren framework of a decadent system. To this must be added that none of the consequences of this misapplication is a genuine creation of Protestantism. All the 'heresies' Protestantism may have fostered, far from being its creations, even creations warped in their nature by the dead weight of a routine, unreformed system, appear already to be taking shape in the nominalist thinkers before the Reformation.

Whether we take the theory of extrinsic justification, or the completely subjectivist view of faith (shutting faith up in itself, instead of seeing it as the means enabling the human mind to be drawn to God and to transcend itself), or that of the sovereignty of God confused with an arbitrariness fundamentally due to anthropomorphism, or a conception of the Word of God that both opposes it to any ecclesiastical institution and makes it incomprehensible, and even incapable of formulation—none of this is a Protestant innovation. All these strange, in a sense unhealthy, monstrous conceptions, to be so soon applied to the religious principles of the Reformation, disfiguring them at the outset, had been elaborated long before the Reformation. The Reformers merely took them over as they found them.

Occam, and following him Biel, thought out the idea, without precedent in tradition, that justification, properly speaking, consists only in the acceptance of man by God, and that this acceptance in itself is independent of any change in the person justified. If they go on to admit that justification is accompanied by regeneration, by the restoration of charity to the soul of the justified, they deny any connection between the two. They affirm the fact, since it seems to be contained in Scripture and tradition, but maintain that God could also 'justify' the sinner and leave him in his sin.[1]

At the same time, for them and for the whole school of Occam, faith adheres to the truths contained in Scripture and proposed by the Church, but does so not for any objective reason beyond itself, whatever one might think. Their whole line of argument goes to show that such a motive, in fact, could only be illusory. Never has so strict a 'fideism' been put forward; never, in other words, has faith been so conceived as depending entirely on itself, as being its own justification. If, however, as the Reformers were to do later, they allow it a content already fixed, derived

---

[1] *Cf.* P. Vignaux, *Justification et prédestination au 14ᵐᵉ siècle*, Paris, 1934, pp. 119–22, on Occam. Feckes, *Gabrielis Biel quaestiones de justificatione*, Münster, 1929.

from Scripture or the Church, that is because what they actually envisage is Christian faith; there is nothing at all in their principles in favour of this more than any other faith, nor, in fact, anything that justifies in the least its apparent possibility of orientation to an object above itself, outside the consciousness of the believer.

Moreover, the idea of a *potentia absoluta* is the key to the whole Occamist theology, which amounts to saying that it is the negation of any possible theology. In such a system, God is only God in so far as he is beyond the true and the false, good and evil. Truth, falsehood, good, evil, are no more than hypotheses he has actually adopted; there is no reason why he should not have taken them in the contrary sense, or why he should be prevented from reversing them.[1]

No more suitable expressions could be found to add the finishing touch to the system worked out by Barth with the aim of withdrawing the Word of God from what he considers its contamination by the words of men. Nothing, either, seems more radically opposed to the scriptural idea of the 'truth', that is to say, God's fidelity to his own Word, or of the 'sanctity' of God, which the Bible is far from reducing to the level of morality; on the contrary, it raises 'justice' in its most exacting form, to the centre of the 'sacred', so that ultimately the two are inseparable.

Finally, whence comes this opposition of the Word of God, in its scriptural form, to all the other authorities, to tradition, to the magisterium, to ecclesiastical authority as well as human reason, while at the same time its affirmations are said to be incapable of 'harmonising' with any truth acquired by other means, the result being either the idea of a double truth, or the idea that truth is unattainable by the human mind? This opposition is most characteristic of nominalist theology, perpetually balanced, as it is, between an inevitable agnosticism and the argument from scriptural authority as a *Deus ex machina*. As to the latter, nominalism itself shows how illusory it is, since the initial assumptions of this philosophy are carried to their extreme consequences, without any but a verbal deference to what is most prominent in the teaching of Scripture,

---

[1] *Cf.* Gilson, *op. cit.*, pp. 653–4 for Occam and Biel; also Humbert, *Origines de la théologie moderne.*

while this remains a dead letter as soon as it comes into conflict with the philosophy.

Our conclusion from this chapter is that the negative, 'heretical' aspect of the Reformation neither follows from its positive principles, nor is it a necessary consequence of their development or vindication, but appears simply as a survival, within Protestantism, of what was most vitiated and corrupt in the Catholic thought of the close of the Middle Ages.

This latter point, the utter corruption of Christian thought in nominalist theology, quite uncritically retained and applied by all the 'orthodox' Protestant thinkers, should by now be thoroughly clear. But the matter is so important that we must dwell on it a little further, and define the relation existing between adherence to the Catholic faith and acceptance of one or other of the various systems of philosophy and theology erected for its explanation and defence.

Contrary to the opinion of many Protestants, Barthians in particular, the Church neither is nor can be bound up with any intellectual system as such. But, precisely to safeguard, not for her own sake, but for the sake of the revelation entrusted to her, the necessary liberty of the divine Word in respect to the human, it is her duty to pass judgment on systems which offer a framework for the truths of religion. If, then, the Church is mistrustful of systems of a nominalist type, while greatly in favour of a realist system like thomism, without identifying itself with it exclusively, that is not to involve herself in controversy on purely human concerns. She is so, because certain systems of thought, such as nominalism, make the mystery of Christianity, the mystery of a God Creator and Redeemer, either inconceivable or absurd. Once this system is admitted, as it was by everyone at the end of the Middle Ages, either we reject the God, 'Creator and Father of Our Lord Jesus Christ', or, if we still admit him, we do so on such terms that he appears a monster repugnant both to common sense and to moral feeling, affronting in either way the truest of our instincts, God's trace left intact in his creature, even when impaired and blinded by sin. Such a system can only be condemned by the Church; the true reform to be unceasingly sought within her body should be to work unremittingly to eradicate it—a thing, unfortunately, that never occurred to the Reformers of the sixteenth century.

Other systems, though human and so limited, incapable, therefore, of comprising all the perfection of the revealed deposit, admit the possibility of mystery. Not only do they bow before it, but they welcome it, since their chief aim is absolute docility to the whole of the real. In this aspect alone does the Church give them its encouragement, without overlooking the fact that they are human and imperfect, necessarily inadequate to the expression of the Word of God in its fulness. It may be said that it is just because they recognise it themselves, not only in an introductory rhetoric, but in reality, at their very heart and centre, that the Church receives them. In blessing thomism, far from raising up a human system as judge of the Word of God, she blesses its very submission to this Word. The tragedy of Protestantism, on the other hand, we see to be its remaining a close prisoner of a system which prevents God communicating with us, or unconsciously claims to dictate to him what to say at the very moment it aims at restoring the sovereignty of his Word.

CHAPTER VIII

The Decay of the Positive Principles of the Reformation

WHAT the Reformation took over from the Middle Ages was just what it should have criticised and rejected; in fact, it led the positive principles the Reformers had brought to light to assume a negative and polemical aspect. This was the origin of the heresy and schism which Protestantism was fated to become.

This unhappy association of the great religious affirmations of the Reformation with the disastrous *a priori* principles of nominalism not only led Protestants to a one-sided development of their own insights to the neglect of the complementary aspects of Christian truth; it ended by strangling in Protestantism itself its own finest principles.

This is so important that it deserves a chapter to itself, for, if it is true that the positive principles in Protestantism were not responsible for its rupture with the Church, but rather the negative elements from which the Reformers could not free themselves, how striking it is that the anti-Catholic system built up from these elements came to suffocate the very principles they claimed to support!

Lucien Febvre, in his very original essay on Luther,[1] has clearly set forth the personal drama of the Reformer who saw, in his own lifetime, the principles he wished to reinstate opposed and hindered by the very structure his protest had created. But M. Febvre does not bring out sufficiently that it was Luther himself, and not only the stupidity of his followers, who provided all the elements of the system which was to imprison, rather than protect, the original doctrine.

Two phases may be distinguished in the gradual suffocation of the positive principles of the Reformation within the rigid yoke imposed by the negative elements it could not get rid of, but rather used as its chief and most accessible material for its distorted structure. In the first phase, characteristic of the various

[1] *Un destin: Martin Luther*, 2nd edition, Paris, 1949.

Protestant 'orthodoxies', the system, by its own weight, stifled the views it claimed to serve. In the second phase, typical of those movements which place liberty before orthodoxy, the most remarkable example being the 'liberalism' of the nineteenth century, the desire to reject that crushing weight led to the rejection of the views so imprudently attached to it. In this way, Protestantism, by a very logical process, has paradoxically come to carry to an extreme all the errors it had begun by attacking. The religion of the *sola gratia* has arrived at the extreme of Pelagianism; that of *sola fide* has become a type of regimentation or ecclesiastical officialdom surpassing anything of this nature which the clerical corruptions of Catholicism can furnish; the religion of *Soli Deo gloria* has become a 'humanism' firmly closed to anything transcendent; the religion of the Word of God, a religious philosophy that is purely immanentist. The study of this dialectic of history is of extreme interest; it establishes that the institutions, created by Protestantism in its lapse into heresy and schism, have culminated, by the logic of events, in destroying its reason for existence; and it makes us see why this came about.

What happened first was that orthodox Lutheranism, that of the theologians known as Gnesio-Lutherans, since it made extrinsic justification the crux of the entire system, came in less than a generation to make it the reverse of what Luther desired. His fundamental intuition, as we have seen, was accompanied with joy, even rapture, in the experience of the liberation, of the victory brought by Christ to sinful man. Their religion, on the contrary, has the appearance of a pure cerebration, dried up and empty of any religious or mystical life. Melancthon had already observed with disquiet that the preaching of salvation by faith alone, as an abstract truth, led only too easily to a general condoning of the indulgence of animal instincts, freed from all restraint. Later on, what strikes us more is the withdrawal of religion from contact with ordinary life, which is left to a statecraft with purely mundane views, or to the pursuit of private interests without regard to anything higher. What is even more significant than this mutual disregard of religion and life, called Lutheran quietism, is the suspicion and mistrust of orthodox Lutheranism for any kind of mysticism. In every case,

whether that of libertarian mysticism, an offshoot in seven-
teenth- and eighteenth-century Germany of the medieval sects,
or the theosophical mysticism inspired by Jacob Boehme, or the
very moderate and quite traditional mysticism in the *Collegia
pietatis* of Arndt and Spener, we find the same attitude of suspicion and disapproval among Lutheran ministers. All that presupposes grace to be a living reality in the Christian, or that even
tends to stress this aspect of religion, is suspect in their eyes.
Extrinsic justification, devised originally to assure the absolute
domination of grace, came to prohibit it from giving any sign
of its presence; so it excluded God from both the public and
private life of man, and made even of the interior life a sphere
closed to his intervention.

It can be easily understood that this bondage provoked an
almost immediate reaction. Official Lutheranism might well
call in the forcible argument of the temporal power, whose
absolutism was assured by the doctrine of non-intervention; it
failed to bring the 'heterodox' to heel. Meanwhile, the identification between *sola gratia* and extrinsic justification was so well
established in current opinion that the triumph of a living religion
brought an invasion of semi-Pelagian or frankly Pelagian ideas.

Melancthon had already introduced a co-operative idea of
salvation, man and God working together for justification, without making it altogether clear whether he meant to teach a
response independent of grace, or prompted by it.[1] Pietism, in
spite of excellent intentions, culminated in a moralism and a religion of experiences, largely sentimental, which slowly degenerated into the 'natural religion' of the eighteenth century,
at the furthest possible remove from the *sola gratia* of Luther.
This evolution towards a conception of the Christian life in
which what are called 'good feelings' is the essence, if not the
whole, was bound to happen, once the mind was conditioned to
confuse the religion of grace with one where man had nothing
to perform. For it was impossible to bring in the doctrine
of man's personal action against that background, without
admitting, at least by implication, that grace was not all, and so
ultimately making it only secondary, or even unimportant.

More clearly even than in the moral sphere, this reaction

---

[1] *Loci communes*, 1548 edition, Ch. IV.

is shown in that of the interior life. To resign oneself to extrinsic justification seemed obviously to resign oneself to asphyxia. But the opponents of that doctrine kept the idea that grace is fundamentally something juridical; consequently, what they evolved was, at any rate largely, a natural mysticism. The mysticism of the Anabaptists, of Schwenckfeld and of Valentin Weigl, was increasingly one of the 'inner light', innate in every man, independently of Christ's redemption. Closely connected with this, the theosophy of Böehme, all through its occultist or neo-platonist offshoots in seventeenth- and eighteenth-century Germany and England, invariably confused mystical experience with intellectual illumination. Pietism itself looked to the stirrings of the imagination and emotions for its clearest insights. The 'conversion' whose formula it gradually worked out, and which was taken over by Methodism, seems often enough the result of human effort on the psychological plane, rather than that of grace working in the recesses of consciousness.

The final outcome of this Pelagianistic mysticism was the religion of Schleiermacher, a religion of the 'religious sentiment', viewed as a human endowment analogous to artistic talent, or to the 'sensibility' so much in vogue in the eighteenth century. Having reached this point, we have not only attained, but gone beyond, Pelagianism; for, in spite of a Christian veneer, the structure is no longer Christian at all. Christ has ceased to be the Redeemer sent by God, but is merely the supreme example of a man endowed with the sentiment of the divine.

It would be extremely unjust in us to see in this spiritual progeny only the branch which led to Schleiermacher. In the next chapter, we hope to indicate the authentic rebirth of Christianity, both in Lutheranism generally and in German and English pietism in particular. It remains, however, that the semi-Pelagian, or Pelagian, or even purely 'naturalist', tendency to overlook grace in favour of some 'inner light' inherent in everyone, or the 'natural goodness' of Rousseauist man, is undeniably present all through. Equally so is the fact that its force arises from the disastrous equating of grace with extrinsicism, of religion as a pure gift of God with a moral or spiritual life devoid of any religious content.

This process, in spite of the precautions Calvin took to avoid what we have called Lutheran quietism, is no less evident, though with certain differences, in the other Protestant countries as well as in the strictly Lutheran ones. But in those, the initial distinction between justification and sanctification enabled Pelagianism to be introduced, not only as a reaction against Calvinist 'orthodoxy', but often enough under cover of its principles. Puritanism, extremely Calvinistic in its intentions, is distinguished from authentic Calvinism precisely in this. The religion of Cromwell's Roundheads, and of the emigrants to New England and of their descendants especially, simply confused the 'heavenly Jerusalem' with the city made by man under the impulse of primitive Calvinism, while admitting it had been adulterated with too human elements. This was even more true of the countries where Arminian theology prevailed, that is, in the great majority of the Reformed Churches.

It was in connection with the doctrine of predestination, as conceived by Calvinism, that is, the positive predestination of some to salvation and of others to damnation, that Arminius launched a protest from within Dutch Calvinism, and from the beginning of the seventeenth century he rallied to his side almost all that part of Protestantism hitherto dominated by Calvinism proper. But Arminius, in making the efficacy of grace depend on its acceptance by the autonomous human will, reduced predestination itself to a simple foreknowledge of decisions freely made, in which grace only intervenes subsequently. In other words, he adopted, as regards the sovereignty of God in the work of salvation, an even more minimising view than that of Molina in the Catholic Church. In consequence, through its failure to detach the positive affirmation of the sovereignty of God from negative statements inadmissible to the Christian conscience, the section of Protestantism originally most tenacious of the divine sovereignty came to adopt a moralism which grew more and more explicit. It soon culminated in that religion of efficiency, of worldly success identified with the blessing of God, and ultimately in the almost complete pragmatism which constitutes the religion today of so many Americans. Hence the close connection noticed by Troeltsch between capitalism and what he improperly terms Calvinism, but which is in reality a strict application of the formula, 'Heaven helps those who help themselves'—a corruption, in fact the exact antithesis, of true Calvinism, though proceeding logically from its principles. For, on the assumption that man must be nothing so that God may be all, it is impossible to restore man to his right place without creating a 'humanism' (the name adopted by the religious pragmatism of modern America), in which the tendency is for man to treat God as an equal, even to domesticate him into no more than a source of energy.

Even 'social Christianity', which in Anglo-Saxon Protestantism, attempted a courageous reaction against plutocracy and the capitalist idolatry of wealth, far from escaping this monstrous idea, unwittingly carries it to the extreme. A strong trend may be discerned running through modern Protestantism, not merely to make use of Christianity to improve the conditions of life, to obtain or ensure the greatest happiness of the greatest number, but to justify God to man on the sole ground of utility. With that, the circle is complete. One may say that Protestantism, while still claiming the inspiration of Calvin, has arrived, by the evolution of what was always immanent in it, at the point where it reverses all that Calvin stood for. Instead of God being the sole end of the world and of man, man becomes the sole reason for God; instead of a world of which God is the absolute ruler, we have a world which admits religion only as a means to the absolute dominion of man. But we have to recognise that this reversal was bound to come sooner or later. Once the principle was laid down that the greatness of God supposed the nothingness of man, man could not be raised up again without God being proportionately lowered, and it belonged to the logic of the system that man should dream of domesticating God, so as to reach the fulness of his own development.

The dialectic of the principle of justification by faith, in its subjective aspect, has naturally followed a different course. Yet it testifies just as clearly to the strange power of Protestant institutions, built up on the original system, to eliminate altogether the religious insights it was considered to subserve. Here, as we have already observed, the reaction against its negative possibilities came much sooner than elsewhere, since it was aroused in Luther himself by the anarchical excesses of the Anabaptists of Münster who, however, had only taken literally some

of his expressions on the subject of 'faith'. Hence his insistence
on a Church where the authority of the temporal ruler should
replace that of the bishops, and whose laws, framed in the spirit
of the purest absolutism, should replace the canon law of
tradition. In this way the Lutheran Church soon became a
wholly bureaucratic Church, one among other departments of
the modern State, with the absolute ruler directly governing
men's souls. The Calvinist Church, for its part, escaped that
danger. But, to the extent that Calvin or his imitators in Scotland and Holland succeeded in what they aimed at, it represented a form, no less severe, of spiritual regimentation. In
order to restrain the anarchy and counter the dispersion of the
various subjectivisms, it simply tried to authorise and impose
on all the subjectivism of the founder. The Calvinist Church,
an artificial construction to ward off the effects of the dissolution of the Church of tradition, where Protestantism, on plea
of reform, had destroyed it, was but a particular ideal of Christianity, stamped in every detail with the genius of Calvin, and
made a norm for all.

However, this is not true only of those systems erected as
a result of a reaction, prompted by prudence, against the element of anarchical subjectivism introduced by Luther in his
preaching of personal religion. It applies equally in cases where
this reaction was not present, though in forms less obvious or
at any rate less naïvely displayed. In fact, apart from the extreme case of absolute subjectivism, resulting immediately in
the rejection of any organised Church, whenever a Protestant
Church is set up, it must be on a basis of subjectivism, particularly when organised in opposition to another and to the
traditional elements it retains. A person who makes his own
ego the ultimate norm of his religious beliefs and practice can
obviously not feel at ease in a Church that holds to any objective criterion. The Church, however, that he himself founds
will soon become far more oppressive for other people, being
based on his particular brand of subjectivism. This is the reason
for the ceaseless multiplication of Protestant sects which, once
started, gathers speed, since each new foundation is as a rule
established on a narrower base than its predecessor. Hence, too,
those doctrinal formulations, carried to the extreme of theo-

logical subtlety, that the Churches, desirous of putting a stop to
this crumbling process, come to impose on their members. The
two processes seem antagonistic and are so, historically; but
they both alike spring from an individualism which either carries
the protest against any form of objectivity still further, in the
name of freedom, or else creates an *ersatz* objectivity out of
tyrannical individualism. Experience shows that the human
mind is prone to oscillate continuously between these two
tendencies; the ego is correspondingly less respectful of others
as it is more preoccupied with itself. The extreme Protestant
'liberalism', systematised by Schleiermacher, for example, was
no less despotic than the old orthodoxy, rather the reverse. In
the 'evangelical' Church of Prussia, where the sovereign tried
forcibly to amalgamate the Lutherans with the Calvinists, it
became the apologist of the most intolerant ecclesiastical
authoritarianism. In general, the Protestants most hostile to
dogma, to any objective truth of tradition, while decrying more
than anyone the intolerance of the Catholic Church, are often
themselves the most intolerant of all; they refuse to admit any
union between Christians, unless based on the universal acceptance of their thoroughly immanentist philosophy of religion.

But it is when we examine the historical fate of the principle
of the authority of Scripture that Protestantism best reveals its
congenital tendency to reverse its own affirmations.

During the seventeenth century especially, orthodox Protestantism strove to set the Bible in a 'splendid isolation'. The
sovereign authority of the Word of God became in effect the
sole authority of the books of the Bible. Then it was that Protestantism made itself, or attempted to make itself, 'the religion
of the book'. That implied a double process. On the one hand,
the human element was neglected and even formally excluded
from Scripture. Fantastic theories of scriptural inspiration were
constructed, which equated it with dictation from on high, no
scope being left to the human instrument. The culminating
point was the theory of the inspiration of the vowel signs in the
massoretic text. The most serious result was the kind of apologetic which arose from these theories and which did not stop short
of any absurdity, in order to uphold what amounted to a divinisa-
tion of the sacred text. They demonstrated the grammatical

perfection of the Greek of the Apocalypse, the scientific exacti-
tude of Genesis, the literal accuracy of the genealogies (even
when in flagrant contradiction), the perfect morality of the
daughters of Lot, and the high spirituality of the Proverbs.
In face of this, people felt obliged to discredit tradition, the
authority of dogmatic definitions and, in general, to emphasise,
not only the discontinuity between the people of God and the
Word of God entrusted to it, but the absolute opposition of the
two which this conception of the Bible seemed to require—a
sort of spiritual meteor suddenly discharged on to our planet,
which must be, at the same time, innocent of any geological traces.

The immediate result was evidently the desiccation of religion, since it was reduced to being nothing but a continual recourse to a fixed and petrified text, necessarily so, since lacking
any living medium of the same nature with it.

In this state of affairs, the inevitable reaction was more
grossly exaggerated than on any other point. Even where, as
with the fundamentalists, the unique authority of the Bible was
still upheld, an illuminist interpretation practically emptied this
'authority' of all objective reality, and reintroduced, in the form
of an allegorical bias or some other fantasy, an unrestricted subjectivism. Above all, the obvious artificiality of the idea of the
Bible fallen from Heaven quickly became so untenable that the
authority of Scripture, bound up with a conception as fragile
as it was fictitious, was jettisoned with it.

When, in the eighteenth century, the human element in the
Bible came to force itself on the attention of Protestant exegetes,
the divine element disappeared correspondingly. The whole
development of exegesis and Biblical criticism proceeded on
lines more and more purely historical. They became incapable
of seeing in the Bible anything but a witness to the 'religious
genius' of the Hebrews, a document of the 'varieties of religious
experience'. The faculties of Protestant theology, originally intended as schools of Biblical theology, became at the end of this
development no more than workshops of comparative studies,
exclusively employed in the work of reducing Scripture to a
purely immanent product of human psychology, until not the
slightest room was left for any supernatural intervention.

Once again, with an evidence more telling than anywhere else,

the evolution within Protestantism of what Melancthon recognised as the sole formal principle of the Reformation resulted
in its absolute denial. From the sovereign authority of the Word
of God, from the inspiration, as literal and comprehensive as
possible, of the Bible, men came to reduce the Bible wholly to
the status of a piece of human literature, and so to deny, not
only that the Word of God was authoritative, but that there was
any such thing as the Word of God, strictly speaking, at all.

At this point, nothing is more interesting than to consider
the reactions of 'orthodox' Protestantism to the opposition
stirred up against it. It comprised many different elements.
The most profound of these seems to have been a fairly clear-
cut perception of the positive Christian value of the principles of
the Reformation, so completely misunderstood by the rest of
Protestantism in its ultimate development. The easiest course
to take was a simple return to original Protestantism, to take
over its affirmations and its entire system of thought. Unfortunately, if it is true, as we hope now to have settled, that the
gradual stifling of the positive principles of the Reformation
within itself originated in their complexity, both in their
enunciation and their systematisation, an uncritical return would
only turn back the process to its point of departure, leaving it
free to continue. Worse still, such a return would necessarily
involve a simplification or a new structure, against which the
reaction, it is to be feared, would as a result only accelerate and
harden the trend towards disintegration.

There we have a fact constantly present in the history of Protestantism. 'Neo-lutheranisms' and 'neo-calvinisms' regularly,
and very promptly, usher in a counter-offensive of 'neo-liberal-
isms' and 'neo-rationalisms', or 'neo-naturalisms', more bitter
and negative than ever. The most reactionary of the Protestant
Churches invariably bring up in their fold 'immanentists' and
'humanists' most intolerant of anything transcendent. Edmund
Gosse's own experience, told with such cruel lucidity in his
autobiography, *Father and Son*, is only one example among
countless others. If 'orthodox' Protestants regularly beget
'liberal' Protestants, the 'neo-orthodox', whom liberals en-
gender in their turn, only bring forth atheists, who view, no

longer with hate, but merely with scorn, any religion claiming to be transcendent. 'God is in heaven, and thou art on earth,' the Barthians are constantly repeating. They run a grave risk of being answered by their former followers: 'Let God stay in heaven, the earth is good enough for us.'

An uncompromising return to the theological principles of original Protestantism, in so far as it refuses to analyse them and acknowledge their irreducible complexity, or even praises this complexity as being a divine paradox, can only result in the end in making it less defensible or tolerable. The sort of dialectical intoxication in which a man may revert to and refine upon the preaching of a grace which saves the sinner without changing him in the least, a faith which depends on nothing outside itself, a God who can only be acknowledged as Creator by the annihilation of his creatures, of a divine Word whose authority is supreme as long as it is unutterable, lasts only for a time. After the first factitious enthusiasm, he will inevitably come to recognise beneath these revived 'affirmations' that the negations they claimed to overthrow have in fact returned.

Meanwhile, along with these periodic swings of the pendulum, which can only result in further crashes, and often mixed up with them, we see the efforts of Protestantism to escape this vicious circle. To these movements we must now turn; we shall call them, not 'reactions', but, a term dear to Protestants, 'revivals'. The study of them seems to us of capital importance, for we believe that it could lead Protestantism out of the permanent state of crisis in which it is imprisoned, and help it to surmount for good and all the death throes we have just described, not just to suspend them a moment, only to intensify them immediately after.

CHAPTER IX

Protestant 'Revivals': the Positive Principles of the Reformation Bursting its Negative Bonds

THERE is one general observation which we made at the beginning of this book, and which at this stage we must repeat and apply in detail. We said that abstract formulas rarely exhaust the living reality, and we can only come to know and form an opinion on a religious movement if we go beyond its theoretical description and study it in its life. So it is, as we have made abundantly clear, that, though Luther's statements about extrinsic justification are entirely unacceptable, he none the less expressed and effectively propagated a religion in which the whole life of man was illumined and actuated by grace.

Similarly, it would be quite wrong to see in the history of Protestantism nothing but the dialectical system which we have expounded in the last chapter. This system is one of the elements, but it is not the whole, and in our opinion not even the most significant part. Luther himself forged—or rather, as we have said, simply made his own—the conception, fundamentally nominalist, of extrinsic justification. But in his own spiritual life and for those under his care, he had recourse to a totally different conception, and we ought to expect the same cleavage, more or less conscious, with his successors. In fact, as we have shown, we do find it; it is this survival in the interior life of Protestants of a view of grace very different from that contained in books of controversy, that is the only possible explanation of the continuous Christian life of Protestantism.

A whole anti-Catholic scholasticism has been worked out by Protestants, and has occasioned the disastrous reactions we followed in the last chapter. Nevertheless, side by side with it, and often among those who worked on it, we constantly find a reality which contradicts it, souls who live by grace which, for them, is far from being a cloak hiding their death in sin from the sight, even, of God. The same may be said, as we have seen, about the sovereignty of God, even about the subjective aspect of justification by faith, also, and especially, about the sovereign

177

authority of Scripture. A dialectic of ideas may well have arisen, only to destroy itself afterwards, which would appear to make all these principles mere negations. Along with it a real, or living, dialectic has maintained in the soul their positive value that minds, imprisoned in a decadent philosophy, had striven to deprive them of. This is so true that it is common to see candidates for the ministry lose practically all positive faith during their theological studies, only to recover it slowly when the work of the ministry has brought them back into contact with the unsophisticated believer.

However, it is true that the notional dialectic of Protestantism is the exact contrary of its dialectic of life. There is, therefore, a danger that those who have passed through the stages we have described will return to a merely blind faith, anti-intellectualist, and constantly menaced by the theology which ought to sustain and strengthen it. The survival of Protestantism, the maintenance and periodic renewal of its vitality, rest on something more than that. It would long since have ceased to radiate an authentic and vigorous spirituality, if it did not possess at least the germ of an effective critique of the fatal process whose implications we have shown, not in the principles themselves, but in their early polemic forms and their first theological expressions. This critique, realised in varying degree, but always undertaken with courage—not for mere intellectual reasons, but under the impulse of a strong and genuine Christian sense—is, we believe, the source of the Protestant revivals, as distinguished from what were no more than sterile reactions. These revivals, we maintain, have up to now saved Protestant Christianity, in so far as they more or less completely broke the shell in which the original Protestantism had imprisoned its most positive principles, and so doomed them to extinction.

One of the most remarkable things in the history of Protestant spirituality is the appearance, along with controversialists who oppose, in a fatal sequence, radical transcendentalism to an immanentism no less radical, which raises up in turn a neo-transcendentalism and so on, of men who are first and foremost men of God, spiritual writers or ministers, generally both, who instinctively elude this barren cycle. But, when these are obliged to defend before their co-religionists what is often at first an instinctive reaction, their justification, when brought to light, is seen to lie in a rejection, more or less direct, more or less lucid, but always decided, of the dilemma in which early Protestantism had involved both itself and its successors. They remain faithful to the religion of the *sola gratia*, but they do not consider themselves bound irrevocably to extrinsic justification. They do not cease to uphold the ideal of *Soli Deo gloria*, but they have discovered anew the meaning of the words of St. Irenaeus, *Gloria Dei, vivens homo*. More than anyone they desire personal religion, but they escape the chimera of a person built up on autonomy and subjectivism. More ardently than all the rest they believe in the Bible, in the Word of God in the Bible, as *the* source of light and life; but the very truth of their practical obedience to the divine Word is what preserves them from bolstering it up with philosophical assumptions which would prevent its being heard whenever it said anything different from what the system warranted.

Protestantism has never lacked such men; if it had, it would have died away altogether. That being so, it ought above everything else to examine the meaning of their protest within its frontiers. For, if there is any way of escape for it from the fatal cycle we have described, it can only be along this road.

The pietism which arose in Germany in the seventeenth century is the first religious movement expressly opposed to Protestant 'orthodoxy'. It arose, not in order to reject the positive principles of the Reformation together with the frame applied to them, but, rather, to free them from it. The first timid and uncertain attempt in this direction was that made by a minister in Brunswick, Johann Arndt. His *True Christianity*, published in 1599, asserts categorically that the true faith which justifies is that which bears fruit in justice and sanctity. In his *Theophilus*, Valentin Andreae (who died in Strasbourg, where he had been the Court chaplain, in 1654) developed on the same lines the ideal of an active piety, nourished on the Scriptures. The works of J. Gerhardt,[1] of Jena, the most celebrated dogmatic theolo-

---

[1] *Cf.* his *Loci communes* (9 vols. 1610–21) and *Doctrina catholica et evangelica* (3 vols. 1634).

G

gian in Germany in the seventeenth century, are full of this conception. But with Philip-Jacob Spener, president of the seminary of Frankfort on the Maine from 1666, it acquired its full vigour and influence. He himself, while maintaining his allegiance to Luther, called Arndt the 'father of the faithful', and considered him the real founder of pietism, placing him, for this reason, 'immediately below Luther'. He declared his conviction that justification by faith in divine grace was the main principle, but he set himself against confusing it with extrinsic justification; on the contrary, he put all the emphasis on its association with practical sanctity, expressly including voluntary effort. Faith alone justifies, he said, but only living faith, working by charity. Essentially a minister, Spener formulated his teaching in order to animate and justify the *collegia pietatis*, those informal meetings for edification by which he sought to inspire real piety in his students and hearers. In his *Pia desideria* (1675), he opposed the exclusively polemical use of the Bible in the Lutheran scholasticism, and advocated a living meditation on Scripture, whose model was to be found in the German mystics. The *collegia biblica*, which practised this at first in the university of Leipzig, then in Saxony, and soon after in the whole of Germany, really created the movement, called by its opponents 'pietist'.

After attaining considerable influence, inspiring in particular the first foreign missions undertaken by German Protestants, pietism was watered down into the moralism and sentimentalism of the eighteenth century, and lost its distinctive character. Count Nicholas-Louis of Zinzendorf—a strange figure, combining pathological traits with very pure flights of mysticism and an unequalled ardour for the apostolate—was born in Dresden in 1700. A pupil, at Halle, of the Institute directed by Francke, a centre of pietism, he was won over permanently to a life of intensive prayer, dominated by affective meditation on the sufferings and love of Christ. He himself attributed his conversion to an image of Christ crucified which overwhelmed him with the words: 'Look at what I have done for thee; and thou, what hast thou done for me?'

However, it is to the confrontation of this interior life, so extremely personal, with an apparently chance happening that the renewal of the pietism associated with his name was due. In 1722, a group of Moravians, that is, of disciples of John Huss hitherto living in Bohemia, came to him to ask for asylum. He gave them, out of his property, the estate of Hutberg where they built their village of Herrnhut. Above all, he took a deep interest in their community, seeing in it a providential opportunity to realise one of those *ecclesiolae* which, in the pietist conception, was destined to regenerate the Church by recalling it, without creating a schism, to its primitive fervour. The statutes he gave in 1727 to the community which took the name of the Society of the Brothers of Unity (though they are better known as the Moravian Brethren), made of it one vowed to a quasi-monastic ideal, in spite of the marriage of its members. They practised an almost complete community of goods, seeking always the presence of God, animated by a tender and joyful devotion to Christ, the Lamb of God, which, they held, necessarily involved an active fraternal charity.

It is worthy of note that the community adhered in 1749 to the Confession of Augsburg but, in accordance with the original intention of Zinzendorf, now its 'bishop', aimed at promoting the return to Christian unity and at avoiding all sectarianism. The idea, perhaps chimerical but certainly generous, of those modern Protestants who wished to become 'evangelical Catholics', no doubt owed its origin to Zinzendorf and his followers.

The Moravians, for their part, spread throughout the world by reason of their missionary zeal. But it was by touching in one of these missions the soul of a young Anglican clergyman that they prepared the really universal extension of a Protestant revival issuing from 'pietism'.

In 1735, John Wesley, with his brother Charles and two friends, all four later ordained priests of the Church of England, had left for Georgia where they intended to evangelise the Indians. This enterprise was the outcome of the pious meetings organised in the year 1720 by Wesley at Christchurch, Oxford, where he was a student, from which he gained the nickname of 'methodist'. The mission he undertook met with only indifferent success, but his meeting in Georgia, and later in London, with the Moravians, especially with Bishop Spangenberg, the successor of Zinzendorf, was to change his whole life and his whole idea of the life of religion. In reaction against the slackness and immorality of his fellow-students, even those studying for the ministry, he had been sincerely pious, but somewhat rigid in his piety, which consisted of external practices rather than an inspired and living reality. In a Moravian assembly, whose date, May the 24th 1738, he noted, he tells us that on hearing a 'Brother' describe how God transforms man interiorly by faith in Christ, he 'felt his heart strangely warmed'. This he accounted for in his Journal by the assurance that 'Christ had taken away all his sins, and saved him'.

Then he went to spend three months at Herrnhut. But his own personality, so strong and independent, changed almost completely the spiritual tradition that had thus moved, awakened and 'converted' him. Indeed, the greatness of his work is enough to give him a place in the history of Protestantism comparable to that of the sixteenth-century Reformers, and the character of the work itself makes him truly a Reformer of the Reformation.

Before the end of the year 1739, when Wesley on his return from Germany started his work in England, he had preached more than five hundred times. His life, up to the very end, was consumed in an itinerant ministry which knew no respite. But it was the end he set himself directly, rather than the range of his work, that makes it so admirable. In the eighteenth century, when all classes of society were so profoundly dechristianised, Wesley, the contemporary of the Industrial Revolution that started in England, instinctively betook himself to the workers whose miserable condition had turned them into neo-pagans. He was, perhaps, the first Christian to grasp the new problem set before the Church, that of the infidel community newly created within a devitalised Christendom by the birth of a proletariat. His work, carried on at first within the Church of England whose minister he was, and which he never wanted to disown, and then, in spite of him, more and more apart from it, not only preserved England from a decline into materialism, but developed there a popular Christianity such as it had never before known, at least since the Middle Ages.

Through the intermediary of a Scottish layman, Haldane,

living in Geneva at the beginning of the nineteenth century, the
Wesleyan Movement came to reanimate continental Protestantism, particularly the French-speaking part in France and
Switzerland. That is what Protestants know as the 'revival' *par
excellence*. It is perpetuated in the memory of its followers by
such names as Felix Neff, the popular 'evangelist' of the High
Alps, Adolphe Monod, the minister of whom we have already
spoken at length, Alexandre Vinet, the religious thinker. Even
if their movement is criticised by some moderns, no one can
deny that it is owing to them that Protestantism has survived,
and especially that it has remained always a religious and
authentically Christian force.

What made this whole movement so akin to that of Wesley
is the vigour with which it propagated the doctrine of gratuitous
salvation, and its decisive rejection of the whole complex of
theological and philosophical tenets which had reduced it to
extrinsic justification. Wesley himself claimed to teach nothing
but justification by faith. But he was not satisfied, like the
pietists before him, with bringing sanctification and justification into the closest possible relation, after the Calvinist formula
he was fond of recalling. More penetrating than any of his pre-
decessors, he criticised Luther's opposition of faith to works as a
sophistry. As early as the year 1739, when he started on his new
course of action, he denounced what he called Luther's 'mania
of solifideism'. Luther's commentary on the epistle to the Galatians, with its unbalanced depreciation of the divine Law, was
in his view more likely to be pernicious than beneficial in its
results. His reason was that the holiness of Christ should by no
means be opposed to the holiness accessible to the Christian,
but, rather, be represented as its unique source. Far from admitting, therefore, that the epistle of St. James deserved to be
called an 'epistle of straw', he called it 'the great antidote
against the poison' of a justification which required no moral
change in the Christian.

He went still further. His fellow-worker, Whitefield, like
many of the popular Protestant mystics who reacted against the
sixteenth century formulas without being able to escape from
them, admitted certainly that grace ought to change the one
'converted'; but he assumed that this change, if it was to be

gratuitous, had to be instantaneous, as if miraculous, and that the individual should contribute nothing. Wesley, on the other hand, taught more and more clearly that since the great effect of conversion was the regeneration by grace of the human will, the human will ought to work for its own salvation, and make daily progress, otherwise, even if the conversion was real in the beginning, it would become ineffective, through want of perseverance.[1]

Against all this must be set the intense subjectivism of the Wesleyan 'faith', no less than that of the Lutheran 'faith'. The Methodist 'conversion' is essentially the attainment of a personal, direct conviction of 'having been washed in the blood of Jesus Christ'. As may be seen from this expression, taken from the Moravians, it takes place in circumstances where the sermon, the singing, the whole atmosphere of the meeting, unite to create an emotional, sentimental tension. . . . All this is undeniable, but it does not dispose of the fact that Wesleyan 'faith' supposes, in the most explicit fashion, at least the two doctrines of the divinity of Christ and the unique redemptive value of his death. The weakness of the 'revival' and the whole Methodist movement comes from the failure to incorporate these two truths in a harmonious theology. Its strength, incontestable after two centuries of history, derives from Wesley's firmness in restoring these two objective and fundamental elements of faith, not as abstract beliefs, but as real convictions, necessary to the life of the soul, and all-powerful to produce and sustain it.

All that such a faith means to a receptive soul, a faith centred on the living person of Christ, on God made man and Saviour of man, a faith restored to its true function as source of, rather than excuse from, personal sanctity, is expressed, better than by any commentary, in a celebrated passage of Vinet. This 'hymn' to Christ suffering, taken from his *Théologie pastorale*, expresses all the sweetness and strength of which Protestant devotion is capable and which is precisely the endowment it received from the Revival animated by the ideal of Wesley.

[1] The essential texts are to be found in Lelièvre, *John Wesley, sa vie, son oeuvre*, Paris, 1924 (4th edition).

'O King of glory and man of sorrows! Whoever loves thee has suffered, whoever loves thee consents to suffer. He is promised both to glory and to pain.

'Man suffers, on thy account, even in his dreams; so suffered, though she did not know thee, the wife of the judge who condemned thee. Who loves thee a little, or mourns for thee, has only to realise he follows thy way; he is made to partake, like Simon the Cyrenian, the hard burden of thy cross.

'Those who bless thee are cursed; mankind casts them out from its communion; and, in this place of exile from the human family, they are, themselves, doubly exiled.

'All those who loved thee have suffered; but all those who have suffered for thee, loved thee all the more. Pain unites to thee, as joy unites to the world.

'Pain inebriates, like a generous wine, those thou invitest to thy mysterious banquet, and forces from their anguished hearts hymns of adoration and love.

'Happy is he who, like the Cyrenian, has stooped to take his share of the cross thou drawest! Happy is he who wills to endure, in his body, that which remains, will remain to the end of the world, to suffer, of thy sufferings, for the Church, thy body!

'Happy is the faithful minister who continues, in his flesh, thy sacrifice and thy conflict! While he strives and groans, I see him, in vision, leaning on thy breast, like, on the day of the funeral feast, him whom thou didst love.

'For himself, while charity bears him, dusty and bleeding, from place to place, from suffering to suffering, he, unknown to the world, reposes on thy breast, in a sacred retreat, and tastes, in silence, the sweetness of thy words.

'Happy the faithful minister! His charity multiplies his sacrifices, and his sacrifices augment his charity; love, which is the soul of his work, is, also, its great reward.

'Happy the faithful minister! What every Christian would desire to be, he already is. That cross which everyone tries in his turn, he carries without ceasing. This Jesus, with whom the world ceaselessly disputes our gaze, is himself his world, and the object of his unceasing contemplation.

'Happy, thrice happy, if all his desire is to add a few voices to the concert of the blessed, and to remain hidden in the joy of all, keeping only in his heart the invisible regard and the eternal "Well done!" of his Master and Father!' [1]

What strikes us in this passage is its fully Catholic tone. Yet it would be hard to find another equally expressive of all the characteristics of the piety of the Revival. After reading the life of Wesley, his Journal, his sermons, the hymns of his brother Charles, one cannot imagine a prayer more exactly suited to a minister as he wished to be, and most certainly was.

This illustrates perfectly a fact we hold to be indisputable, namely, that the Protestant Revival, by its very fidelity to the great principles of the Reformation, and primarily to the *sola gratia*, a fidelity clear-sighted enough to detect the jewel hid in so much dross, recalls the best and most authentic elements of the Catholic tradition. This is even more interesting in that the leaders of the Revival, generally speaking, Wesley first of all, Vinet even more, not only lacked any pronounced sympathy for Catholicism, but lived in a prodigious ignorance of its real nature, and held most extraordinary views on its hierarchy, sacraments, and doctrine. However, though they knew it so little, they did not fail to be struck with the coincidence between the principles by which they lived and those that sustained the spiritual lives of the great Catholics. They accounted for this as well as they could, sometimes by very strange reasoning, to prove to themselves that the Catholic saints had been such in spite of their Catholicism, not because of it. But honesty obliged them to admit that, in these and their teaching, they found their own ideal expressed and realised. The author of the Imitation, St. Francis de Sales, M. de Renty, were those most familiar to Wesley, and most loved by him. He was always engaged in compiling extracts from their works and publishing them in popular form, to be circulated among his followers. St. Francis Xavier, he wrote in a letter of the 30th of May, 1772, strikes him as the very image of a life given to God in the service of his brethren. 'There is a martyrdom,' he said, 'that seems to me more glorious than that of St. Peter.' As for Vinet,

---

[1] *Théologie pastorale*, 2e édition, Paris, 1854, pp. 22–3.

he considered Pascal and St. Bernard as the teachers and living examples of the Christianity a Protestant ought to realise in virtue of his Protestantism.

Moreover, both the Moravians of Zinzendorf, and even the first pietists (Luther too, for that matter), had recourse to the great medieval mystics, notably of the Rhenish school, as both sources and living examples of the Reformation and the Christianity it ought to produce.

It is also certain that the entire movement, pietist as well as Wesleyan, which we have described, profited by the vast mystical trend apparent from the beginning of Protestantism, sometimes in anarchical forms, but often at the heart of the most conservative movements in thought and action.

We have already mentioned that succession of German mystics who, in sixteenth- and seventeenth-century Protestantism, continued the teachings of Tauler as well as that of the more or less pantheistic mystics of the medieval sects—Sebastian Franck, Valentin Weigl and, greatest of all, Jacob Boehme, the theosophical cobbler of Goerlitz. They undoubtedly prepared the way for pietism and, while alarming it perhaps, helped to arouse it. In addition to them, we have what remained of the Anabaptist movement, so prevalent in the Low Countries, where it was the direct inspiration of Rembrandt.

In a form at first quite popular, but soon refined and intellectualised without ever losing its first simplicity, the Quaker movement in the seventeenth century recreated, in England and America, an original mystical tradition, destined to a remarkable permanence and continuity. George Fox, a young shepherd, son of a Presbyterian weaver, set out in 1649 on an itinerant prophetical ministry at the instance of an interior voice, seeing in the Word of the Bible, not only an exclusive revelation, but the fuel and the stimulant of the 'inner light' which ought to be kindled in every man. The historic Christ himself was in his view a reality for us only in so far as he brings us to his presence within us, which constitutes the whole of redemption. We have already emphasised the boldness of the Quakers in acknowledging the presence in Catholic mystics of their own ideal. The Carmelite saints, in particular, St. Teresa, St. John of the Cross, Blessed Laurence of the Resurrection,

soon became their favourite writers. To them were later added
Ruysbroek, Tauler, and also Fénelon and Madame Guyon.

It is true that, in the eighteenth century, the mysticism
originated by Boehme and the Quakers, for example in the
latitudinarianism of the Cambridge Platonists, or the illuminism
of Hamann, Lavater, and Madame de Krudener, degenerated
into a hotch-potch of sentimental rationalism and occultism.
Yet, even within the apocalyptic gnosticism of Swedenborg,
there ran a vein of authentic mysticism, since the strange vision-
ary of Sweden so powerfully inspired Oberlin, who, at the height
of the Revolution, created in the valleys of the Vosges one of
the purest Protestant Revivals.

If the Catholicism latent in the Revivals is thus attested,
if not strictly speaking by their sources, at least by the affilia-
tions they acknowledged, it is made still more evident by some
of their later developments. For we see in every Protestant
country Christians who owed their religion to the movement we
have called, in general, Revivalism, attain a more or less complete rediscovery of Catholicism.

The case of Newman is the most famous of these. It must be
clearly distinguished from that of the majority of his Anglican
friends, who were turned towards Catholicism by the tradition-
ally anti-Protestant element that the High Church party had
always kept side by side with its Protestant trends. Newman, on
the contrary, was brought to a living faith by the influence of the
Evangelicals, who preserved in the Church of England the best
elements of Wesley's movement. It was not at all by a denial
of his first 'conversion' at the age of fifteen, but by a deeper
realisation both of what it had brought him and of what it
further required, that he arrived at his second conversion, which
in 1845 brought him to Catholicism. More exactly, he discovered that the living faith in the Redeemer, Christ, the Son of
God, if it was not to founder in illusion or take refuge in a sectarian paradox, accepts the Church, her Sacraments, the living
tradition of faith according to which the Bible is to be understood. One of his books which was the least understood, but
today appears the most lasting and valuable, the Lectures on
Justification, shows with an admirable lucidity and breadth of
view that the living faith of Protestantism, in spite of its con-

troversial expression, only attains its full sweep in a renewed and deepened adherence to the traditional Catholic doctrine.

The present Lutheran Archbishop of Upsala, one of the best historians of the Oxford Movement, published on the occasion of its centenary a small but excellent work, where he maintains that this process was neither unique nor exceptional. The contemporary Revivals most valuable and lasting in their results all present a striking analogy with this process of rediscovery of Catholicism as a result of a deeper insight into the principles of Protestantism. This, Brilioth shows,[1] is equally true of the Bavarian, Wilhelm Löhe, the Lutheran minister who fought so vigorously against the official Church in which the Prussian king intended to fuse Lutherans and Calvinists, and of the Swede, Henric Schartau, who prepared in his own country the Lutheran renascence which is so striking at the present time, and even of the Dane, Frederik Severin Grundtvig, anti-Roman though he was. We may add to these two French Lutherans, Hornung of Strasbourg and Louis Meyer of Paris (already mentioned). Both understood perfectly among other things, and taught on the same lines as Löhe, that an ecclesiastical basis, dogmatic and sacramental, was the objective element necessitated by Revivalist mysticism, if it were not to go astray and die of inanition.

No less important than these very different personalities, united in a common aim, though for the most part unknown to one another, is that of Archdeacon Frederick Denison Maurice, whose work, at first misunderstood, is seen now to have been of greater influence in the Church of England than any other of the nineteenth century. A contemporary of the Oxford Movement, Maurice never joined it, revolted as he was by the deliberate scorn and ignorance shown by most of the Tractarians for all that was best in Protestantism. Having come to Anglicanism from Quaker surroundings, he never ceased to uphold the validity of the fundamental principles of the Reformation. At the same time, he constantly maintained that the logic of these principles, far from requiring the overthrow of the Church of tradition, with its sacramental and doctrinal structure, ought to lead to a completely fresh understanding of them, and could

[1] *Cf.* Brilioth, *Evangelicalism and the Oxford Movement*, Oxford, 1934.

not be followed out fully outside that framework or, rather, outside the living organism willed by God. His principal work, *The Kingdom of God*, dedicated to this thesis, is certainly of capital importance in the evolution of Protestant thought. That is not to say that it is exempt from prejudices or misunderstandings in detail, both in regard to the ultra-Protestantism it starts from and to the Roman Catholicism it stops short of; in fact, it abounds with them. This only makes the depth and sureness of his thought all the more remarkable. If there is anyone within Protestantism who saw with clarity and depth into the principle needed to resolve the crisis endemic in Protestantism, it is certainly Maurice.

After taking account of all these different facts, we must, it is evident, not fail to consider the judgment passed on them by the movement of rebirth which in the last generation was the most conspicuous factor of Protestant vitality, at least in the sphere of theology. We allude, of course, to Barthism. But first of all, what place is to be assigned to Barthism itself? It seems to be unquestionably a true renascence of Protestantism and, both in the richness of the positive elements in its theology of the Word of God and in its attempt to overcome the subjectivism manifest in the Reformation teaching on faith, it constitutes a real 'revival' of what is most Christian in Protestantism. On the second of these points, Barth was in fact the first to distinguish fully between faith in the Redeemer, in salvation as coming from him, and faith directly in our own salvation as such. Rightly or wrongly, he denounced the confusion of these as the error out of which came 'pietism'. We must note also his formal dissociation from the whole system of extrinsic justification, his insistence on the character, fundamentally creative, not juridical or simply declaratory, of the Word of forgiveness. However, on this point, as soon as his thought is examined closely, the progress made appears quite illusory, for the creative reality of the forgiveness remains so bound up in the Word that he is obliged to deny it any stable existence within ourselves. That is to return, in a more extreme degree than Calvin or even Luther, if we except some polemical instances, to the substance of extrinsic justification under another name.

Whatever the case with this particular question, in spite of the way Barth extols some of the most positive aspects of Protestantism, in spite even of his strong distrust of all subjectivism, he has no hesitation in rejecting the whole of pietism and its consequences. He himself was fully aware of its fundamental accord, especially from the time of Wesley, with the traditional spirituality of Catholicism. But he emphasised at the same time the decadence and compromises with naturalism which we have already admitted, both of the Revivals and of Protestant mysticism in general, in the eighteenth century and at other times, whether it took the form of a platonic rationalism or a sentimental illuminism. In his view, the issue of Modernism out of Catholicism is a revelation of a common basis of agreement between it and the most negative kind of liberal Protestantism. This basis would be Pelagianism, the religion of immanentism; in a word, a return to the idea of a salvation acquired by man for himself, instead of one given by God, to a purely natural religion replacing that of the pure grace of God.

Moreover, he denies aiming at a mere return to the old Protestant orthodoxy. That, he considers, unconsciously prepared the deviation both of the liberal scepticism and of the Catholic credulity, both ultimately amounting to the same thing, the putting of man in the place of God. The orthodoxy of the sixteenth and seventeenth centuries led to this upheaval through its failure to exorcise Catholicism entirely. The true solution, then, of the crisis of Protestantism would not lie in the rejection of the negative elements present from the outset within Protestant transcendentalism, but rather in their accentuation. Far from acknowledging that grace, to be truly grace, has to be effective, able to be effectively received, we are to deny this possibility more radically than the Reformers did, even in their most anti-Catholic passages. Nor is it a matter of acknowledging a real value belonging to man, even if only to man saved, whether or not that is revealed as the sovereign will of God. On the contrary, we are to consider it the worst blasphemy to suppose that God could possibly will that. Hence arises, not only the impossibility of interpreting the divine Word, in any way, by any kind of ecclesiastical tradition, but, in spite of all that can be urged against liberal subjectivism, the impossibility also of confining this Word in any human word, idea, or definition.[1]

Obviously our study is completely opposed to this criticism. It is evident too that our conclusions are justified or not according as Barth's judgment of Catholicism is valid or otherwise. We have, therefore, to turn to an examination of Catholicism, and to compare it with the idea currently held by Protestants, which Barth makes his own and sets out systematically. If their objections are seen to be unfounded, the Revival, in so far as it converges with Catholicism, will be freed from the reproaches addressed to it by Barth, and we shall be compelled to recognise in Barthism, in so far as it is opposed to Catholicism, simply a Protestant neo-orthodoxy. For it only accentuates the confusions we have seen present at the origin of Protestantism between the authentic truths of Christianity and what is merely the product of a decadent medieval philosophy, which the Reformers were incapable of criticising. The energy the Barthians display in refusing to admit this inevitable criticism may well be the energy of despair.

---

[1] These subjects were developed to the extreme by Barth himself; to Brunner, attempting, in connection with the Oxford Group, a reconciliation between revivalism and Barthism, he answered: *Nein!*

CHAPTER X

The Catholic Church Necessary to the Full Flowering of the Principles of the Reformation

THE title of this chapter may sound like a deliberate paradox. None the less, it expresses the conclusion to which all the preceding logically leads, if our study, as we hope, faithfully corresponds to the reality in all its aspects.

It will be useful at this point to go back, step by step without deviation, over the way we have gradually cleared through the entanglements of controversies, of systems, of numerous schools of thought and spirituality.

We began by affirming that the essence of Protestantism lies, not in any negation, but in certain great positive assertions of Christianity. That is the standpoint from which the great principles of the Reformation must be interpreted, those we see present in Protestantism as lived, those we find immediately we seek, in the abundant production of the Reformers, what they considered essential. Next, we established that, from this point of view, the principles of Protestantism are not only authentically and essentially Christian, as is shown by revealed data, but also that they are corroborated by Catholic tradition, not only prior to but subsequent to the Reformation.

The question then naturally arose: how could a reform which set out from such principles end in schism, even in heresy? We answered that, in the actual development by the Reformers of these principles, there were inserted at the outset negative elements having no intrinsic connection with them, in fact, in formal contradiction with the Scriptural teaching the Reformation claimed for itself. These negative elements, we established, were the presuppositions of the nominalist thought of the fifteenth century, that is, of what was the worst of all the too real corruptions of medieval Catholicism. Brought up on these lines of thought, identified with them so closely that they could not see beyond them, the Reformers could only systematise their very valuable insights in a vitiated framework. Actually, not one of the errors the Church was led to condemn in their

193

teaching was of their own creation; extrinsic justification, faith shut up in subjectivism, purely negative transcendentalism (God beyond reason and morality, or rather beyond the true and the good), the flat opposition of the authority of Scripture to that of the Church—there were so many theses of nominalist theology which had up to then escaped condemnation, simply because they did not leave the sterile playground of the dialectic of the schools. The Reformation, however, to its misfortune as much as the Church's, brought them out into the pulpit and the public square.

This connection of the principles of Protestantism with the worm-eaten framework of a decadent medievalism, far from serving them, simply suffocated them, as we saw from the history of Protestantism from its second generation onwards. In orthodox Protestantism, which only systematised the unfortunate statements uttered by the Reformers under the stress of a too hasty polemic, what, with Luther and Calvin, had been the source of a real spiritual renewal, became a yoke effectively stifling all spiritual life. The misfortune is that, when the inevitable reaction occurs, as long as one maintains the alternatives created fallaciously and develops the principles on nominalist lines, it is impossible to oppose the fatal negations of orthodox Protestantism without denying or misunderstanding what was wholly positive in it. This alone accounts for the strange paradox that the Reformation, begun to extol the work of grace, arrived at a Pelagianism never equalled before; begun to exalt the sovereignty of God, arrived at an immanentism absolutely closed to all the transcendent (strangely enough, not without getting rid of that spiritual liberty it had wished to promote, as Catholicism had never done); begun to establish beyond dispute the divine authority of Scripture, ended by reducing it to a purely human document and by denying even the possibility of revelation.

In view of all this, it seems to us evident in itself, and confirmed by history, that returns to Protestant orthodoxy or to an uncritical adherence to the principles of the Reformation as expressed by the Reformers, cannot possibly resolve the crisis of the internal conflicts of Protestantism, but only accentuate it. For, if the whole evil arises from the bond forged, unawares at the outset, between the positive principles of the Reformation and the negative elements which had nothing to do with them, to return to this bond, and attempt to tighten it still further, could only result in bringing back to its starting-point an evolution, necessarily disastrous, and to make it more fatal than ever.

On the other hand, we have seen that if Protestantism has been able to retain and renew its vitality, that was due to a series of 'revivals' closely related to one another, which succeeded in some degree in separating the Reformation principles from the conceptual mould in which the Reformers had begun to encase them. However, in view of the traditional and Catholic nature of these principles in their original tenor, it was impossible to do this without at the same time, even unconsciously, drawing nearer to Catholicism. We have seen that this was in fact the tendency of the revivals, that it was furthered by all that remained of Catholicism in the Protestant tradition, and that it ended up, in some of their most distinguished exponents, with a genuine rediscovery, at least in part, of the Catholic Church in its essentials.

Arrived at this point, we came up against the reply of Barth. It ignores, or tries to, the historical criticism we made of the principles of Protestantism, not in themselves but in their formulation from the sixteenth century onwards. None the less, confronted with the undoubted trend of Protestant revivalism towards the Catholic Church, and moved by the obvious degeneration of the revivals into a natural religion, either rationalist or sentimentalist, the school of Barth rejects both Protestant pietism and Catholicism. It denounces, in fact, both of them as victims of the same error that lies at the root of liberal Protestantism, that dechristianised religion; namely, the denial, though concealed, of really gratuitous grace, the confusion of the work of God with the work of man, the setting of man in the place of God.

The only way of meeting this objection is to examine the idea of Catholicism considered to be self-evident, according to which it either denies or misunderstands any grace worthy of being so-called, the sovereignty of God and the unique authority of his Word, and is at the same time an organism designed to destroy the liberty of the children of God. In discussing this objection, we shall at the same time be discussing the idea that the Protestant revivals, in drawing near to Rome, betrayed the true principles of the Reformation.

We hope to be able to show, on the contrary, that, in the view of Protestant prejudices which Barthism merely intensifies, Catholicism in so far as opposed to the principles of Protestantism, only opposes a systematisation of them that rests on fallacies and leads to their destruction. In reality, the real tenets of Catholicism, if seen as they are and not through a distorting lens, bring the Reformation principles the support refused to them by the structure actually made for them, and which it is bound to go on refusing so long as it is not itself reformed, that is, until the decision is made to return to those essentials of the Church it caused to be misconstrued and rejected. If this is the case, the instinctive orientation of the revivals towards the Catholic Church, so far from being a betrayal of the Reformation, is a sign of a more perfect allegiance to it. We shall be led to conclude that complete allegiance would bring about in its full splendour the Reformation only begun, would bring in that way a reconciliation between the Protestant movement and the Church, in a Reformation at last achieved.

In the Protestant preconception, first expressed in the *De Captivitate Babylonica* and reaching with Barth its ultimate development, Catholicism is the negation of the *sola gratia*, in its account both of the source of salvation and of its effect. It sees the Church substituting for grace the action of man, in the sacraments which work *ex opere operato*. At the same time, in canonising saints and, in particular, attributing to Our Lady certain special privileges, it is said to canonise human effort and to ascribe to the merit of man the salvation that is a pure gift of God.

On the first point, it must be obvious that the prejudice is such that it makes the phrase concerned say exactly the opposite of what it really means. Yet, as regards the sacramental doctrine and practice of Catholicism, it is so deeply rooted that no Protestant controversialist, Barth less than anyone, takes any serious trouble to verify it. It is taken for granted that *opus operatum* means magic, man claiming to subject the divine power to his own will. The thing is taken as self-evident and anything Catholics may say in rebuttal is held to be null and void.

The fact is, however, that the phrase *ex opere operato*, applied by Catholic theology to the working of the sacraments, is always expressly opposed to the idea of their working *ex opere operantis*. What does that mean other than that they derive their value and efficacy, not from the man who administers them, but from their very nature, independently of any human agency? And what do we mean when we say they have this value 'in themselves'? We mean, as St. Thomas expresses it with the utmost clarity, in so far as the sacraments are signs given to us by God in his Word, and in so far as this Word has ordered certain men to administer them in his Name. In other words, the efficacy of the sacraments *ex opere operato*, and not *ex opere operantis* (not even *ex opere operantis Ecclesiae*), means that they are efficacious by the express will of God, not only in general, but in each individual case, in so far as administered by this or that person, here and now, who has received from God the express vocation to do so.

Obviously it may be questioned *a priori* that God willed this or that sacrament, that he in fact charged certain men to administer them, but, unless one declines to study the Catholic teaching or to make any effort to understand it from within, it cannot be denied that Catholics believe the sacraments to have been instituted by Christ and that their ministers were sent by Christ. They believe, therefore, that each sacrament acts *ex opere operato*, precisely because they believe that it is the sole grace of God, in this case the sole free and loving will of God, that gives the sacrament its being and value, and by no means anything human or created. The sacrament, of course, may be administered in surroundings conducive to devotion or not in a way that inspires reverence or the reverse; it may conduce to a real sense of the presence of God. Catholics are convinced of the importance that everything in the externals and the action of the minister should correspond with the dignity of the sacrament. Canon Law holds any defect in this to be a grave sin in those responsible. It goes so far as to forbid any celebration, unless certain minimum conditions are satisfied. But once these

are assured, Catholic faith holds that the sacrament is effective
or fruitless, not on account of the good sentiments or conduct
of man, but according as it is or is not a sacrament willed by
God, administered or not by one whom God has entrusted to
do so in his name.

If that is so, and it is enough to read any Catholic manual on
the sacraments, or to question any Catholic child on his catechism, to assure oneself on the point, the Catholic idea and practice of the sacraments, far from making the *sola gratia* meaningless, gives it the fullest recognition and the most complete
application imaginable.

In recalling all that Barth shows us in his theology of the
Word, a Word creative, efficacious of itself, and so implying
the personal Presence, behind the Word, of the God who
speaks, anyone must recognise that for the Catholic the celebration of a sacrament is precisely the occasion of the utterance
of this living Word, this personal Word of God in Christ,
whence comes the sole reason of its certain efficacy, *hic et nunc*,
an efficacy which is always purely an object of faith, inaccessible
to sense. The whole question, then, is whether the Catholic is
justified in holding that God is present when the minister claims
to act in his name, and if what he does in administering the
sacrament is really what God wills him to do. Once this is
admitted, the efficaciousness *ex opere operato* of the sacrament
is simply a strict application in practice of the scriptural theology
of the Word of God so ably constructed by Barth and, therefore,
the acknowledgment, not only in the abstract, but in the concrete and in practice, of the *sola gratia* without any compromise.

What, then, is to be thought of the idea that the sacraments
of the Catholic Church are signs ordained by the Word of God
itself, and that those who administer them do so, not in their
own name, but in the name of God alone, in virtue of the command given by this Word?

The Protestant, prejudiced against the Church, will retort
that this manner of binding grace to a particular sign or of
attributing to men a power to act in the name of God, amounts
to undermining the sovereignty of God, to fettering him to the
things of the world, to subjecting him to an authority of this
world.

Let us come to the crux of the matter. Must the sovereignty
of God be considered something purely abstract, the sovereignty
in fact of an idea certain theologians entertain about God, of
what he may or may not do? Or is it sovereignty in the concrete,
demanding the effective and unconditional obedience of man?
In other words, is it to be the sovereignty God has taken the
trouble to affirm in his Word, or simply the sovereignty of an
idea we may have formed about him, if necessary, discarding
his Word? Surely Protestants who take their own principles
seriously could not hesitate in their answer. The sovereignty
of God is but an illusion, if it is no more than the sovereignty of
our ideas (or imaginings) about him, and not that of his own
Word.

On this point, there has gradually been formed an impressive
unanimity among exegetes. They agree, first of all, that Baptism and the Eucharist are presented by the New Testament as
formally prescribed by God through Christ. Secondly, these
are conceived by the New Testament writings, those of St. Paul
especially, as admitting the individual to participation in the
Kingdom by continuous communion with the risen body of
Christ, in virtue of his own institution. On the real presence,
absolutely objective, of the crucified and risen Christ, in the
Supper as described by St. Paul and St. John and proclaimed
by the apostles as contained in the Word of God in Christ,
there is now a practically unanimous agreement among all
exegetes of note, free-thinkers and Protestants as well as
Catholics. The same may be said of our incorporation into
Christ by Baptism, as taught by St. Paul, and of our new birth
with Christ, as described by St. John.

Equally striking is the practical consensus of modern exegesis in recognising apostolicity as the fundamental note of the
Church of the New Testament. That is to say, the Church and
all its activities, in particular the way it transmits to men the
Word of God as a living Word, are shown to be conditioned,
not only by the fact of its apostolic mission, but by a very exact
idea of what this implies. The 'Apostle' is primarily the Christian equivalent of the Jewish *Schaliach*, which means, not any
kind of envoy, but one the rabbinical law expressly held to be
in practice equivalent to the one sending him, or, rather, to his

presence itself. 'The *schaliach* of a man is another self', is repeated ceaselessly in the rabbinical texts. This is the context in which we are to understand the words of the Master: 'As my Father has sent me, I also send you; he that receiveth you receiveth me, and he that receiveth me receiveth him that sent me.' (John XX, 21; Matt. X, 40. *Cf.* John XII, 44, and XIII, 20.) In other words, in the 'apostolic' Church, he, whoever he be, on whom the 'apostolate' rests, whatever his personal merits or defects, when he does what Christ has charged him to do, is simply allowing Christ to do it through him and, in Christ, it is God who does it.

If this is so, and if also the Catholic Church is the same as the apostolic Church, possessing this essential character of the Apostolate (which is the presence of Him who sends in those he sent), it must be acknowledged that the Catholic Church, in its celebration of Baptism and the Eucharist, giving them the significance it does, far from opposing the sovereignty of God as expressed in his Word, simply bows down before it, obeying it in the adoring submission of faith.

Here we come upon a final objection which is not confined to Barthians or other anti-Catholic extremists, but appears fundamental even to such moderates as O. Cullmann, the great exegete of Alsace.[1] The Church, after the time of the apostles, in particular that of today, can only be said to be apostolic in the sense that it has to preach always what they preached, as transmitted to us by the New Testament. But it neither is nor can be apostolic in the sense that it possesses within itself the apostolate. This function was of its nature incapable of being transmitted, for it applies to the foundation only of the Church, not to its continuation. To think otherwise would be to confuse the history of the Church which receives and propagates salvation with the history of salvation itself, to confuse the revelation made once and for all with tradition, the Word of God with the words of man which cannot do more than comment on it and explain it.

This objection is certainly of the highest interest, for it compels us to make clear in what sense the apostolate is a permanent

[1] *Cf.* his article on *La Tradition et le Nouveau Testament*, in *Dieu vivant* 23, and the theological part of his *St. Pierre*, Neuchâtel-Paris, 1952.

quality of the Church. However, it involves in its turn a prejudice against the Catholic Church which seems to us to rest on a simple mistake of fact (supported, moreover, by so many vague and misleading expressions often used by Catholics). When the Catholic Church maintains that the apostolic function is always living in her, she does so because otherwise it would have to be said that the Church of the apostles died with the last of them, and it is another Church that has succeeded to it, not the same that has continued, though in different conditions and a more or less altered form. But, in holding this, she does not by any means misconceive what in the function of the apostles was unique and incommunicable. Theirs was the duty of founding the Church. To this end, the revelation had been made to them and they possessed the charisma of positive inspiration, making all that they taught the teaching of God, his own Word. The Catholic Church is the first to proclaim that, if she is apostolic, that does not mean that those she considers the successors of the apostles (the Pope and the other bishops) have the power of laying a foundation other than that they laid, could receive a different revelation from theirs (or even enlarge it in the slightest), are endowed (even in exceptional cases) with the same inspiration as they had. All this the Church not only does not pretend to, but today with greater precision than in the past, when the theology on these points was rather vague, repudiates and condemns. A Catholic, seriously maintaining any one of these propositions, would now be held to have lapsed formally into heresy.

St. Thomas Aquinas explains that the title 'vicar of Christ', given to those who rule the Church in succession to the apostles, does not mean that they can modify in the least its essential structure or its basis, but that their power is so dependent on what God has done, once and for all, in Christ, and entrusted to his apostles, that it is restricted to preserving this legacy, without altering or adding to it. The Church they govern is 'constituted by the faith and the sacraments of the faith. Consequently, just as they are not allowed to set up another Church, neither may they hand down another faith or institute other sacraments'.[1]

[1] *Summa Theologica*, III, 66. 2, ad 2.

The decree *Lamentabili* formally condemned the modernist proposition which said: 'The revelation, which constitutes the object of faith, did not come to an end with the apostles.'[1] In so doing, it only repeated and gave precision to the teaching of a decree of the Vatican Council, itself derived from one of Trent: 'The supernatural revelation, according to the faith of the universal Church declared by the holy Council of Trent, is contained in the sacred writings and the unwritten traditions which, received in the time of the apostles from the very mouth of Christ, or transmitted, as it were, from hand to hand, by the apostles under the inspiration of the Holy Spirit, have come down to us.'[2]

We see in this text how narrowly the word tradition is understood. Those traditions which the Councils admit as capable of containing any part of revelation are only those which are not simply human, even simply ecclesiastical, but apostolic traditions in the strict sense, that is, those which preserve what the apostles themselves handed down as coming from Christ. These, moreover, are not important as additions to the facts and truths contained in Scripture, but as maintaining these clear and precise in the living Church. As St. Irenaeus says, the apostolic writings, considered in their content, can be appropriated and applied with great brilliance, even by a heretic or pagan. The Catholic Church alone, in its living tradition received from the apostles, knows how to interpret faithfully and respect them, not only in the letter, but in the Spirit which dictated them and expresses itself in them.

Once more we must insist that this permanence of the Spirit and its action in the Church, especially in those who are responsible for maintaining the living fidelity of the revelation made once and for all, is not by any means the 'inspiration' proper to the apostles. Before the Vatican Council, there had been attempts on the part of some to teach this, but the Council rejected them formally and made them permanently inadmissible. According to its teaching, which confirms that of all the great theologians, the way in which the Holy Spirit keeps alive the revelation made to the apostles, whether in the apostolic

[1] Prop. 22 (Denz. 2021).
[2] Session III, ch. 21 (Denz. 1787).

tradition itself, preserved in the ordinary teaching of the Church, or in the most solemn definitions of the extraordinary magisterium (of Pope or Council), is not at all the same thing as the inspiration of the apostles which produced the last books of the Bible, and which is something unique and unrepeatable. It is no more than a negative assistance, preserving the Church from ever officially teaching error, that is, from adulterating revelation. In other words, the Church, in her ordinary and extraordinary magisterium, is assured by the Spirit of never teaching anything not taught by the apostles. But none of the formulas, even the most solemn, in which she may convey or elucidate this teaching, is or will ever be strictly speaking the 'Word of God'. Only the inspired books of the two Testaments are that; that is why there is not, nor will there ever be, any definition (or still more, any ordinary teaching) of the Church which does not refer to these books of the 'Word of God', in the strict sense, that is, the only word of whose existence God can be said to be the literal author. He is not the author, in this sense, even of the most solemn definitions of the Church, and he guarantees them, with the charisma of infallibility, only as guaranteeing their conformity, both in the letter and its meaning, with the Word given once for all by the apostles.

All that we have just said cannot be stated better than by St. John of the Cross in a passage we have already alluded to and which we now quote in full:

'. . . God has said all to us in giving us the all who is his Son. For this reason, anyone who now asks or desires any kind of vision or revelation would not only be acting foolishly but would be doing wrong to God, in not turning his gaze entirely to Christ, but desiring something else, something new. For God could answer him after this fashion: "If I have said all to you in my Word, who is my Son, I have no other in which I can now answer or reveal anything over and above that; look only to him, because in him I have spoken and revealed all to you, and you will find even more than you ask, more than you could wish. You want a word or a revelation that is merely partial, but, if you look well upon him, you will find there all; for he is my whole word, my reply, my whole vision and revelation, that I

H

have already addressed to you, answered, shown forth and revealed, giving you him as brother, companion, master, your ransom and reward. From the time when I, with my Spirit, came down on him on Mount Thabor, saying: 'This is my beloved Son, in whom I am well pleased, hear ye him', I have stopped all these different ways of instruction and answer, and have committed all to him; listen to him, for I have no other faith to reveal, nothing else to make known. Beforehand, if I spoke, it was to promise Christ; and if men questioned me, it was but to ask, and hope, for Christ, in whom they should find every kind of good (as the teaching of the apostles and evangelists has now made known). But now, anyone who questioned me likewise, and wished me to answer and reveal something, would be, as it were, asking me again for Christ and asking for a further faith, as if something was lacking in the faith already given in Christ: and so he would be doing great wrong to my beloved Son, not only lacking faith in him, but seeking to make him become again incarnate and go through his past life and death again. There is nothing more for you to ask of me; you have not to desire visions and revelations from me. Look well upon him; you will find all that, and even more, given and accomplished." ' [1]

It could not be better said that the Catholic Church is called 'apostolic', not to add to or change what the apostles said and did in the name of Christ, but solely to preserve it.

However, there is one thing most important to clarify. How is this deposit to be kept? Simply by human conservatism? Or by the ecclesiastical authorities confining themselves to compel respect for the letter of the apostolic writings? This would be quite ineffective since, as St. Irenaeus has already observed, heretics excel in keeping the letter, while losing the Spirit. Above all, it would be to fall back under the law, and to lose the Spirit who is precisely the great gift of the New Covenant. It is absolutely unthinkable that the Church is to be 'apostolic' merely by keeping the writings of the apostles as the only source of her teaching. That would be for her to fall back into the Old Testament, and to a purely rabbinical and pharisaic under-

[1] *Ascent of Mount Carmel*, Book 2, Chapter 22.

standing of it. The Church cannot preserve the 'doctrine of the apostles', if all her members have not living in them the Spirit which filled the apostles. And, since the Word they brought us is a living Word, the Son of God entering human history, it will only be the same Word within the Church if it remains an actual happening, part of the life of each of us. That is exactly what is realised in the sacraments of the faith, in which God commits himself freely but truly, not in an abstract, general covenant with a people of God which would be only an impersonal mass, but in a living, individual covenant with a people of God which is but one heart and soul shared by all. The sacraments themselves are such, only because they are not only signs once instituted by Christ, but signs given here and now by Himself, actually and in person, through those who act in his name, since he remains always present in those he has sent to do his work; which supposes that they are only instruments acting always in direct dependence on him. Further, all this is kept alive in the consciousness of the Church and each of its members, only because those who have the responsibility for the divine Word are preserved by its continual presence from adulterating it and, what is more, do not present it in a lifeless form, but as a Word which continues to be uttered, through those who speak in his name, by Him who has 'placed them, as bishops, by the Spirit, to rule over the Church of God, which he has purchased by his blood' (Acts XX, 28).

This is the sense in which the Church is apostolic, not only materially but spiritually, not only as being once founded by the apostles, but as having the Spirit of the apostles and the living actuality of the Word entrusted to them. She is apostolic because she has present within her, through the successors of the apostles from whom they received the charge of continuing their work, not as a different work, but as the same, living with the same life, Him who is always the Lord of the Church, being 'with her to the consummation of the world'.

This view, far from being an innovation, is what appears with the most perfect clarity in the same post-apostolic Church to which we owe the New Testament, without this Church having the slightest inkling that her view could be inconsistent with it; rather, she was evidently convinced that only so could she be the Church of the apostles, the Church of Christ, and not some other Church substituted for that later on.

Once all this is set in a clear light, it becomes manifest that the Catholic Church, in the principle of her constitution and ordinary life, is the Church where, not in theory but in fact, grace is all. She is the Church where God, in Christ, remains actually sovereign, the Church where the Word of God, the same which was entrusted finally to the apostles, and is kept literally in the Bible, is always speaking. The Word is there, always living, always creative of the new man, because always directly uttered by Him who willed to be present in his Church, and who so disposed that she herself should be for the eye of faith the enduring sign of his presence.

In the light of these various points, we may finally inquire if the Catholic idea of 'merit' and in general of the sanctity declared by God through his Church to be possessed by the faithful members of his Son, amounts to a denial of grace, as is assumed by the Protestant conception and by the whole system which Barth raised upon it.

We will take first the case of the Virgin Mary. It is certainly the one which best reveals the Catholic idea of sanctity, since to Protestants it appears the height of the idolatry which underlies the whole idea of the worship of saints.

The eminent privilege attributed to Mary by Catholic doctrine, one which asserts the uniqueness of her sanctity and reveals its source, is the Immaculate Conception. Now, it would seem that, provided one takes the elementary care necessary to understand what those who use these words mean by them (which unfortunately seems to be as a rule the last thing any Protestant controversialist thinks about), if there is any Catholic belief that shows how much the Church believes in the sovereignty of grace, in its most gratuitous form, it is this one. It is remarkable that the orthodox controversialists, contrary to the Protestants, reproach Catholics for admitting, in this one case of Our Lady, something analogous to what strict Calvinists admit for all the elect—a grace that saves us absolutely independently of us, not only without any merit of our own, but without any possibility of our co-operation. This reproach naturally seems to us erroneous, but it has some colour of justification, whereas the Protestant view seems, not merely against reason, but completely absurd. To say that Mary is holy, with a super-eminent holiness, in virtue of a divine intervention previous to the first instant of her existence, is to affirm in her case as absolutely as possible that salvation is a grace, and purely a grace, of God. We will add that to present Mary, not so much as an unheard-of exception, but as the masterpiece of grace, which is the central and unvarying theme of Catholic preaching about her, is to indicate sufficiently that the Catholic idea of grace in general, far from depreciating it by affirming that man can attain in Christ to sanctity or simply to merit, presupposes behind all this a pure gift of God, unmerited and unable to be merited.

The very foundation of the Catholic idea of sanctity and of merit is this: grace, being the principle of all merit in the supernatural order, cannot itself be merited. 'Merit', in the sense in which Catholic theology takes it, is the property of an action which, being wholly the product of faith, itself purely a gift of God, is, therefore, entirely the product of grace in us. Obviously, to speak of merit supposes the act to be ours, and ours entirely, of our intellect and will; but this act is, not only completely subordinated to grace, but also originated by it, so that the act belongs wholly to God before it is ever ours; or, better still, so that, precisely in the act, we belong no more to ourselves, but, through faith working in charity, we deliver ourselves wholly to God, or, rather, are completely reconquered by grace.

This is admirably shown in the thomist doctrine of the concurrence of habitual, or sanctifying, with actual, grace; in its turn, this doctrine is as a rule made to mean exactly its opposite in the works of Protestant controversialists. In the first place, the fact that sanctifying grace is a *habitus*, in the thomist sense, does not mean that it gives us a separate, independent power of acting supernaturally without further need in every instance of a special intervention of God; the exact opposite is the case. Sanctifying grace does not cancel the necessity of a particular actual grace for each meritorious act. The *habitus* of sanctifying grace, far from establishing us in some sort of autonomy in regard to God, involves precisely a permanent hold of God, not only on our actions, but on the source of our being, in so far as this could have been alienated from God by sin, and has to become his again, in the strictest possible sense, in Christ.. In consequence, sanctifying grace, so far from conferring any power of our own to perform independently supernatural acts, is simply a disposition maintained in us by God to act no more but under the impulse of actual grace. Each of such acts accomplished by the Christian is itself the product of a special grace, immediately given and indispensable, and presupposes that in each case he puts himself in the hands of God, not indeed on his own initiative but on that of God alone.

When the Church declares someone a saint, she simply affirms that his life in her judgment reached the point of total abandonment to grace, in virtue of a faith that had come to dominate his whole life. She never does so before his earthly life has come to an end. For she holds as a dogma of faith that, whatever the degree of fidelity to God a soul may have attained in this life, perseverance, especially final perseverance, is itself a grace impossible to merit in the strict sense; it can only be asked for with humility in prayer and faith, never taken for granted as due.

Nor is this all. Just as sanctifying grace is by no means an independent faculty of performing acts of virtue, but the re-establishment of the depths of our being in a voluntary dependence on God, neither is the merit of the faithful on the way to heaven, nor the intercession of the saints in glory, ever something autonomous. If the Church has rejected the doctrine of extrinsic justification, according to which Christ alone is, properly speaking, holy, and covers with his holiness our indelible sinfulness, she has not thereby proclaimed a holiness inherent in the just, which they would possess independently of Christ, however this word, independently, may be understood. On the contrary, if the justice of the justified is real, not imputed, it does not exist, is not even conceivable, in Catholic theology, apart from our incorporation with Christ by Baptism and our actual adhesion to him by living faith in his grace. For this reason, the merits of the saints are not, either *in patria* or *in via*, by any means additional to the merits of Christ in his Passion, but are a participation in these and nothing more. The holiness of the saints and that of Our Lady, just as what holiness there may be in the least movement of faith and love in a soul still sinful, is and cannot be other than the holiness of Christ communicated; and this holiness is not communicated by being broken and divided, but only in 'gathering into one the children of God that were dispersed'.

This description of the real attitude of the Catholic Church towards what were in fact the guiding principles of the Reformation manifests, by contrast, the unsatisfactory place to which they are inevitably condemned in the 'Churches' apparently formed to uphold them. In the beginning of this chapter we drew attention to the apparent paradox of the intimate harmony existing between the Catholic Church in its inmost nature and the authentically Christian inspiration of the principles of Protestantism. Now we have to conclude it with the establishment of something equally paradoxical: just as the process of reducing these principles to a system stifled rather than promoted them, so the separated 'Churches', born of this process, are actually the greatest obstacle to their realisation.

According as the Protestant sacraments are other than a continuation, more or less impoverished, of the Catholic ones, or as they are quite different, deliberately contrasted with the Catholic sacraments, they are, whether one likes it or not, a practical denial of the Protestant doctrine of grace in its most positive aspect. While the sacraments in the Catholic view bring grace, not in virtue of any contribution of ours, but by the free gift of God who gives them to us over and over again without ceasing; in the usual Protestant view, one could say of them exactly what St. Teresa said of purely human mystics, comparing them to the poor Spanish inns of her time: 'You can only eat there what you bring along.' In fact, the sheer confusion, in the minds of Protestants, between the action of the sacraments *ex opere operato* and some kind of magic causes them to see in the sacraments nothing more than what faith puts there, rather than finds there. Even in the Calvinist system, itself everywhere riddled by the Zwinglianism which simply denies any real presence, the presence of Christ in the Eucharist is admitted only for those who believe in it. In other words, it is their faith which gives the sacrament its content. It only brings them a confirmation or, more exactly, a more vivid awareness of what they already had independently of it. So, although orthodox Calvinism persists in describing it as a sign given by God, in the actual reality of Protestant devotion, it is only a sign, given by the faithful themselves, of what they have within them, and in this lies for them its whole value. This being so, it can only be insisted on as necessary in a purely exterior way, like the law of Judaism. Interiorly, no need for it is felt, since it brings nothing that is not already there and, as is shown by daily experience, one needs it less the more advanced one is in the spiritual life. For the less spiritual, this exterior act, by what it expresses, is a psychological support or stimulant to faith. But, as soon as they have made some little progress, it is only natural for them to think it childish to need this play-acting in order to believe. The more 'spiritual' Protestants are, the more they tend in fact to neglect the sacraments; it will be remembered that the Supper is ordinarily celebrated only four times a year in the Reformed Churches. If they keep them all the same, it is only through a sense of obligation to something purely exterior, and those whose feeling of interior liberty is strongest, like the Quakers, boldly abandon them altogether, leaving the others with a feeling of regret or uneasiness at not being able to follow them to that extent.

The principle of this development had already been laid down by Luther, although in deference to the words of the Bible he kept the Catholic teaching of the objective presence of Christ in the Eucharist. In the *De captivitate Babylonica*, the idea appears that grace is not given in the sacrament, but that this is simply a psychological help to faith, given by God only in view of our weakness. If that is so, it is impossible to see at all what the real presence in the Catholic sense can mean, being condemned on principle to inaction, since the entire content of faith proceeds from itself, and it is refused all possibility of a supernatural nourishment coming from outside. In fact, in his colloquy at Marburg with the Zwinglians, Luther did not hesitate to admit this, maintaining his belief in the Eucharist only because he did not see how he could escape the force of the Gospel words, but without disguising his regret. After this, it is not surprising that, wherever Lutherans have come up against Calvinists, they have

quickly given in to them, while the latter in their turn yielded to
the pure subjectivism of Zwingli, and this showed itself in the
end incapable of maintaining any real interest in the sacraments.
No one could ever take a serious interest in a sacred ceremony
which is only an exterior representation of what he has just as
much without it—in fact, he has more, for a recollected faith
seems to spiritual persons always more living and profound than
a faith which displays itself uselessly in more or less theatrical
fashion.

All this reveals an actual Pelagianism which ought to astonish
those Protestants who have remained true to their original
principle. The whole sacramental system of the Protestant
'Churches', except where the Catholic system survives in them,
is but a juggling with signs of divine objects to which in the most
favourable hypothesis, that of Calvinism, man has to give
whatever reality they may have. More often their sacraments
are reduced to signs of a subjective faith itself, content not to
appear a mere redundancy for a faith wholly satisfied with its
subjectivity, and conscious of no need to complete it from outside. Nothing could be imagined more capable of introducing,
in the psychology of Protestantism as maintained by its institutions, a current more directly opposed to the spiritual impetus
proper to the *sola gratia*. What in fact is more contrary to the
principle of a religion in which the gift of God is all than the
reality of a religion in which there is nothing beyond what is
brought by the personal devotion of each? That the Protestant
'Churches', solely by their natural development, in so far as this
took them away from Catholicism, arrived at such a flagrant
contradiction, is perhaps the best implicit witness to the fact
that they themselves are not the product of the main principle
of Protestantism, but of its being stifled by the negations of the
system.

This inexorable verdict passed on the fallacious claims of the
system by the course of its actual development applies to them
with equal force in connection with the doctrine of the divine
sovereignty, the *Soli Deo gloria*.

In its rejection of the true 'apostolicity' of the Church,
through misconceiving or denying the apostolic succession, the
Protestant system, which gave birth to the Protestant 'Churches',

involved itself in practice in a constant denial of that divine
sovereignty it had willed to set up as a principle. Three different
possibilities were open to Protestant organisations, once the
rupture with the Church of tradition was accomplished. Either,
as with the Anabaptists at first, or later with the Quakers, the
rejection of all visible authority, resulting in an absolute,
anarchical individualism; or else, as in the Lutheran reaction,
the handing over to the civil authority of the organisation and
direction of the Church; or, as in Calvinism and the sects following and opposed to it, the artificial construction of a new
Church, created in all its elements by the genius (or fantasy) of
an individual, according to a system of his own contrivance. In
the three cases, the result was the same; in the place of divine
authority in the Church Protestantism set up purely human
ones, with the inevitable consequence of an enslavement of man
to man, stifling the idea of personal religion and Christian
liberty.

It must be obvious that, after relegating the authority of God
to an inaccessible heaven, the pure individualism into which the
Reformation was from the beginning in danger of falling, ended
by establishing the authority of the individual in religious
matters as the sole authority on earth, making his private experiences, ideas, tastes or reasonings the one criterion; and indeed it is so evident that all the Protestant churches merely continue in order to put a stop to the disintegration of the Church,
recognised by believers as the disintegration of the sovereignty
of God himself.

But the Protestant churches could only oppose human
authorities to this religious anarchy. Lutheranism, where it has
not kept, as in some countries, especially Sweden, some elements of the Catholic Church, has only succeeded in hurrying
to its extreme a tendency already threatening the medieval
Church, which the Gregorian reform had sought to counter.
That is, it made the Church merely a department of the State
and subjected it to the pleasure of its rulers, making the up-
holding and organisation of the Church's life depend on the
whim of a purely civil authority. The rapidity with which this
devolution of ecclesiastical authority to the civil ruler, brought
about by a feverish reaction against the excesses of Anabaptism,

was to end in such a fundamentally anti-Christian principle as *Cujus regio ejus religio* is once more a self-condemnation which rules out any need for further argument. A Church which from the outset renounces any possibility of independent 'witness', which dissociates itself, as it were, from the 'martyrdom' in which the Christian Church was born, which renders to Caesar what belongs to God alone, is so flagrant a repudiation of the divine sovereignty that it is not surprising that Calvin exalted this principle as much as he did, in the effort to turn aside Protestantism from such a fatal surrender.

In spite, however, of what he intended, can we say that he did any better than Luther in this matter? We think not.

For, though he had the great merit of rediscovering that the whole ecclesiastical organisation ought to be established in obedience to the sovereign will of God, manifested in his Word, he yielded in fact to a narrowly legalistic conception of this obedience, amounting to a Judaic or Pelagian idea of it. He thought it possible to take over, from the New Testament, a particular design for an ecclesiastical organisation, and to realise it by political action, to which he devoted his best efforts. Apart from any criticism of the design he sincerely believed to have borrowed from the Bible, it seems to have entirely escaped him that the Church, to be the 'body of Christ' in St. Paul's sense, 'the pillar and ground of truth', is not simply to be made or remade by man, with his eyes fixed on a model supplied from above, but must have been created and kept in being by the intervention of God himself. The Calvinist Church, supposing it realised its own ideal, would be a human structure on a divine plan. But it would not be, and never seriously thought of being, the work of God.

This astonishing inconsequence in practice of a work aiming at establishing the one, absolute divine sovereignty was itself due to a misconception inherent in the idea of the Church Calvin believed himself to have taken from the Bible, and to his failure to see that he was neglecting the essential element of apostolicity, in the sense in which we have defined it. The Church of Calvin is a Church where everyone is a priest, directly in contact with God, without any other intermediary than the purely material one which brings him the letter of the

Word of God. But the idea that the knowledge, not only material and exterior but living and interior, of this Word, and above all the knowledge that its actual creative power for the Christian, are all elements of 'apostolicity'—pertain, that is, to the fact that God is in Christ whom he sent, and Christ in the 'apostles' he sent—this idea, or rather fact, object of faith, source of the reality of the Church, as seen in its development in the New Testament and in Christian antiquity, does not seem ever to have occurred to him. In other words, the Calvinist Church can only be an organisation human in origin, even if it claims (wrongly, in the almost unanimous opinion of contemporary exegetes) to be modelled on a divine plan. In fact, it supposes a complete misunderstanding of what the divine plan really was, as made known to us in the Incarnation; that is to say, of God's design that his Word should affect us, not only as an ideal left to us to realise, but as a creative event in which God himself, in Christ, the chief actor in our history, realises in us what he has decreed.

The Calvinist Church has never known more than a precarious and unstable existence. In the different forms of congregationalism, opposed almost from the outset to Calvinist presbyterianism, or in presbyterianism itself when it has been actually preserved, we see a succession or aggregate of systems, in which the individual believer simply delegates an authority of which he is convinced he is the only real holder. So, the Churches known as 'Reformed' oscillate between mere anarchical federations where each individual recognises no other authority than what he is prepared to canonise himself, and real dictatorships, such as those of Calvin in Geneva, and Knox in Scotland, a strong personality imposing by his own ascendency his subjective views on those around him. Hence the fact we have already noted: the splitting up of the Reformed Churches—the liberty claimed by each new founder over against a system he judges oppressive of his own personality becomes unconsciously the source of a new oppression for those who for a time enter his system.

But through all this the divine sovereignty is no more present than in the Lutheran Churches. Always it has to make way for subjectivity, whether that of unbridled individualism, or that

of the reaction against it, which invariably occurs in the name
of the domination of some other individual's system.

The history of the Churches of the Reformed type abounds in
illustrations of this. Whenever they refuse to dissolve themselves in practice into simple associations for worship, without
any other doctrinal, moral or liturgical law than the whim of
each, they tend immediately to become rigid frameworks in
which a particular type of religious mentality or feeling unconsciously results in the oppression of the others.

Moreover, in practice, even where the ministers do not wish
or claim to be other than delegates of their own communities,
Churches of this type always end by delivering over their members to the subjective views of each minister.

The Reformed 'confessions of faith' are extremely characteristic of this authoritarian subjectivism which was in fact substituted from the beginning for the authority of God it claimed to
restore. The 'Helvetic Confession', that of Westminster, the
articles of Dordrecht, are so many attempts to confine the
thought of all the believers more and more closely in the mould
of a particular theology. While the Catholic 'definitions' of
faith, even when utilising the thought of a particular school of
theology, with its local and temporal characteristics, only impose truths which transcend these limitations, and so leave other
schools perfectly free to continue within the Church; these 'confessions', being attempts to impose in detail a more and more
particularised view of Christianity, have resulted, as might have
been expected, in breaking up the Church they were intended to
unify.

Still more revealing in this respect is the history of the reformed worship. While Catholic worship, even where a particular rite prevails, is formed, and continually renewed, according to the spirit of the people and the time, it is impossible to
imagine anything more rigid and uniform, whatever the time
and place, than the meeting for worship in the Reformed
Churches. Where Catholic traditions have disappeared and
have not been reintroduced, Protestant worship follows the in-
variable pattern of a place centred round a pulpit, where someone comments, in almost unchanging fashion, on readings from
the Bible, interspersed with hymns and prayers that reflect at

the most one or two types, practically always the same, of religious feeling and expression—either the severe transcendentalism of the Calvinist type or the conventional imagery of revivalist sentiment; generally an amorphous mixture of the two.

The sole element that offers any possibility of renovation is the Word of God, in its inexhaustible richness. However, an instinctive horror, purely negative in effect, of the Catholic tradition has in practice left to the presiding minister the choice of readings from the Bible, and of the hymns to be sung. As to the prayers, generally he improvises them himself, just as he likes. Ultimately, then, everything normally centres on the ideas or forms of religious sentiment he has decided to impress on the congregation in his sermon. The scriptural passages are chosen with this in view. The hymns are those which will in his opinion best prepare his audience to accept what he has decided to say to them. The prayer itself is simply a second version of the first sermon, but addressed to God.

The final result is that the Protestant who seeks, in his Church, food for his faith finds it only in the form of a total subjection to all the peculiarities, the momentary idiosyncrasies, of his minister's personal devotion.

One cannot imagine any system more completely effective in replacing the authority of God by that of the individual minister, at the same time subjecting to him the religious personality of each participant in the worship of his Church.

Moreover, when Protestant Churches try to react against this by setting up liturgies—which, as experience shows, are never adopted without being everywhere adjusted and made subservient to the judgment or tastes of the minister using them— all they do is to impress on a greater number of persons the formulas, the feelings, the private opinions, of a minister or group of ministers, and the remedy is soon found to be worse than the disease.

Even when Protestantism has not gone to this extreme, and has kept some remnant of the Catholic liturgical tradition, as is the case especially with the Lutheran Churches, nothing is more characteristic than the 'reforms', imposed on this tradition, of the rule of the subjective, which is the real substitute of historical Protestantism for the sovereignty of God proclaimed in principle. By the same token, it is always spiritual liberty which is the sufferer under a system bearing the imprint of a particular time and place.

In the liturgy of the Eucharist in particular, the Lutheran innovations, far from returning to what was primitive and essential, the direct product of divine authorship in Christ, have to make predominant the latest, most adventitious elements. So much so that, strangely enough, historians have been obliged to conclude that the Lutheran liturgy is by no means what it claimed to be, the Catholic liturgy restored to its origins, to the purity of its divine institution, but, rather, a medieval liturgy, in which elements of alien growth, or warped in their development through the centuries immediately before the Reformation, had overpowered the rest, or altered its original significance. The *Formula Missae* of Luther reduced the whole Canon of the Mass to the words of institution. In their turn, the reformed liturgies reduced to the same practically the whole of the Eucharistic service, the remainder being no more than a theological commentary on these words, of the sectarian type we have already described.

Today it is perfectly clear to all liturgical scholars that this was simply the final term of a disastrous tendency in the medieval theology of the Eucharist—a tendency to deal more and more exclusively with the words of consecration alone, isolating them from the rest of the Mass and contrasting them with it. The older theology, on the contrary, had interpreted them only in the context of the great prayer of thanksgiving for all the gifts of God, itself derived from Judaism, a context in which the primitive Church, following the example of Christ, had seen the true meaning of his sacrifice. In tearing these words from their context, the Reformation, so far from returning to the primitive sense and the fundamental reality of the Eucharist, simply rejected what still remained of it in the Middle Ages, which had already begun to misconceive it.

The conviction, widespread in orthodox Protestantism, that the Eucharist is validly celebrated by anyone who pronounces the words of the Gospel account over the bread and wine, is itself only a hasty endorsement of an erroneous opinion running right through the Middle Ages. Besides, it is obvious that this opinion only rests on a quite openly naïve idea of the Mass as a piece of magic. The orthodox medieval idea, rejected by the Churches of the Reformation, made the efficacy of the words of consecration depend on their utterance by a validly ordained minister, that is, one 'sent' by Christ, and so upheld the principle that the sacraments derived their effectiveness from their being the sovereign acts of God himself in Christ. It was, then, this principle that the Reformation denied, whether consciously or not, in rejecting the necessity of an ordained minister. In doing so, it left no alternative but a sacramentalism having a magical content, or else no content at all.

In general, it follows from these considerations that the Protestant Churches, in spite of their reaction against Catholic 'sacerdotalism', have in fact given rise to a pure 'clericalism', one which emasculates the 'universal priesthood' of the faithful which the principles of Protestantism should have fostered, and eliminates completely the effective sovereignty of God over the Church.

From the moment of their creation, the Protestant Churches were merely the works of man. In so far as they manage to attain any authority at all, it is always the authority of a man, either of a founder or organiser or of a simple minister, and, if that fails, they break up into fragments, to the sole profit of the authority of each individual, his private views, tendencies or experiences.

This being so, it is not surprising that the *Soli Deo gloria*, so magnificently affirmed in principle by Calvinism, is so completely ignored by Protestantism in its organised practice. The fact is, although French Protestants like to call their services *le culte*, that there is nothing which resembles so little the worship of God, or is more like the cultivation of a religious humanism, than the general practices of Protestantism, unless they happen to be simply a survival of Catholic worship itself.

The very appearance of a Protestant Church is revealing; it is dominated by the pulpit, which is the centre of everything, showing that all that takes place is the teaching of religion, more or less enlivened by prayer, chant and ceremonial, all strictly subordinated to the sermon. Admittedly, in theory, it is the Word of God that should be conveyed in the sermon, but we

have just seen that the reality is quite different, and that the
sermon has come to make everything else, even the scriptural
reading, revolve round it, round a purely personal discourse.
Even where this is not the case, when there is a real 'worship',
properly so called, it is a purely interior worship given by each
one individually to God. The people are united as members of
a Church, only on the level of an association for mutual religious education; their 'Church' in fact is never anything else;
it is a centre for the religious culture of man, not a centre for the
worship of God. How characteristic of this is the restriction and
disappearance of the elements of praise and adoration from
Protestant worship! The 'thanksgiving', in the Eucharist itself,
so much minimised in the course of the Middle Ages, has entirely disappeared in Calvinism. Along with this, the element
of penance, of purification, in which the attention is focused
more on the worshipper than on the God he worships—an element that gradually extended in the Middle Ages, but is only
marginal in the Mass of the catechumens and the Mass of the
faithful—has engulfed practically all that subsists of either in the
Protestant liturgies. How could it be otherwise, if it is true that
Christ alone is the true adorer, being God made man, since God
is absent from the Protestant ecclesiastical organisation, it
being a purely human creation, even when, as in Calvinism, it
aims at least at being conformed to divine command?

The sphere, however, in which the actual reversal of the principles of Protestantism by its institutional reality is most evident, is undoubtedly that of the authority of Scripture.

The Protestant Churches set themselves up in contrast with
the Catholic Church, as Churches aiming at total submission
to the Word of God, over against a Church they accused of
replacing it by tradition. In actual fact, the history of the Protestant Churches, and of their disputes on doctrine, is all comprised in the history of their impotence to maintain, even in their
ministers, either submission to the clearest and most solemn
affirmations of Scripture, or a practical belief in its authority,
even the simple recognition that God has in truth revealed himself, 'spoken' to man, except in a wholly metaphorical sense.
The Protestant Churches either spend their energies in endors-
ing, and vainly attempting to impose, particular systems of

theology, which seem to their authors alone a true reproduction of the divine Word, or else yield to the force of things and give up teaching any definite doctrine, even that of the inspiration and authority of Scripture, however much it might seem to be the only serious ground of their opposition to the Catholic Church. After trying to form themselves into theological schools, whose authority is oppressive because wholly human, they all end up by resigning themselves to be merely in the words of one Protestant, 'associations of old pupils of Christ', without any definite principles.

All this experience makes it plain that the authority of the Word of God cannot be only the authority of a book, because no book is capable of exercising authority on the interpretation men put on it, when there is no living authority to govern its readers. More exactly, since the Word of God is really sovereign only in so far as He himself continues to utter it, with all the creative power that belongs to his Word only when pronounced by Him, this Word can keep its sovereignty only where the divine presence continues to be; in other words, where the Church is not merely an abstraction drawn from the ideas contained in scriptural texts, but a reality created and kept in being by the 'apostolate' of the Son of God, of the living Word made flesh, prolonging himself in all times and places, in human form, by the 'apostolate' of those the Son sent in his turn, as he had been sent by the Father.

Apart from this fundamental condition, all precautions against the temptation, only too natural, to humanise the divine Word, immersing it in the word of man, will be ineffectual, because it will be attempting the impossible: to make the divine Word remain divine, after it has ceased to be uttered by God; whereas 'God alone speaks truly of God'.

CHAPTER XI

Conclusion: The Protestant Movement, Protestant 'Churches', and the One Church

IF the analyses contained in the last chapter are accurate, we have to conclude that the Barthian criticism of the 'Revivalism,' which arose out of the pietist movement, and the attempt to refute it along with Catholicism, is without foundation. Not only, we believe to have established, did the revival not betray the purest Christian elements in the original Reformation principles when it reorientated itself towards traditional Christianity, that of the Catholic Church, but it thereby indicated the only way of freeing the living soul of Protestantism, once and for all, from the corpse in which the sixteenth century imprisoned it, in the belief that it was incarnating it.

No doubt Protestant mysticism, of which the Revival was the flower, was adulterated with elements of immanentism and naturalism, which often transformed and paralysed it and ended by stifling it. But, we may now say, the blame for this lies principally with the false transcendentalism of orthodox Protestantism which virtually necessitates a plunge into the merely human, once an attempt is made to recapture the truth of divine creation, the reality of divine salvation. That is why Barthism, in so far as it is and aims at being a reaction, a simple return to the original formulas of Protestantism, without criticising them but, rather, tautening them still further in their original and unintended complexity, far from helping to resolve the internal crisis endemic in Protestantism, can only in the end blind it to itself and infatuate it.

Barthism and the other forms of Protestantism akin to it, whether the theology of Brunner or that of Nygren, have concentrated their attacks on what they call 'the mystical', as the element of pagan, merely human religion, with which Catholicism adulterated the Word, and so replaced the way of God by grace to man, by the way of man to God, in a religion of merit and human striving which aims at making him the equal of God and able to do without him.

221

What really distinguishes true Catholic mysticism from the ill-defined forms in which Protestant revivalism gropes after it, is contained in the final word of St. John of the Cross, the doctor of mysticism *par excellence* in the Catholic Church, when he affirms the nothingness of all human effort to reach to God, and the need for the all-sufficiency and omnipotence of the God who has spoken to us in Christ to lead us to him by *his* way, that by which he came to us—the Cross. None the less, the Cross of Christ, in the traditional view of the Church, which is obviously in perfect conformity with the New Testament, as illumined by the entire Bible, means man, not simply brought back to the nothingness of a creature and a sinner, but recreated out of this nothingness by the Spirit in the image of God, to live as a son in the only Son of God become man.

The system of Barth, particularly as directed against the Church, in spite of its magnificent reaffirmation of the divine holiness proclaimed by God himself in his Word, is more incapable than any other form of Protestant thought of embracing this paradox, and so of preaching a salvation that is something real. This being so, it is impossible to see in it anything but a striking accentuation of the fundamental defect of Protestantism. This defect, it can now be seen, does not consist in a too extreme application of the positive principles of the Reformation; it is, on the contrary, part of the original and unconscious compromise—a compromise with the very corruption the Reformation should have swept away. That hopeless entanglement of a human philosophy, fundamentally opposed to religion, with the affirmation of the divine Word inflicted a fatal wound on Protestantism at its very start. The *a priori* refusal to pass judgment on that confusion, the deliberate accentuation of that internal contradiction, constitutes the supreme mistake of Barthism, and risks making it the poison, rather than the remedy, of the faith of Protestantism. For Barth's own reassertion of the divine transcendence within this confusion in which he surpasses all other Protestants is in danger of being compromised in the view of the world of today, even more than the divine sovereignty was by Luther and orthodox Protestantism of the sixteenth and seventeenth centuries, in the world of the Renascence.

The source of the evil, today as formerly, remains exactly the same. Just as Luther, while proclaiming to his contemporaries the Gospel which should have been their salvation, compromised it irremediably by setting it in a philosophy closed to the living God, which he had taken over from an exhausted Christianity, Barth compromises this same Gospel once again, burying it even more deeply in a thoroughly godless philosophy, the latest offspring of nominalism.

To understand Barth intimately, we have constantly to bear in mind the intellectual world in which he was brought up, which he reacted from but never escaped. It was the world of post-Kantian religious philosophy, particularly that of Ritschl. It takes as a fundamental axiom that the 'noumenon' and the 'phenomenon', transcendental reality and immanent experience, are irreconcilably opposed. This gave rise to Ritschl's attempt to make it once more possible to use the statements of the Bible and the dogmas of traditional Christianity in a world rigorously shut off from any contact with the transcendental; he wished to call by the names of God, revelation, salvation, the wholly immanent religious experience of man. Christ would be said to reveal God, and save man, merely in the sense that he expressed, and enables us to express, by the image of him immortalised in the Gospels, the highest mode of man's self-awareness. . . .

In his commentary on the epistle to the Romans, Barth has described better than anyone else could the brutal awakening he experienced when the human crisis, caused by the war of 1914, tore him from this artificial dreamland, and made him see the absurdity of its verbalism. Unfortunately, in rediscovering the transcendent God, he never thought of criticising the concepts of radical immanentism which had always governed his thought. The result was that, for a 'phenomenalism' wholly enclosed in itself, he could only substitute a 'noumenalism' exactly corresponding with it. The God of Ritschl was only the super-ego of man, when he has definitely given up all hope of going beyond himself, and resorts to the ingenious (or puerile or senile) consolation of adorning himself with all the attributes and even the name of what is above all. The God of Barth is but the exasperated negation of this negation, disguised as an

affirmation. It is the vindication of the 'noumenon' by someone
who refuses even to discuss either its essential distinction from,
or its incommunicability in principle with, the 'phenomenon'.
In other words, Barth's 'faith' is reduced in the end to an affirmation, in complete darkness, of a God who can no more
approach man effectively than Kantian man can attain to God
in himself. No one has ever before tried to express a transcendentalism so absolute; but neither has it ever been so firmly
entrenched in the inexpressible. However magnificently Barth
has developed the Protestant theology of the divine Word, his
principles, accepted without criticism, condemn him from the
outset to perpetual silence. His omnipotent God is prohibited
a priori from ever acting outside himself; his Creator is forbidden to create, his Saviour to save, anything outside himself.

Once again it is the intellectual drama of the Reformation,
but carried to its highest intensity. An affirmation of the reality
of God, if expressed in terms designed precisely to avoid any
real contact of God and man, is bound either to contradict
itself or to deny unrelentingly any gift of God to man, any real
relation between God and man. For that reason, Barth, far
from liberating the divine Word from enslavement to the
human, as he intended, either shuts it up in complete silence or
condemns it *a priori* to total degradation. He can no longer
avoid the idolatry against which he had rebelled, except by
adopting in fact, whatever his intention, a complete nihilism.
His God remains God only in being for us another word for
pure nothingness. Whence those fatal paradoxes and in the end a
new verbalism, even worse than that of Ritschl, of a sovereign
Word, but whose statements no one can know; of a creative
God, who may not create any reality that exists; of a God who
is Saviour, but who can only save, while leaving what is lost to
its own perdition.

The adherence of Bultmann to the theology of Barth—that is,
of a Biblical critic and exegete for whom nothing of the historical content of the Gospels is certain, nor any of the teaching
attributed to Christ, except the radical cleavage between the
'present world' and the 'world to come', on condition, however,
of placing it outside of history—is the most embarrassing possible threat to the system, for it testifies to the ultimate empti-

ness of the verbal affirmations on which it is built. Apart from
the desperate logic of a negation simply attired in affirmative
terms, the dogmatic theology Barth has worked out is, in spite
of the considerable interest of many of its elements, only a continuous oscillation between a doctrinaire agnosticism, the only
natural conclusion of the system, and a Protestant neo-orthodoxy merely jerked into movement, not reanimated, because
obviously incapable of being so.

What is the explanation of the striking temporary success of
Barthism? Without any desire to judge or even question Barth's
sincerity and his genuine desire of obedience to the Word of
God, we are compelled to say that he offered the uneasy and
nervous conscience of institutional Protestantism a momentary
escape which was bound to meet with resounding success.

Between the Scylla and Charybdis of Protestant orthodoxy
and liberalism, whether rationalistic or sentimental, the Revival movement, with its authentically Christian elements,
cleared the way, within Protestantism, for the recognition of the
innate error through which, in opposing Catholicism, it fatally
wounded the Christianity it wished to reform. But it is never
pleasant for a man to admit his mistakes; most painful of all to
recognise is the mistake made at the very moment of discovering
a truth, that prevents one applying it. At a time when institutional Protestantism hesitated on the verge of acknowledging its
original error, Barthism appeared as a providential means of
avoiding or at least postponing the acknowledgment. A religion which had set out to reinstate God as sovereign, and was
actually moribund in its self-sufficient humanism, was to be
allowed once again to attribute to itself a high-sounding rôle,
to arrogate to itself the right to judge and condemn its ad-
versaries, in the manner of the prophets, without confessing its
own faults, but exalting them as high distinctions insufficiently
admired hitherto.

For, if Barthism is always reminding the Christian of his sinfulness, it is invariably in consideration of what remains or
might remain of Catholicism in the breast of the Protestant that
he is urged to say, *mea culpa*; yet it never acknowledges, does not
apparently admit the possibility of, any fault in Protestantism,
in so far as it is an anti-Catholic system, the most narrow and

abortive. This newly-found and apparently imperturbable good conscience restored to contemporary Protestantism by Barth is accompanied by a doctrine that cannot be seriously examined, apart from controversial aims, without being seen to be terribly deceptive and empty. Like the teachings of Ritschl, but carried to a higher pitch, it simply puts an affirmative colouring on the negations from which Protestantism was dying, without giving them any positive content at all.

Barthism has only postponed the day of reckoning, put off for a time the task, supremely repugnant to natural man, of drawing up the balance-sheet of his catastrophes. On one side is the Protestantism we have called institutional, worked out in the different Protestant Churches, starting from the polemical systems drawn up in the sixteenth century and never radically criticised; on the other side there is Protestantism in its principles, that Protestantism which is no sociological complex irremediably burdened with a misdirected past, but a spiritual movement, authentically Christian in inspiration, which has made continual but unsuccessful efforts to free itself from the non-Christian or anti-Christian casing which had held it from the beginning.

To sum up, the conclusion of all the preceding is that the problem Protestantism has never resolved is the problem of the Church: never resolved in fact, because never clearly stated.

In its first phase, up to the Confession of Augsburg, which was the first synthesis of Lutheranism, Protestantism had no idea of developing into a Church other than that of all time, the Catholic Church centred on the See of Rome.

Next, after it had seen all its complex affirmations condemned by the See of Rome and then by the Catholic Church as a whole, being incapable of understanding the reason for this condemnation, because unable to criticise its own expression of its principles, the movement was tempted to take refuge in the chimera of an invisible Church. Faced with the results of Anabaptism and with the purely destructive anarchy to which this chimera was obviously leading, Luther took the irrational course of invoking the secular arm; in other words, to maintain the reform of the Church, he left it without defence to the most formidable threat of corruption the medieval Church had known. Considering the remedy worse than the disease, Calvinism then tried to recreate by an individual effort, in virtue of a system hastily authorised by a very disputable and subjective interpretation of the Word of God, an authoritative Church. But this Church, never absolutely conformed with its ideal, stirred up other subjectivities in reaction to that of Calvin and its imperiousness, and these were no less individual, unjustifiable and tyrannical. Hence the perpetual tension between Churches, which are only dictatorial attempts to impose a particular school of thought and spirituality, and rebellious individuals, who can only escape from anarchy by setting up new dictatorships of their own.

The course of institutional Protestantism cannot come to an end. The various Churches of Protestantism were built up on a basis of opposition to the one Church of all time, an opposition latent within the Protestant synthesis, but deriving from its infidelity in practice to the profound principles of the Reformation. They are, therefore, incapable of ceasing to paralyse these principles, or of ceasing to oppose the only Church postulated by the commission given to the apostles by the authority of the Incarnate Word of God. The two things are in fact bound up with each other, as we hope to have made absolutely clear. The Catholic Church, in those elements which contemporary historians and exegetes agree in recognising as continuous with the Church of antiquity, the Church of the New Testament— and continuous, too, with the Incarnation, is the main target of the factitious opposition of nominalism, and of all those philosophies, antithetical though they be, of transcendence and of immanence that actually flowed from it. But these strike also at the very essence of the Gospels. In binding up its Christian principles within the categories of such a philosophy, the Protestant Reformation impaired at once the Catholic Church and its own principles. The Protestant Churches, set up in opposition to the Catholic Church on the base of an eclectic system, constructed with insufficient reflexion by Protestantism at its origin, and warped by Protestant 'orthodoxy', far from serving the essential cause of the Protestant movement, has placed it in a state of permanent crisis.

The only real issue from this crisis would be, not a toning

down of any of the positive principles, but a radical criticism
of what the first Protestants kept of a decadent medieval system,
without noticing it, which from the outset distorted their fundamentally most legitimate affirmations, and continues to do
so today. Such a criticism should convince Protestants of the
futility and harmfulness (to what is rightly most dear to them)
of their attitude of hostility to the Church. Its result should be
a rediscovery of the true countenance of the one Church, un-
recognised ultimately because of the same prejudices which
have made their own principles barren. Thence should come
their agreement to return and form part of this Church as an
indispensable condition for the full expansion of those insights
in which consists the entire, authentically Christian value of
Protestantism as a spiritual movement. As its failure was due
internally to what caused it to be expelled from the Church, its
success can only be assured by a fully conscious and deliberate
return.

The final conclusion of this essay can only be a reminder to
Catholics of their own part in making this return possible; of
the need for understanding the original profound meaning of
the Protestant movement, which we have tried especially to lay
bare; after that, the necessity of grasping afresh the nature and
significance of the Catholic Church itself, with all that it implies. In this way alone can they legitimately aspire to show and
prepare for their separated brethren the way to a return which
would be for them not a denial, but a fulfilment. Catholics are
in fact too prone to forget that, if the Church bears within herself, and cannot ever lose, the fulness of Gospel truth, its members, at any given time and place, are always in need of a renewed effort to apprehend this truth really and not just, as
Newman would say, 'notionally'. The very generosity of certain
unbelievers can often be, for our own sloth or negligence, a reproach, or a positive sign that God is summoning us to make
that effort. If other Christians strive towards the living truth of
Christ, we ought even more to do so, we who, without any
merit of ours, have at our disposition so many means of grace
that they lack.

That is the kind of reaction incumbent on Catholics in the

face of all that is best in the Protestant movement. 'This word is hard,' many will think, and some will add: 'Who can endure it?'

Let them remember that this word must appear infinitely harder to even the best of Protestants. To Catholics, lukewarm and unaware of their responsibilities, the Protestant movement, when rightly understood, recalls the existence of many of their own treasures which they overlook. But to the best among the Protestants, the very movement which bears them along imposes the duty, if our interpretation be correct, of leaving, like Abraham, their country, their family, what they call their 'Church', and love as such. What could be more painful for a Protestant, brought up in allegiance to great and holy persons like Alexandre Vinet, Adolphe Monod, Louis Meyer, Auguste Lecerf, to come to the point where he has to say that 'real fidelity to what they had so much at heart, to the divine Word, salvation by faith in the gift of God in Christ, which proclaims it to us, compels me finally to be in appearance unfaithful'? It is not pleasant for the sons of the house to be reminded of the respect due to the holy table where Wisdom has placed for them bread for which they have but a moderate appetite, wine they are in no hurry to taste. Can they, then, think it pleasant to feed on the crumbs which fall from this table? And can those who display themselves in the nuptial garment, without stopping to consider what it cost Christ to acquire it for them, consider as negligible the suffering of those invited to strip themselves of all, in order to receive it in their turn?

Note by G. de Broglie, S.J., on the Primacy of the Argument from Scripture in Theology

THIS brief note is far from being a complete treatment of the complex problem of the relationship between Scripture and Tradition. Still less does it question the fact that the argument from Tradition has a certain *logical priority* to the argument from Scripture—in so far as our belief in the inspiration of Scripture rests on the authority of the Church. Nor does it maintain that every dogma can be proved by the argument from Scripture, without recourse to Tradition. It does not call in question the infallibility of the Magisterium, or its indispensable rôle in the interpretation of Scripture.

Neither does it ignore the fact that the theological argument drawn from ecclesiastical documents is, in a number of cases, the *most clear and cogent* that could be imagined. All it aims at is to emphasise the classic recognition of the argument from Scripture as holding an *inalienable primacy of importance and value* among all the arguments used in theology.

The reason for this is easy to understand. Even in cases where in the Catholic view the teaching of the Magisterium satisfies all the conditions for infallibility, the Church is obliged by her own teaching to acknowledge that an ecclesiastical document of the sort is an entirely different thing from a text of Scripture. True, the Church's teaching is divinely guaranteed to be free from error; none the less, it remains, in the various acts which constitute it, an aggregate of testimonies which are merely human, bearing on a past revelation made by God to men: whereas the sacred text presents us with a formal and direct testimony from God himself, in the very form in which it originally appeared.

Consequently, Scripture has always had a place apart in the teaching of the Church. For, if the essential function of a theologian is to transmit the divine message in its entire purity, and, if Scripture is in fact the sole *immediate* source at his dis-

230

posal whence he can derive that message in the very words of
the God who sent it, his primary concern must needs be to recur
continually to that source to the fullest possible extent, and so
to refer in the first place to the testimony of Scripture in preference to any other. So it is that Pope Leo XIII (whom no one
will accuse of underestimating the importance of the Magisterium!) could well observe that recourse to Scripture should
be, as it were, the 'soul' of all theology; and he continued:
'This was, in all periods, the doctrine of all the Fathers and the
greatest of the theologians, one which they followed out in their
own practice. *They set out to establish and confirm, primarily by
the sacred books, all the truths of faith as well as those which
follow from them.*' [1]

It seems needless to insist that the argument from Scripture
was the 'soul' of the whole Patristic theology; the fact is so
strikingly evident. St. Thomas Aquinas himself, as Pope Leo
pointed out, conformed with the utmost fidelity to the same
principle. Not only does the argument from Scripture appear
throughout the whole of his work as the fundamental argument
from authority, but he bases his whole concept of theological
science on the primacy of the sacred text in questions of doctrine. In the 4th book of his *Summa Contra Gentes*, where he
undertakes the defence of those truths which are the specific
object of the Christian faith, he declares plainly that he will take
as his 'principles' *the teachings of Scripture* (*C. Gent.* IV. 1); and,
in the first question of the *Summa Theologica*, he seems at first
sight to go still further, since, according to the literal meaning
of the text, it could appear that the argument from Scripture is
the only 'necessary', absolutely rigorous, argument in theology
(I, q. 1, 8 ad 2. See above, page 130).

We hasten to say that it would be erroneous to interpret the
passage in such an extreme sense. For, though St. Thomas may
not have had a fully elaborated theory of the Magisterium and
its various rôles, it is certain that he possessed at least a very
clear idea of *infallible ecclesiastical documents*, and of the decisive character of the arguments that could be drawn from
them. That is shown clearly enough by his teaching on the

---

[1] Encyclical, *Providentissimus Deus.*

Creeds elaborated by the various Councils.[1] But, though he does not question in any way the normative authority of these documents, or their extreme usefulness, it is a striking fact that he always sees in them simply a *means of defence* of dogma against heresies, or an *auxiliary* which makes more accessible to the unlearned the content of Scripture and Tradition. . . . If then, for St. Thomas, the fundamental aim of theological science is to establish the truths of revelation by having recourse (as far as possible) to *the very sources* whence the Church derives them, it becomes clear that the argument based on ecclesiastical documents (even infallible ones) cannot be considered by him as having a right, in theological 'science', to a superior or an equal rôle to that of the argument from Scripture (even to that from Tradition). For, to say that the purpose of 'definitions' is not to create or reveal new dogmatic truths, but simply to attest with clarity and certainty truths *already possessed by the Church's faith and already discernible as such*, implies that the theologian discharges his office imperfectly if he confines himself to the establishment of dogmatic truths *by means of* 'definitions'; whereas he would fulfil it in the best possible way by establishing all the 'defined' truths *without direct recourse to the argument drawn from the definitions themselves*. The 'definitions' lose none of their value by being considered by the theologian in the light of 'confirmations' which he could, strictly speaking, dispense with; on the contrary, that would be the best way to justify their existence, to arrive at their proper understanding, and to shed the clearest light on the study of the meaning and application of each. Seen from this standpoint, 'infallible definitions' in no wise affect the primacy which the argument from Scripture enjoys and must retain in the science of theology.

However, the recognition of this primacy should by no means lead to undervaluing the argument from Tradition and its necessity. For, unless we take a singularly narrow view of 'inspiration', we are obliged to acknowledge that the apostles were not 'inspired' only when they took up the pen. Does not St. Paul assure us that his *oral* teaching, once given, is to prevail

[1] See, for example, IIa IIae, 1, 9, ad 1 et 2; art. 10, ad 1.

over any other? (Gal. I, 8). Does not St. Peter expressly state that it was 'inspired by the Holy Ghost that the holy men of God *spoke*'? (2 Peter, I, 21). In general, all goes to show that the apostles were 'inspired' every time they aimed expressly at fulfilling their task of teaching the faithful and forming them, whether by word or in their writings or even by their acts and example. One may say in consequence that the Word of God, in the fullest sense of the expression, flowed from them con-tinuously as from its living sources. What Catholics do not admit is that all this flood of the divine Word, which issued from them into the world, subsequently disappeared, except that part which they committed, or caused to be committed, to writing. All the rest of the Word they uttered remains equally living and effectual; but it is such through the tradition of the Church, whose rôle it is to transmit to us its authentic and com-plete echo.

The position of the Catholic Church, it will be seen, is perfectly clear and precise. It admits, on the one hand, as traditional doctrine, that the apostles (and their associates, the evangelists) have in fact expressed in their writings *all the principal part* of the message they possessed to hand down to us; and it follows that tradition, by its essence, is obliged always to gravitate, as it were, round Scripture, guaranteeing to us its divine origin, in-terpreting and commenting on it, clarifying and completing its teaching. Yet, on the other hand, the Church can never forget that, if we desire, by the exercise of our faith, to make contact with the divine Word as it springs from its source, it is not enough to question the text of Scripture alone; we must interro-gate, too, all that conveys an exact and authentic reflexion of the unwritten teaching of the apostles. History shows well enough what abuses Scripture may occasion, once it is viewed in isola-tion from this organic, living environment, charged both to transmit it and to maintain for ever its right understanding.

To sum up the matter, we may say that the whole attitude of the Church is explained by her sole and constant concern for the Word of God, as communicated to us by the apostles. Her attachment to this Word makes her refer on every occasion to Scripture, both in her solemn definitions and in the exercise of her ordinary Magisterium. And whenever, on one point or

another, her teaching goes beyond what is clearly and explicitly contained in the text of the Bible, this procedure of hers,
far from indicating a certain indifference to the original Word of
God, testifies in another form to the same rigorous care to preserve it in every part, and to transmit it in its entirety to her
children.

CPSIA information can be obtained
at www.ICGtesting.com
Printed in the USA
BVHW050018140223
658395BV00021B/288